DO IT HERSELF

DO IT HERSELF

Women and technical innovation

Edited by
HELEN APPLETON

INTERMEDIATE TECHNOLOGY PUBLICATIONS

DO IT HERSELF

Women and technical innovation

Edited by
HELEN APPLETON

INTERMEDIATE TECHNOLOGY PUBLICATIONS 1995

Intermediate Technology Publications Ltd
103–105 Southampton Row, London WC1B 4HH, UK

A CIP record for this book is available from
the British Library

ISBN 1 85339 287 1

Illustrations by Debbie Riviere unless otherwise credited;
flow-charts and maps by Eric Apsey;
photographs from the Intermediate Technology photo library
in Rugby, UK
Typeset by J&L Composition Ltd, Filey North Yorkshire
Printed in the UK by SRP, Exeter

Contents

Acknowledgements

This project was made possible by the Ford Foundation, NORAD (Sri Lanka), and UNIFEM, who funded the research and workshops. We are grateful to these organizations and to the Overseas Development Administration, UK, for funding.

Many thanks are also due to the following women—representatives of invisible technologists in communities all over the world:

- Herminia Pinilla Melillanca, part of the group in Nuevo Amanecer that worked with TEKHNE.
- Candelaria Orocillo Montana, a resident of the township of Las Americas in Tacna.
- Migdalia Orellana, a resident of El Trompillo who became involved in the hydroponics work.
- Isabel Lozano Díaz, one of a group of *cecineras* (porkcurers) in Tarapoto.
- María Sanabria Guerra, a member of the food processing group *La Asunción* in Huancayo.
- María Sóliz, a member of the community of San Miguel Afuera.
- Cecilia Renault Manríquez, a member of the group of women in La Chimba who built their own houses.

Dedication

To Dolores . . .
Thanks for giving us
the chance to know you

María Dolores Mateo Montero, who worked with Lourdes Perdomo in La Zurza in Santa Domingo, died during the workshop at the end of their research. Aged only 35, she was a victim of the poor health facilities that she was working to improve.

Introduction

HELEN APPLETON

Over the last few years, research has begun to challenge the traditional (Northern) view that poor producers are tradition-bound and resistant to change (see, for example, Gamser, 1988, and Bhalla and James, 1988). Studies have highlighted the fact that in countries of the South, small-scale producers make logical choices based on their own perception of their needs and on the resources available to them (Gamser *et al.*, 1990). It has been argued that these local solutions are technical innovations at grassroots level, and represent a vital though largely untapped resource for understanding what constitutes an appropriate technology in any context, and a firm basis upon which to develop further technology in ways that genuinely reflect local skills, priorities and needs (see, for example, Lemonnier, 1993).

The development of these arguments has depended on more critical discussion about what constitutes technical 'efficiency' in any context. Traditional evaluations of technical hardware were often based on criteria assumed by technology designers rather than on criteria developed in consultation with intended beneficiaries (Anderson, 1985). Such criteria are usually perceived as being in some way 'objective' or 'value free', and may reflect, for example an assumption that increased output or improved productivity are the only priorities.

Little or no recognition was given to the socio-economic reality in which any technology is conceived, designed and used, the wide range of priorities and expectations which people may have in relation to technology, or the ways in which they are already using existing skills to achieve their ends. However, given that any technical solution is the result of a complex interaction between processes of technical design and non-technical and wider social logics (Lemonnier, 1993), an understanding of how people make decisions is crucial to the planning of technical assistance (Stewart, 1977).

HELEN APPLETON is a Policy Researcher for IT UK.

1

The subject of this book derives from an interest in the relationships between people, technology development and technical innovation within communities in countries of the South[1]. 'People', however, comprise both women and men who have different, and widely varying, roles and responsibilities across different societies. The sheer range of what constitutes 'men's work' and 'women's work' in different societies indicates that biological sex is not an absolute, but rather represents a social construct— the social interpretation of a biological fact. Gender research thus focuses upon the different ways in which sex is used as a principle of social organization.

Over the last 25 years there have been many studies investigating the different roles of women and men. The overwhelming conclusion of the research is that women and men do not benefit equally from the sexual division of labour. Across countries and regions, women have fewer resources, fewer legal rights, less political voice, less education and more responsibilities than their male counterparts, and although they often work longer hours, their contributions are less valued and of lower status. The evidence also indicates that women do not automatically benefit from aid programmes, even when 'household incomes' apparently increase (Ostergaard, 1992; Mazza, 1987), and an increased collection of statistics on a gender-disaggregated basis has shown that poverty is not gender neutral: according to the United Nations, women comprise 70 per cent of the world's poorest people.

Most of such studies have been carried out from a general development perspective; the aim in this book is to examine a specific area—that of grassroots technical innovation—and to focus on the roles of women within it.

Technological innovation at the grassroots

There has been some work done on the gender aspects of industrialization (Baud and de Bruijne, 1993; Carr, 1988), and previous investigations of technology use, small-scale production and indigenous innovation have indicated that many of the users of small-scale technologies are women (Carr, 1984; Baud, 1983; Gamser et al., 1990). However, as Baud (1993) notes, there has been only limited research on technology development and the impact of technological change at local level, and, with the exception of Carr and one or two others, the information that is available is rarely gender disaggregated. Within a general context of lack of recognition

---

1 'The South' will be used in this book in preference to 'developing countries', 'less developed countries' or 'Third World'. 'The South' is a geographically inaccurate term, but at least does not imply that there is a universal understanding of what constitutes 'development', or that all countries are pursuing the same kind of 'development'.

given to local technical environments, there is thus a particular lack of understanding among governments, aid agencies, universities and research and development institutions of differences in the technological contexts in which men and women live and their different expectations of, and contributions to, technical change. In relation to technical assistance, women particularly are viewed as passive recipients of home economics-oriented aid packages, rather than active participants in technical processes (Whitehead and Bloom, 1992).

In order to find out more about this apparent gap in existing knowledge, a research programme, *Do It Herself*, was designed specifically to investigate the contributions of women to technical innovation at grassroots level. The work was based on the assumption that women as technology users have specialized technical knowledge which they employ daily in the operation of production processes. This was extended by the hypothesis that women use their knowledge and skills to develop, modify and adapt the techniques and technical processes in which they are involved. A further objective of the work was to explore the ways in which technical development agencies can work with women in order to ensure that technical assistance is appropriate to and in the control of the intended users of technology.

Methodology

A major challenge for the research was to be the obtaining of information about an area—women and technological innovation at local level—that was to some extent invisible, and therefore unlikely to be easily accessed by conventional research methodologies. Three factors were identified at the outset of the *Do It Herself* programme as being key to production of good information: the involvement of the technology users in the research and the creation of space for their views to be heard; the identification of researchers who had good community links, and support to their research skills; and, in the longer term, the strengthening of regional capacity with regard to women's contributions to technical innovation.

In each region a list of contacts—non-governmental organizations, universities, appropriate technology organizations, women's networks and individuals—was compiled. The proposed work was then described and the contacts were asked to assist with the identification of researchers who had good links with women technology users at grassroots level and the ability to represent the women concerned. Extensive research experience was not regarded as essential: the programme was structured around using existing capacity in the organizations involved to support and develop the skills of investigation and analysis among the researchers.

The prospective researchers met together in a workshop in one of the countries of the region before the research was done. They each had an idea of a possible case study (or studies), which they shared with the rest of the

3

group. The group then spent a day identifying what they felt were the main issues arising from both the potential case studies and their own experience, an exercise which provided terms of reference for the research. Next, possible research methodologies were discussed. The researchers expressed a feeling that conventional research methodologies and approaches were inadequate in the identification and analysis of issues arising in the lives of grassroots women, and different approaches would be needed if the perspectives of women technology users were to be fully reflected. Proposed methodologies varied according to the different circumstances of each researcher, but the unanimous emphasis was on involving technology users as much as possible in the work, planning activities and identification of priority areas for investigation.

The researchers then spent time in pairs, with the support of facilitators, working each other through the terms of reference for the research with relation to each individual case study, so that each person had a clear understanding of what she was going to do, and how and when she was going to do it. This was shared with the rest of the group. A seminar, at which the completed work would be presented to a regional audience, was then discussed, objectives and dates decided upon, and possible participants identified. Each researcher was encouraged to think about nominating one resource person to accompany her to the seminar (this was covered in the budget) in order to provide support, to reflect different perspectives and to provide an extra communication link back to the women involved in the research. In Central/South America, where Spanish is widely spoken and understood in rural and urban areas, all the resource people were grassroots women.

The researchers themselves emphasized that the investigations should provide information that would be of use primarily to those who were working in the technical area concerned, and that the sharing of research information with the informants—women technology users—was essential. In order to facilitate this, a small workshop was held in each area towards the end of the research period, at which the findings were discussed with technology users, and modified to reflect their views.

The researchers carried out their investigations over about six months, and communication by post was maintained during this time. A seminar was arranged in a second country of the region to enable the findings to be presented to a regional audience of representatives from NGOs, governments, donor and aid agencies and development organizations. A week before the seminar, the researchers met again in a small workshop, the objectives of which were: to share the information obtained by each researcher; to assist with the analysis of the work; to identify key themes arising from the investigations; to decide how the work would be presented in the seminar and to assist each researcher with her own part in the presentations.

4

In each region the decision was taken not to focus the presentations on individual case studies, but instead to use the case study material to emphasize the key issues identified by the research. This way, it was felt, would present a whole that was greater than the sum of the parts, and that participants would leave the seminar with a grasp of the main points. In order to assist this, time was spent in the pre-seminar workshop compiling and practising the presentations so that they would be as clear as possible. This time was valuable for many of the researchers who had not previously had the opportunity to present work in front of an audience.

The support that each individual derived from the group was important to the personal development of the researchers. The mixture of skills, backgrounds, nationalities, perspectives and experience strengthened and encouraged each researcher, and carried her (occasionally him) through a process that all regarded as challenging.

Definitions

Technology   A clear understanding of the word 'technology' was crucial to the research, particularly as researchers recognized from the outset that some of women's technical expertise was derived from their reproductive activities. The definition of technology used was therefore one that identifies the four elements of technology[2]: the *hardware* (machinery or equipment) of production; the *software* (knowledge and skills) needed to produce something, including the concepts and thinking processes linked to production; the *organization* needed both to produce a product and to enable production to take place, including social organization[3]; and the *product* itself.

Innovation Within the formal sector, technical innovation is regarded as a proactive process, where opportunities are sought or created, and risks taken or supported. The importance of maintaining an innovatory edge in products and processes is recognized, and research and development departments and institutions have the responsibility of identifying, creating and responding to new markets. *Do It Herself* researchers felt that this understanding did not adequately reflect the definition of technology identified above. In order to examine processes of technical innovation within a broader band of activities which are not necessarily linked to the market or to changes in machinery or equipment, the following definition of technological innovation was adopted: *any change, however small, in*

---

2 This is an accepted broad definition of technology, see Hillebrand *et al.*, 1994.

3 See Sen (1987) for a detailed discussion of the relationships between social organization and the organization of a production process.

5

the skills, techniques, processes, equipment type or organization of produc-
tion, that enables people better to cope with or take advantage of parti-
cular circumstances. This definition was seen as relating both to the
detailed content of innovation and to the broader factors which stimulate
a particular type of response.

Through the processes of research, these definitions became key elements in furthering the understanding of women's relationships with
technology. The definition of technology was examined, and questions
asked about whether its four component parts are equally reflected in the
allocation of funds to technical assistance: are skills and knowledge and
organizational processes, for example, supported equally alongside the
development and transfer of machinery and equipment? Further questions
arose about the different involvement of men and women in hardware and
software aspects of technology, and whether there were differences in
status and recognition between these elements. This raised issues around
the values accorded to different types of knowledge and the ways in which
gender relationships contribute to these values. It became clear that women
are not generally high-profile users of technical hardware, but have
important technical skills and knowledge and are engaged in complex
production processes. They constantly adapt and innovate, or contribute
to the adaptations and innovations of others, but their expertise is unrecognized and less valued. A particular issue that emerged, therefore, was the
apparent invisibility of women's technical contributions, and the need to
examine the factors implicit within this.

The invisibility of women's technical knowledge

Four factors contribute to the lower visibility of women's technical knowledge and to the lower profile of women overall as technology users and
producers.

First, at national and international levels, is the consistent failure of
compilers of Gross National Product and Gross Domestic Product figures
to accord an economic value to unpaid work, much of which is carried out
by women. Unpaid work comprises, among other things, the subsistence
activities on which the lives of most rural people depend, and the taking
care and servicing of all community members: producers, workers, children
and the elderly. Such unpaid activities, which have been calculated as
representing between 25 and 30 per cent of any country's current and
future output (UN, 1991), also represent the areas in which many of
women's technical contributions are made. National and international
planning, policymaking and resource allocation are based, however, on
available figures, which means that work whose value is not measured or
estimated is not invested in. Thus technical assistance policies inevitably

6

ignore many areas of women's activity, compounding women's technological invisibility.

A second factor contributing to invisibility of women's technical knowledge is the cultural perception of what is 'technical' and what is 'domestic'. Women carry out a considerable number of technical activities, or activities with technical components, often within a single day. They may, for example, farm, process crops and food, weave, sew, collect wood and water, cook, fish, tend animals and care for children and for the sick. However, some of these activities may be part-time or seasonal, and, as noted above, many are unpaid. As much of women's unpaid work is oriented around family welfare, it tends to be classified as domestic rather than technical, as, for example, has happened with women's subsistence farming in relation to men's cash-crop production in many parts of Africa. Domestic work is rarely regarded by outsiders, or by women themselves, as having technical components, requiring technical skills and knowledge or as being an area in need of technical support, inputs or intervention (see Whitehead and Bloom, 1992). This, coupled with the fact that specialists identifying or developing technical assistance programmes are unlikely to have the skills necessary to analyse the technical components of women's work, means that women's technical expertise remains unrecognized, and the focus of technical intervention remains outside the household.

Third, technical assistance is not only dependent on which areas of work are considered technical, but also on perceptions of what comprises technology. Technical assistance by donors is identified and evaluated within a context defined by outsiders. The context usually derives from the commercially oriented provision of hardware, or transfer of technology, through export from the donor country to the recipient country (Mazza, 1987). The status derived from high-spending, hardware-focused technical programmes diverts attention from other areas of activity which may be less hardware dependent or contribute less directly to the cash economy. This has led to the devaluing of technical contributions which are dependent more on knowledge and skill than on the use of machinery and equipment.

Fourth, the fact that few women are involved in extension work, research and development or technical development planning has meant that there has been little challenging of assumptions made about the nature of productive roles and responsibilities, assumptions which have tended to undermine women's roles and technical capacities, and strengthen the view that technical development has to be brought in from outside. For example, a 1987 study on women's access to extension services conducted in Kenya, Malawi, Sierra Leone, Zambia and Zimbabwe, reveals common images of women held by men involved in agricultural extension work (Gill, 1987).

o Women do not make significant contributions to agriculture.
o Women are always tied down with household chores and children.

○ Women are shy and difficult to reach.
○ Women are difficult to gather together in one place, even if their interests converge.
○ Women are unprogressive in dealing with innovations.

Themes emerging from the research

Do It Herself and the Latin American programme, *Mujeres: Tecnólogas Invisibles* (Women: invisible technologists), provide 22 case studies of technical innovation by women from 16 countries in Africa, Asia and Latin America. All these countries and regions have very different histories, cultures, geography, and economic, social and political environments. Certain themes, however, emerged from all the regions as central to women's use, production and adaption of technology.

The technological worlds of women and men differ according to the social, economic, political, cultural and sexual relationships existing between them. These different worlds affect the ways in which women and men perceive technology, and use, adapt and control techniques and equipment. Compared to men, women in all the studies were disadvantaged in the amount of control that they had over their lives: they had less time available and less disposable income, had received less education, participated less in political decision-making, were less able to move about, interact with other technology users and obtain information. All these factors helped to constrain women's access to technological information and to new technologies. They also contributed to a lower self-image for women, which meant that neither women nor men regarded women as producers and users of technology or as having valuable technical skills and knowledge. On occasions, as López points out, this can lead to attempts to promote 'new' technologies, such as ham and sausage production in Tarapoto in Peru, without reference to existing skills in the curing of meat.

When existing knowledge is not recognized, its potential for helping to avert crises is not explored. Dirar describes the many techniques that Sudanese women have for preserving and adding nutritional value to foodstuffs. Nevertheless, drought and famine assistance to Sudan is based around products that are surplus to requirements in countries of the North, rather than the promotion of local skills and knowledge.

The lack of recognition of women's technical contributions also deprives national economies of the possibility of adding value to local production. In Ghana, for example, Wallace-Bruce points out that shea nuts are exported whole, where appropriate policies could instead encourage local production of shea butter for export, and thus improve benefits to small producers.

8

The issue of domestic violence is easily forgotten when work is focused around technology. Technology use and adaptation cannot be divorced from the rest of people's lives, however, and where domestic violence is an aspect of the relationships between women and men it limits women's ability to gain access to ideas and training, and to innovate. In Latin America, it was noted that one of the effects of technical change for women can be to strengthen them and enable them either to prevent violence in the home or to lead independent lives.

Women's knowledge of production processes is rational and is based on a logical framework of understanding. In Kenya and Nicaragua, Mutagaywa and Romeo who show women potters use their knowledge of the proportions of clay and other materials needed to make durable pottery products and fuel-efficient stoves. In Sudan, women produce foods using up to 40 different stages of fermentation but very little equipment. They understand and can explain why they carry out particular processes, and women who live hundreds of miles apart, with no apparent communication between them, perform identical technical steps. Each step can also be expressed in biochemical language.

The understanding that women have incorporates a knowledge of market conditions. From India, Shekar highlights the importance of the draping qualities of *charaka* silk, and shows how the innovations that women silk reelers helped to develop have maintained the fabric's essential characteristics. Government-sponsored innovations failed precisely because they failed to understand the marketable elements of *charaka* silk.

It is important to consider not only the *content* of what people know, but the knowledge systems within which information is used, because such systems underlie processes of problem diagnosis, experimentation and innovation. Women in all the case studies have their own language, understanding and experimental methods, which may differ from those of Northern scientific approaches and language, but which form detailed, logical and internally consistent frameworks of understanding. Colour, feel, consistency, temperature, appearance, sound and taste, are all means by which women test, experiment, explain, predict and adapt. Abeywardene describes how women processing *jak* and breadfruit in Sri Lanka, for instance, use the 'finger-nail' test for readiness before terminating blanching, and Lahai highlights the use of taste by women salt producers in Sierra Leone to judge the stage of crystallization reached when evaporating concentrated saline solution. Shea butter producers in northern Ghana use their hands as thermometers to maintain a constant temperature throughout the long kneading process.

The space in which women live affects patterns of production and modification and use of technology, as do circumstances such as national

9

disasters, conflicts, environmental changes and market demands. Survival in the city may impose a need for more rapid technical adaptation and change due to closer proximity to political decision-making, and changing fashions and market demands. Palao's descriptions of the experience of the women making *mecheros* (paraffin lamps) in Tacna, Peru, illustrate that the ability to adapt quickly to changing circumstances, and to adopt short-term solutions where necessary, can be as important as conventional technical skills.

Sometimes the more drastic the changes, the more innovative the solutions. Mpande and Mpofu show how the Tonga tribe's move to a poorer agro-ecological zone in Zimbabwe led women to start using wild plants in their diets. Similarly, in Uganda, after years of civil war, Simwogerere describes how women made use of the only available raw material, cassava (which had previously been an unpopular and low-status foodstuff), for food and drink, building material, medicine, glue and starch, both for household consumption and for sale.

In less-difficult circumstances, factors such as women's perception of market potential or the search for less laborious and/or more productive techniques may stimulate innovation: Shahjahan shows that women agriculturalists in Bangladesh were concerned to adapt equipment and techniques developed for men. Similarly, Alzuru's and Machicao's descriptions of vegetable production by hydroponics in Venezuela and of dried banana production in Bolivia, illustrate that the end products in both cases are regarded as useful additional sources of income, although neither form the mainstay of household survival.

The innovations which women make are based on their perceptions of the priorities in all aspects of their lives, and particularly on their understanding of the risks which are involved. Women's perceptions, use and adaptation of technology are shaped by their evaluation of risk. Decisions to reject particular technologies are often dismissed as signs of women being 'resistant to change' or 'conservative', but such decisions are based on women's knowledge of their environments, available resources, priorities and *the risks that they can afford to take.* Women have a wider portfolio of responsibilities and activities, including care of family and children, and they balance risks and priorities for technical innovation across all those activities.

For example, women potters in Nicaragua, and Thacker's women carpet weavers in Nepal, continue to sell their produce through middlemen because the income that this provides, though small, is secure. They cannot take the risk of establishing themselves independently. Women salt extractors in Sierra Leone rejected fuel-efficient two-burner chimney stoves because the cost of repairs by a blacksmith could mean the loss of a season's income. Tonga women in Zimbabwe and women working with

10

Ogana in Kenya continue to cultivate indigenous crops around their gardens, despite extension advice to the contrary, because they know that they can depend on the indigenous crops to provide food and possibly income, whereas exotic crops offer a less-reliable harvest. Similarly, the Chilean women studied by Bustamente were not prepared to disrupt family routines to use a fuel-improved cooker, the benefits of which they had not fully appreciated.

Technology development and innovation may mean enabling women to balance the risks of a newly introduced technology, perhaps by basing innovations around products that are known and accepted, such as Canto's and Sanabria's description of the production of sweets and popular snacks in the Peruvian highlands, but using local Andean rather than imported ingredients.

Risks may also be reduced by the organization of women around a production process, which often means a group of women sharing the load: for the women coir producers working with Peiris in Sri Lanka, organizing as a group enabled them to double their income, although the equipment that they used did not change. Arancibia's and Salinas's work with women builders of Santiago, Chile, shows that the women were able to take the risk of moving in an area of traditionally male activity because of the strength that they derived from their trade union. Organization may also support women who take risks by enabling the sharing of technical information and experimentation, as highlighted by women producers of paraffin lamps in Tacna, Peru.

Women's knowledge and skills in food production, processing and marketing play a crucial role in household livelihoods and food security. The importance of women's technological knowledge and skills in ensuring household food security is an issue identified in all case studies. Some of the clearest examples are the Tonga women's adaptations and modifications of local wild foods to cope with food shortages in Binga, as well as Ugandan women's use of cassava in providing their families with enough to eat. Also in Uganda, Wekiya illustrates how women use the *nkejje* fish to fight malnutrition.

There is a lack of focus on gender and indigenous technical knowledge in food security programmes, despite women's extensive role in food security in most countries. With support and encouragement, fermentation techniques in Sudan, and the adaptation and use of wild foods in Zimbabwe, have the potential to improve food supplies throughout the year, even when food is scarce.

Technical information and skills are communicated to women and between women using different channels. Survival of women's technological knowledge and skills depends on informal means of information

11

sharing and training. Information passes from mother to daughter, from grandmother to granddaughter, between friends and neighbours within communities, or between communities through marriage. Information of this type often exists only in local dialects or languages, and is rarely written down. Its dissemination is thus necessarily limited, often staying within a small geographical area except in the case of nomadic or pastoralist people. Many of the informal communication systems which maintain traditional skills are beginning to break down. The comparison from Kenya between the different amounts of information about indigenous plants held by a 25-year-old woman and by her grandmother, clearly demonstrates that valuable traditional information is being lost. There is need for support for the documentation and widespread dissemination of such information, similar to that being done in Kenya with indigenous plants.

The ways in which communities receive information from outside have changed considerably over the last 25 years. Urban areas and even villages may receive national newspapers and radio and television programmes. Women's access to these media will be affected by culture, status, time and literacy, but the information they receive will influence the way in which they perceive, use, adapt and adopt technology. As the Andean foods case study from Huancayo, Peru, illustrates, women themselves may provide a valuable link with other sources of information if they are educated outside of their communities, and subsequently move back to live and work.

The movement of information *out* of communities and, particularly, the potential for exchange of technological information between women in different countries has to be considered. Ugandan women have learnt some of the cassava-processing techniques through exchange visits to Ghana, and there is potential for exchanges of information on the uses of tamarind between Zimbabwe, where the fruit is available but underused, and countries in Asia, Latin America and Africa, where the fruit is used in many different ways.

The national policy environment affects the ways in which women use, adapt and adopt technology. Not one of the case studies is an example of women using and adapting technology in an isolated environment. All illustrate the effects of national, regional or international levels of policies and decision-making, and of information received from different sources. Local production systems will be affected by national decisions, as in the case of the Tonga women in Zimbabwe, whose move to Binga was originally prompted by the Kariba Dam scheme, and who are now threatened by a new proposal to clear the area of native trees and bushes to enable cash-crop production.

In addition to disrupting local production systems, policy decisions may have negative environmental consequences. An example of this is the near

12

extinction of the *nkejje* fish and the unrestricted growth of choking algae species in Lake Victoria.

Policies which are made and implemented regardless of local production systems may contribute to national disasters. Support for the cultivation of exotic crops instead of indigenous vegetables have, in various countries contributed to food security crises by helping to destroy the diversity on which people depend.

PART I

Latin America

Banana drying in Bolivia

XIMENA MACHICAO BARBERY

Background: welfare versus development

From the 1960s onwards, social policies (of various political tendencies) began to plan the 'incorporation of women into development' from the point of view of welfare which condemned women to being completely responsible for domestic duties and the family unit, and, therefore, to fulfilling the role of 'pillars of society'. That is why the state, the Church and NGOs (intermediaries) tried different programmes of food distribution in order to alleviate the effects of the economic crisis, and programmes of social promotion which 'tried' to elevate women from their backwardness by means of training them in domestic tasks, literacy courses and an orientation towards apoliticism and obedience to the husband (Montaño, 1992).

This vision remained even more pronounced in the 1970s. The queues for food support programmes were permanently added to by poorer and poorer women, both from rural and urban areas, who have no other alternative, and found, in this wrongly called 'incorporation into development', just another strategy for everyday survival.

Some NGOs or IPDs formed mostly by women start by recognizing the disadvantaged situation of women in relation to men in all aspects of public and private life; the multidimensionality of women as social entities is also taken into account, as well as the fact that the relationships established between men and women determine the situation of both in a society which discriminates for reasons of class, sex and culture.

Women on low income are assuming tasks and roles which are more and more diverse but which, although allowing them to improve the material living conditions of their families, do not necessarily lead to a change in their conditions in terms of economic, political, family and social disadvantage and inequality which they face every day. In other words, what

---

XIMENA MACHICAO BARBERY is a social scientist based in La Paz, Bolivia.

they achieve are slight improvements in their conditions, but without modifying their position. It is within this framework that we will try to analyse the experience of the Centre for the Rural Women of San Miguel Afuera, although, first, we will explain our methodology and present an overview of the situation of Bolivian women.

Methodology

Our method has consisted of investigating general aspects of the community and specifically the subjects related to the history of the Dehydration Plant project, its consolidation and the technology used in the preparation of *kissita* (a banana sweet). Opinions of the promoting organization and of the direct and indirect executors of the project was sought both from individuals and from the group.

The work was based on personal interviews, focal groups of both sexes, and testimonies. Also, a questionnaire called 'self-census' was used to gather information about general conditions in the community. Once the study was completed, the results were presented at a general meeting with the women and the community, in order to carry out a revision and to prepare the final copy of the document.

Social and demographic details[1]

Bolivia is a country situated in the heart of South America, with a maximum altitude of 6550 metres and a minimum depression of 100 metres. It is divided into three natural regions: the high plateau and the moorlands, with a cold climate; the valleys, with a temperate climate; and the plains and forests, with a tropical climate. Each of these regions has its own economic, social, cultural and ethnic characteristics, which distinguish them from each other and which give them their own identity and their particular richness.

The population of Bolivia is approximately six million, with a female fertility rate of 5 per cent. The population is made up of different cultures and ethnic groups: the *Aymaras*, the *Quechuas* and the *Guaraníes* are in the majority; then there are the creoles, the half-castes and the whites, and a number of minority ethnic groups situated particularly in the tropical regions. Although Spanish is the main language, the majority of Bolivians speak *Aymara, Quechua* or *Guaraní* as a mother tongue.

The policies of structural adjustment implemented in the country over the past few years have negatively affected the population as a whole. However, their most devastating effects have been noticed particularly by

1 All the social and demographic details used in the present study have been taken from Montaño, 1992.

poor women, because of their already difficult circumstances, discrimination and social differentiation has worsened. As a result, women are forced to look for, and engage in, new survival strategies (which prolong their already long working day), assuming more and more diverse roles which do not enable them to meet their basic needs completely, especially those related to health, education and leisure.

Health

The state of health of the population in general, and women in particular, demonstrates the great social, economic and sexual inequalities of Bolivian society. It has one of the highest child mortality rates under the age of five, with a rate of 160 per 1000 children born in 1990. Maternal mortality is also high. Another significant problem is low access to antenatal care.

For the most part, women do not use the health services, for different reasons: because these are few in rural areas; the distance; the cost; and the ill-treatment and discrimination to which they are subjected. Other reasons for the poor state of women's health are the difficult access to guidance on sex health issues and contraception; the non-existent prevention services for the control of cervical and breast cancer, sexually transmitted diseases, AIDS and nutritional deficiencies. Added to this, there are cultural and ideological reasons which overburden women with reproduction, work, communal and family responsibilities which undermine their mental and physical health and their right to take control of their lives, their health and their sexuality.

Education and work

In Bolivia, one out of every four women is illiterate. In general, women have less access to education, but the poorest have even more limited access, due to the structural elements of poverty (particularly in rural areas), which ensure that 'educating a women is not profitable'. It can also be seen that malnutrition and poor health are often the reasons for a poor performance at school and for dropping out. On the other hand, low levels of education in the family, and the traditional concept of the role of women as reproducers, mothers and self-sacrificing wives, limits the opportunity for developing their potential, capacity and creativity.

The economic model and the policies of adjustment have made possible, in the last few years, for women to increase the number of things they can do to develop different survival strategies, taking part both in the formal and informal economies, and in the services. In this way, in the period between 1985 and 1989, the female PEA (employment rate) grew 12 per cent a year.

In this respect, Silvia Escóbar, from the Centre for Labour and Devel-

19

opment Studies (CEDLA), says, 'the most significant thing about the case of Bolivia is that the dramatic increase in the female PEA (in the context of a recession), together with a greater segmentation of the labour market by the sexes, have resulted, in most cases, in effective occupation rather than in open unemployment' (Montaño, 1992). This may be explained by an increased involvement of women (especially from rural areas) in domestic services, and by the different existing activities which women can carry out (independently of the family environment) in the hope of improving their economic prospects.

This does not mean, however, that women are not predominantly immersed in the family and domestic sectors of the economy. In 1989, the following details were registered: women in the public sector counted for only 21 per cent; in the business sector they counted for 26 per cent; and in the semi-business sector, 33 per cent. These details indicate that much of women's work is informal.

This situation is basically due to two factors: on the one hand, the inability of the state and of its economic model to absorb the male and female workforce and to train it; and, on the other, as Escóbar points out, 'the division of roles between men and women, which is the basis for the division of labour, by means of which women are assigned a "natural" role and turned into "secondary" workers in extra-domestic production' (Montaño, 1992). Their work, therefore, is not valued or socially recognized, because it is based on the sexual division of labour and on gender discrimination.

Rural women

Peasant families, particularly in areas of colonization, constitute consumer and reproductive production units, whose members take part in the different activities this implies. In this context, women are involved in agricultural, craft and farming activities, as well as the exchange and commercialization of products—tasks which are complementary to their fundamental role as domestic workers. Although rural women are a vital part of this production process, their role is not acknowledged.

Factors such as inefficient education, the division of roles and long working hours, preclude the productive role of women ('as responsible for the family, temporal migrants, tradeswomen, processors of food for the market, producers of craftwork, reproducers of life and family workforces and, finally, as disseminators of culture and of mother tongues' (Montaño, 1992)) from being seen.

In rural areas, women are still unrecognized as 'legal entities', in spite of the laws to the contrary. In practice, if a woman wants access to credit, land and technical training, she must do so through her husband. A vast majority are not included in the national registers. An estimated 800 000 women are not registered citizens, and therefore have none of the rights of citizenship. Their autonomy and, what is more, their role as agents of development, as disseminators of traditional knowledge and technology, are therefore denied. All this results in a great negligence on the part of state, non-state and church policies, in terms of meeting the needs, demands and rights of women, especially regarding their health, education and work.

NGOs' activities with women

From the 1980s onwards, non-governmental organizations (NGOs) and Private Institutions for Social Development (IPDSs) began to be created in Bolivia devoted to the problems of women.

It is precisely through these organizations that analysis and work with women from different perspectives is carried out. On the one hand, there is a predominance of the welfare point of view, but, on the other hand, the gender perspective is stronger. Nowadays, there are 136 NGOs and IPDSs which work specifically with women in the whole country, 78 per cent of them are non-governmental organizations. Of these, 24 per cent are in rural areas, 45 per cent work both in rural and urban areas, and 31 per cent work exclusively in the cities. Their activities are mostly focused on health and education, particularly in prevention and promotion and training.

With the worsening economic crisis, a number of non-governmental initiatives have sprung up, the objective of which is to 'help' women with credits, training and, in other cases, technical assistance in the context of production projects. These have largely had an important social impact with regard to organizational strength and technical training, but not so in terms of profitability and long life. It is in this context that the work in San Miguel Afuera should be viewed.

Characteristics of the group

The Group of Rural Women of San Miguel Afuera has a long history as an organization. According to Señora Hilda Burgos (current president and founder of the group 15 years ago), at the beginning, the women organized themselves of their own accord in order to have a framework in which to meet and also in order to learn how to knit and weave. Later they took part in the well-known Mothers' Clubs, groups organized through the food charity programme, Food for Peace, of CARITAS (an institution for the promotion, action and assistance of the Bolivian Catholic Church).

Dedicated to the subject of food donations, about 369 Mothers' Clubs were created in the 1970s in different communities in eight provinces in the Department of Santa Cruz. The distribution of food was carried out as aid to the poorest social sectors, especially in rural areas.

In the 1980s there was a change in focus. CARITAS introduced a new

21

philosophy to its charity work: the promotion of women. At the same time, the organization started a process of reflection, which determined the new point of view that food donations not only do not strengthen national production, but in fact are more likely to weaken it. In this way, they began to reduce slowly the amounts of food donated and start a process of 'monetization'.

Alfonso Martínez, Director of CARITAS in Santa Cruz, says: 'In 1984 we decided to change from being an institution which only distributed food, to having a policy of people support, meaning orientating them towards managing their own development, improving their quality of life by producing what they can and need, especially in rural areas.'

There is no doubt that CARITAS in Santa Cruz took a qualitative leap forwards when they initiated this important process of reflection and change in their work of help and promotion. One aspect that needs emphasis is the momentum given to organizations so that they could turn from being passive, food-receiving structures to more dynamic structures with the chance to choose their own activities. Another has to do with the organization itself: the only positive result of food distribution in Bolivia in general, and in the area of this study in particular, was that it encouraged the creation of women's organizations. This was the basis for the creation of a new kind of organization geared towards production, with a view to improving the economic resources and to preparing the work-force for increased involvement in the labour market. The new approach of CARITAS began to be implemented in organized zones called sub-centres (meaning the union of several Mothers' Clubs) and areas which did not have the support of other organizations.

Caranda was one chosen area. It had a sub-centre which included 10 mothers' centres deprived of institutional support but full of women prepared to work hard. At the beginning of 1986, a study of the production reality of the area was carried out. The study proved that Caranda is a prime area for cultivation, especially citrus, and it is also a strong region for banana production. Because of the bad roads and poor transport services, the fruit in general and banana in particular goes bad. By the time they get to the market, they have to be sold well under their earlier value. This is how the idea of processing the food came about. Different products were tried: jams, vinegar, juices. Finally the idea arose for making a banana dehydration plant. At the beginning, the project proposed the implementation of three small food processing companies: one dedicated to making banana *kissa* (a preserve made with banana flour), and the other two dedicated to other products, the preparation of which needed a deeper study.

The Catholic Relief Service supported the banana dehydration plant which, from the beginning, incorporated the notion of intermediate technology. The social basis for the project was the women's organization. The project was given the name PROCAL—*Productora Integral Campesina de Alimentos* meaning Women's Integral Rural Food Company. PROCAL was formed by 10 communities from the Caranda area around the banana dehydration plant. It expanded its activities later to include agriculture; nurseries and the improvement of traditional methods to cultivate corn and rice; *urucu* stocks; and a cheese processing plant which started operating in 1991.

Caranda produces different varieties of bananas, and the *hualele* variety is the best for the preparation of *kissa* (banana preserve). It is the one with the strongest flavour, but it is also the most scarce. That is why the idea arose for the members of PROCAL (about 50 families) to begin growing the *hualeles* in their plots, in order to supply the plant, situated in the community of San Miguel Afuera. The plant would buy the produce from them, and the families would generate a direct income. At present they have 20 hectares of *hualele*, which do not yet completely meet the needs of the plant, which is consequently working below capacity.

Organization

The Centre of Rural Women of San Miguel Afuera, as part of PROCAL, gave the project its momentum. The main activities were organized around the group, formed by 13 families, who took part directly in the different stages of the production process.

In order to become members of the dehydration plant, the women must spend, each month, 20 working days of six to eight hours, carrying out activities which range from working at the storehouse to the preparation, promotion and selling of the product. The work is carried out by family groups of four people. Women are normally responsible for the oven and the whole preparation process. Each family group works in turns, up to six times a month, so that all groups take part. If it is a group's turn and they cannot work, another one is called in its place. Many times, work groups have been called from among the neighbours, but the main characteristic is the rotation of groups constituted by members of the same family.

Economy

The dehydration plant started work in mid-1989 with the support of CARITAS. This organization managed the resources for the acquisition of heavy equipment, burners, carafes, a sealing machine, furniture and the co-operative's capital. The community contributed with the local materials and the work-force to build the drier and the plant's outbuildings.

The project has an administrator, responsible for purchasing raw materials, and for programming and calling together the work groups. Also,

23

several improvements to the project were possible thanks to a loan given by CARITAS, which is being paid off at 10 per cent of the monthly profits.

The income

The plant has a total production capacity of 3000 units every 48 hours. Due to the shortage of raw material, maximum production is 2500, while minimum production is 800. There is a pay scale for the groups, depending on the number of units they produce. If they process 3000 bananas, the pay is about US$15: $8 for the group leader and $2.50 for each member of the group. With six turns a month, each group can earn an income of about $87. If production is only 2500 units, however, the pay is only $12, and so on.

Stock is controlled by means of registers designed according to the requirements of the organization. The instruments used are: account books, control of each account, control of raw material purchases, control of processes and a record of sales. As a document to record decisions, there is a minutes book and also the reports by the people responsible for finances, for the production process and by the general administrator of the project.

Education and communication

CARITAS was directly involved in the education activities, from literacy to advice and training in production projects (the use of technology, administration/organization and accountancy) by means of different work-shops designed according to the requirements of the organization.

Starting with the production project, an integral training programme was created, including health workshops and others related to the needs not only of the project, but of the community as a whole.

The production stages

The preparation of *kissa* has six stages:

○ Buying and ripening of the raw material.
○ Peeling, grating and laying in trays.
○ Deyhdration (turning over and temperature control).
○ Cooling.
○ Selection and packaging.
○ Selling.

The purchasing and storing of bananas is carried out once the producers associated with PROCAL tell the Plant what their production of *hualele* has been, so that this is taken into account in the buying plan. Usually a bunch of bananas is sold to the plant for about $0.72.

Next, unripe bananas are put in the ripening room (in ideal quantities of 100 to 150 bunches), taking care to avoid sudden changes of temperature. The product is constantly monitored and later it is selected and processed. Ripening depends, above all, on the climate. The ripening time of unripe bananas is 12 to 15 days, and it is not until the seventh day that the first selection is done. Optimum ripeness can be gauged from the colour, which must be yellow with black spots. The texture must be soft to the touch.

The banana peel is taken off, and then the fruit is scraped with a knife, in order to remove the first layer of pulp so that the surface is smoother when exposed to hot air. The laying is done by arranging 80 to 100 peeled and scraped bananas on each tray. Between four and six women take part in this activity. Complete drying takes about seven to eight hours.

The drier is a small oven made of iron and clay. Inside it there is a metal ladder to hold the trays. Once the trays are in the oven, hot air is circulated by forced convection. This is achieved by means of a fan which sends cold

The peeled and scraped bananas are placed on trays and dried in a hot oven for seven to eight hours

air to the conduit where the burners are. These work by pressurized liquid gas, and heat the air gradually before circulating it inside the oven. The drying process normally takes 24 hours. Two women monitor it all the time.

The temperature is controlled constantly by regulating the flame in the burners. The food must be turned over every four hours, changing the temperature from 45°C to 90°C.

Once the drying is finished, between five and eight hours are necessary for the product to cool. It must be turned constantly in order to facilitate the process.

The selection process consists of sorting the product by size before packaging it in polythene bags. The product is then packed in bags of one, half and a quarter of a dozen. Each bag has a label with the logo of the organization and the packaging date. The packets are sealed with the aid of an electric sealing machine. The process of classification, packaging, sealing and boxing of the product before being sent to the market takes between six and eight hours, and it is done by four to six women. Not taking into account the time used in the buying and ripening of *hualele*, the dehydration process takes 40 hours in total, which, with the time spent selecting and packaging, adds up to 48 hours of continuous work.

Next, the woman in charge of the preparation process hands the product over to the project's administrator, who registers the amounts before the products are taken by those responsible for selling them.

Marketing is carried out through intermediaries, shops and direct selling. CARITAS also helps with distribution by opening markets in other departments such as Sucre and Bolivia's capital, La Paz.

The project's impact

The project has already had a big impact in the area. The production of *hualele* banana has increased in eight communities because the producers now have a direct market for their raw material. Other additional benefits for the people involved in marketing and selling were also created. Finally, by having set up a new activity in the area, the dehydration plant has become an example for other communities to set up similar projects.

In sum, the greatest impact of the project has been on the women. The consolidation of the organization through a job qualitatively different from the ones they had been doing before, and the participation of the women in intermediate technology, was a move forward with regard to the position of women in the community.

Problems and limitations

The main problem is the insufficient supply of raw material, stemming from three main reasons:

26

o The area where the project is does not produce *hualele*. Although PROCAL's members began growing it in order to supply the plant, the amounts produced are not enough so far. This situation is aggravated when a bad year brings big losses in production.

o There is a considerable distance between the deyhdration plant and the plantations. The precarious road infrastructure and the lack of any regular transport aggravate this.

o A third problem has to do with marketing. The fact that there is no permanent production (because of the lack of raw material) prevents the project from having a regular market. As a consequence, economic resources are below expectations, and people are demoralized. This also prevents new members from participating in the project.

It is important to emphasize that Caranda and the community of San Miguel Afuera are areas with a high degree of illiteracy, where notions of training are barely assimilated. This situation explains why a majority of the community does not want to accept responsibilities, and why people with some education keep their managerial positions almost permanently.

Another difficulty lies in the donation of food. For years, the women in the area have been receiving foodstuffs. However, the leap from receivers to producers is a difficult one. 'They always expect to be given something first' before starting to work. Although this feeling was not explicit during the investigation, it is not a coincidence that food donations are still seen as one more alternative in their different survival strategies.

The project three years on

It has been three years and four months since the banana dehydration project began. During this time, significant organizational advances resulted in the consolidation of the Centre of Rural Women as a production unit. The centre gained a reputation in the community and, above all, created a framework for participation, assimilation, technology learning and self-respect for the women who take an active part in it. María Soliz Sosa, a member of the group, said:

'I feel proud of having learnt, because I was already old. I can see good things. This year we'll progress. That's why I'm telling my *compañeras* [fellow workers] we must not lose heart, that we must keep working together for the progress of our project.'

In terms of income, the project has not, according to the people interviewed, generated the expected results. This has resulted in the discouragement of the people involved and in the scepticism of other members of the community who had been interested in taking part in the project. Lately, this has meant that only 13 families are taking part. On the other hand, the production of *hualele* banana increased, which mean indirect benefits for

27

approximately 50 families by providing them with a market and stable prices for their product.

As a 'small company', the project is a member of the Association of Small Businesses (ADEPI), in the food sector. Through this association, the group took part in different regional, departmental and national fairs, in which the quality of their product was commended. In 1992, the *kissa* project won the $3000 national prize, 'Women and Food Technology', which was used to solve some of the problems faced by the plant.

The production of raw material is insufficient, and, on the other, the bad state of the roads and the lack of transport has often prevented the bananas that are grown from getting to the plant, forcing the suspension of production. For this reason, efforts are being taken in order to have a plot with adequate soil in the community, so that a new variety of banana (Cavendish Giant) can be grown. This has better properties for the preparation of *kissa*, and is the same size. They have also tried to solve the problem of transport by purchasing a horse-drawn cart.

Until now San Miguel Afuera has had no drinking-water. Some families have water-wheels and ponds, which have been used by the plant. Because this is insufficient, however, it has been necessary to dig a well, 28m deep due to the groundwater level of the area.

Minor infrastructure repairs have been carried out, such as whitewashing walls, putting bricks on the floors, and repairing windows. Also, the plant has been equipped with utensils and tools (containers, cleaning equipment, thermometers and preservatives) which enable better preparation and control of the product.

A really deficient aspect is that of distribution and sale. There is no coherent policy which guarantees, on the one hand, a permanent production for sale in the markets where the product is known, and which, at the same time, opens new markets with adequate local and national promotion. At the moment, the product does not have a permanent local presence, and only very occasionally it is present at a national level, through the different fairs the plant attends. That is why a promotional campaign has been planned, with improved presentation and packaging, posters and a portable stand to be taken to the different fairs and events.

The plant has a small amount of operating capital and a fund for training expenses, used if the need arises to store raw material. Visits to other projects, and courses in technological training and project administration have been planned, with a view to strengthening and improving the different stages of the preparation and the quality of the product.

Perspectives

The women benefited directly from the project; the institutional promoters and the community in general look to the future with confidence. Solving the problem of supplies will guarantee greater and more permanent income for the families involved. One of the members of the group said, with great optimism, that 'the dehydration plant will improve its situation this year. We plan to grow more bananas so that there are no shortages, since this is the biggest problem. We have already planted, and it is going to give good results.'

As for the difficulties in marketing, Antonio Vargas (a project technician), explains: 'The prospects are good. Although there have been some difficulties with the commercialization part, that has not influenced the overall functioning of the project, and, as soon as the problem of supplies is solved, we can start thinking about improving sales and also about preparing other kinds of products. To this end, it is necessary that the women and the community understand that this is a small business, that our technology ensures a quality, competitive product.' Pepita Hernández, Executive Secretary of CARITAS, added: 'The project can be profitable if they work hard in order to make of it a source of income, not only for the people at the plant, but also for those involved in producing the raw material. . . . In the short run, the economic prospects are low. There will be no big profits. Production must be carried out in stages and in a certain order, thus generating the commercial idea. If there is production and quality, there are sales, and this is very important.'

It will be possible to define a coherent marketing policy by ensuring a capacity for permanent production which adapts itself to changes in the market-place. On the other hand, in spite of the fact that the Centre for the Rural Women of San Miguel Afuera is a consolidated organization, weaknesses have been found in the way they adapt to the new situation, since it is not easy to move from a welfare structure to a production structure without changing its very foundations. The exclusive, authoritarian and non-participative practices which characterized their previous stages are not the best groundwork for the development, training and strengthening of a new kind of 'female' leadership: one that ensures democracy. There is a long way to go in this respect, although this does not mean neglecting the importance of the presence of the women, who have been fighting for years to improve their quality of life and that of their community.

Women and training

In general, it is very rare to encounter projects involving technological innovation (in communities characterized by their poverty) which have resulted in permanent and stable social and economic development. They are rather circumstantial experiences, which, in general, stem from the immediate needs of the population and from what a group of people can do. In view of this situation, the 'use of technology' or 'the implementation of technological innovations' are used in order to improve and widen this set of knowledge. The first option includes, among other things, the dissemination of information, the use of machinery, the structuring of a kind of social organization which guarantees the development of a production process. The second option might mean all the changes be carried out in order to improve specific knowledge and hence to achieve better results. In short, the idea is to introduce a new technological production activity, which recaptures the knowledge of the population for their own 'benefit'.

There is no doubt that an important role is played by the interests of private or public technical/organizational/educative support or financing institutions which are behind the implementation of this kind of project. Such interests are not, in most cases, contrary to the interests of the population. However, they limit development opportunities when they do not take into account the set of cultural, political, social, economic and gender relations (that is, structural conditions) which are defined by a concrete technology, finally affecting the success or failure of its incorporation into the everyday life of the 'beneficiary' groups. 'Technology is then seen as a closed universe, a stranger to the relationship between human beings, social groups, and the economic and political power; or indifferent to the values of the population benefiting. So conceived, this or that technology would be justified by eminently instrumental reasons. This is how technology is presented to the modern world' (Maskrey and Rochabrun, 1990). This is how it is introduced to most of the projects, even where the so-called 'beneficiaries' are vulnerable groups, subject to multiple risks, living in uncertainty and fighting for survival.

Can the organizations using a specific technology guarantee a new exercise of democratic development, of equal relationships, of knowledge dissemination, of collective decision-making and of equality between the sexes, or will they tend rather to become institutions which, by means of 'knowledge', consolidate practices of authoritarianism and the perpetuation of the roles assigned to men and women by society?

Intermediate technology and innovation

CEDETI (Centre for Intermediate Technology) was the organization which CARITAS contacted in order to initiate the training process (with the women of the Centre of San Miguel Afuera) in the use of intermediate technology in the preparation of *kissa* or dehydrated banana. The process was not complicated. It consisted of recapturing the knowledge of the women and the community with regard to the traditional method for the dehydration of banana in big firewood ovens or by exposure to the sun. The technological innovation was the use of a banana drier or dehydration machine, which works as a gas oven, and of the forced convection air flow created by an electric fan.

30

The drier was constructed using local materials such as clay and straw. Only the supporting structure is made of metal. The trays are made of *chuchio* (a local variety of bamboo). Other tools include a metal knife for the scraping and peeling of the bananas, and polythene bags for a more presentable packaging. Manual sealing was substituted for by an electric machine. The dehydration room was constructed by the community with significant help from the women.

Traditional knowledge of the dehydration of different fruits and of bananas in particular, the women's will to work, and the technological innovation which meant the introduction of forced convection, liquid gas and electricity, all allowed them to improve the preparation of an indigenous product with a view to selling it. The time normally taken by the whole process was reduced by a third, and the space needed was reduced to half of what was used before. A quicker, more efficient, more hygienic process was achieved, resulting in increased production.

Intermediate technology used in the area is based on the combination of what the community can do and the use of gas and electricity (which are supplied in the area) in order to improve their capacity. 'Caranda is a gas-producing area and the community uses it as fuel. The cost of a gas bottle does not affect the total cost, and the process is much faster than with solar energy. There was the security that gas would never be lacking and that it was cheap. A drier fuelled by solar energy would have been much more expensive,' say the promoters of the project.

Assimilation and adaptation of technology by the women

The training process was not complicated or long. The women were merely learning to do better what they already knew how to do. 'The women had no problem assimilating technology. They are even improving it, in the sense that they are making it more efficient. If, before, some instruments were used to measure the temperature, they have become so skilful now that they do that by 'listening' to the burner and by watching the drying process'. The practical assimilation of intermediate technology is self-evident. The group assume technology as their own through the training that CEDETI gave to a group of leaders. These women were later the direct disseminators of what they had learnt to the rest of the women.

Their sense of technology assimilation is based on the possibility of 'teaching what they have learnt to other women', and they say that with pride and with the certainty that the new knowledge is not complicated, that it is easy to implement, and besides, that gives status and legitimacy to their leadership. However, due to the fact that the project has, from the very beginning, been implemented with the economic support of outside agents, and that so far it has not been in a position to capitalize in order to become self-sufficient, the direct beneficiaries do not feel the project is entirely theirs, because they still owe money to CARITAS. Fortunately, they think differently about the technology they have learnt to use, because they know they can use it in other situations.

Intermediate technology in the women's everyday life

Technological innovation takes place in a family context which determines the roles and responsibilities socially assigned to men and women. Although it is true that these roles are not as strict nowadays (especially in rural areas), thanks to the activities of women in the public sphere (organizations, the community and the agricultural work), it is also true that their fundamental role revolves around being mothers, wives and domestic workers. The conditions which go beyond the private sphere and extend to other activities benefiting the family as a whole, have not extended to the democratization of domestic roles in the family.

The women in the community of San Miguel Afuera have, as an almost exclusive responsibility, the collection of firewood for the preparation of meals, an activity which requires physical strength, time and certain climatic conditions. With the arrival of gas, firewood is unnecessary in many households. This, by saving time and effort, especially with regard to cooking, has had a positive effect on the everyday work of women. The weather stopped being an obstacle in the supply of fuel, thanks to gas equipment.

The work women do at the dehydration plant has not significantly altered their family and agricultural responsibilities. It has had an effect, however, on the distribution of their time, since they have to complete all their tasks. This means longer working days, and working at night. On the other hand, although the whole family takes part in the agricultural work (in which the women play a 'complementary' role), nowadays it is men (and the children) who many times help with the work at the dehydration plant. In this way, there is an inversion of the 'complementary roles', thus creating a non-traditional framework for family participation which is incorporated in a 'natural' way to the everyday lives of the family members.

Although it is true that the income generated so far has not fulfilled the expectations of the direct beneficiaries, it is also true that the amount they have received by way of salaries has made a significant difference to their lives. This is also the reason for the recognition, on the part of the family members, of the women's work. To the women, this is an important achievement, in the sense of sharing with their husbands: the contribution to the household income, and the domestic tasks, especially with regard to the care of the smaller children, and to the preparation of meals, time permitting.

Technological perspectives

The project is not planning to expand, nor to increase its production capacity. Therefore, the incorporation of new technology will not be necessary. What it aims to achieve, however, is for the intermediate technology used to date to be used in the most efficient way, and be developed under the best conditions in order to gain a stable and permanent market. To this end, they plan to have the plant working to full capacity once the problems described above are solved.

Efficient domestic fuel use in Chile

WALDO BUSTAMANTE GOMEZ

The present study was carried out in Nuevo Amanecer (municipality of La Florida, Metropolitan Region of Chile). In this *población* (a marginal urban settlement), the Centre for Experimentation and Development in Applied Technology (TEKHNE) implemented a development programme for the efficient use of domestic fuel. The first stage took place between November 1991 and January 1992, and the second stage between October and December 1992. Twenty women (10 per stage) took part.

The programme consisted mainly of teaching some techniques and technologies appropriate to the implementation of an efficient use of domestic fuel. These included the making of a solar energy-fuelled water heating device, and of a *cocina bruja* or 'witch stove', which retains the heat and enables the subsequent cooking of pre-heated food. The programme sought to teach the participants how to make an efficient use of domestic fuel in order to improve their living conditions in their homes. The programme included different techniques and technologies, always seeking to investigate those more acceptable to the population.

This study sought to discover whether the techniques and technologies taught have been incorporated into the everyday domestic tasks of the participating women. At the same time, the study sought to discover the incidence of the impact caused by the use of the techniques, and by the recommendations made at the course, as well as explanations for the results obtained.

The methodology included interviews with 10 women in their homes. These interviews were carried out by means of a questionnaire, which investigated how and why the techniques and technologies taught were being used, and how (if at all) they had been changed. The professionals from TEKHNE who were responsible for the programme were also inter-

WALDO BUSTAMANTE GÓMEZ is director of TEKHNE—the Centre for Experimentation and Training on Appropriate Technology—based in Santiago, which aims to improve the development of technology based on existing resources.

viewed, with a view to analysing the programme's contents and the results expected from it.

Background

In Latin America, the consequences of economic crisis affects mainly women (especially in poorer groups). This could be due to the fact that economic crisis has a great impact on the living conditions of families—altering them quite dramatically in some situations. As a result of this, women adopt a pro-active attitude in trying to meet the basic needs of their families—something which requires a great deal of effort.

Although, in the case of Chile, the social and economic situation has been showing signs of improvement in the past few years (by comparison with the previous decade), the effects of the crisis among poorer people still persist. The 'social cost' has left deep marks on the faces of the poor which will be difficult to erase.

During the military dictatorship (1973–90), unemployment was high in the country. Under these circumstances, women had to make a greater effort to be able to take care of their children's education, health and well-being. This situation has remained substantially the same for the mass of the poorest in the population, because the social and economic changes of the past few years have not affected them significantly. At the beginning of the present democratic regime (March 1990), there were five million people living in poverty. According to official records, this figure has now decreased to 4.2 million, of whom 1.75 million live in a state of abject poverty. Chile's present total population is estimated to be around 13.5 million.

Women have assumed vital responsibilities (cooking, cleaning, washing, and the like) in ensuring their households' upkeep with generally scarce resources. They have also been forced to look for new ways of generating income, which is the origin of popular economic organizations such as labour workshops, communal shopping and health groups. One immediate consequence of this activity is a much longer working day for the women.

There is, however, a positive aspect to this. Great strength is evident in the women who, due to the unfavourable economic situation, knocked down the 'four walls of the house' and took an active part in the tough social and political activism of the military regime years.

Although this cultural change is difficult to quantify, it has to be taken into account when trying to appraise the changes in the women's roles (in the context of the family) which took place as a consequence of the economic crisis. It must not be forgotten that women, especially poorer ones, have historically been 'confined' to carrying out domestic-related duties, with two exceptions: parents' meetings at the schools, and participation in church activities. These are considered to be women's activities.

It was in this dual context (economic crisis and the role of women) that TEKHNE's Programme of Development for an Efficient Use of Domestic Fuel took place. It has always been women who have shown the most interest in these kind of programmes, because they saw new possibilities of improving their families' quality of life.

Energy consumption

The country spends about 3000 million dollars a year in fuel. In 1990, 32 per cent of this fuel was used by the Commercial, Public and Residential sector. Energy efficiency in this sector is only 35 per cent. The fuel used most by this section is firewood (52.8 per cent in 1990), followed by liquid gas (18.2 per cent) and electricity (12.7 per cent.)[1]

Surveys carried out in 1977 determined that, for the two poorest sections of the population, energy spending came second in importance after food. It should, however, be pointed out here that all food-preparation activities are related to the use of some kind of energy.

Table 1. Distribution of family spending by social sectors

Expense	Sectors (%)				
	1st	2nd	3rd	4th	5th
Food and drink	59.4	56.1	53.2	47.7	32.1
Fuel	7.6	5.6	5.4	4.4	3.1

Source: National Institute for Statistics, 1977.[2]

In the poorest areas of Santiago, between 8 and 30 per cent of total family income is estimated to be spent on fuel.[3] Other studies of similar population sections in the city showed that '30 per cent of the families surveyed spend 60 per cent of their income on fuel.'[4] The types of fuel most commonly used by the poor are liquid gas (for cooking), kerosene (for heating) and firewood. Energy consumption depends on whether the families live in urban or rural areas.

In cities, especially those areas inhabited by the poorest families, the consumption of firewood is changeable, and apparently depends on the level of income of the families and on the location of their homes. If the families live near trees or bushes, building sites, or wooden huts, their consumption of firewood is higher. In Nuevo Amanecer, for example, a 1986 survey showed that the families in the area consumed on average 1.6 tonnes of firewood a year.[5] This has probably changed in the past few years. The poorest sections of the community can, however, still be seen carrying wood from the nearby huts to feed their wood and coal stoves.

It can be concluded that families spend according to their income and not their needs. A survey carried out in Santiago observed: 'The amount spent on fuel changes radically, depending on the level of income of the families, and not on their size (and their food preparation needs), or on the size and quality of their homes (and their heating needs)'.[4] According to this, a programme aimed at improving the efficiency of domestic fuel use may result in an improvement in the living conditions of the participating families.

Despite the many possibilities afforded by programmes of cost-effective fuel use for the poorest sectors of society, it is only in the past few years that the government has begun to implement these programmes—with very few resources earmarked for the purpose.

The programme of training in domesic fuel saving

A development programme of this nature confronts three important elements: first, the fuel-consumption habits of the poorest sectors; second, the women's traditional (and expected) behaviour; and third, making sure that assimilating the new technologies does not mean an additional burden to the duties and responsibilities already assigned to women by society. Any change in habits can only be attainable in the long run, and can hardly be achieved in the course of an intensive, or a one-day-a-week, development programme.

La Florida

The details presented next were obtained by means of a study carried out by the Community Planning Secretariat of La Florida. This study was published by the Municipality of La Florida in the 'Pladeco Community Prognosis' in January 1993.[6] The Community of La Florida, belonging to Chile's Metropolitan Region, has an area of 7350 hectares, of which 3596ha is classified as urban. The community has 334 366 inhabitants, according to the April 1992 Census.

Conditions and history

In La Florida the past few decades, there has been an important increase in the urban population, with a subsequent decline in the traditionally more dominant rural population. The Population and Housing Census of 1960 showed that 37.2 per cent of the population (of a total 18 734) was rural. By the 1992 Census, however, only 0.04 per cent (of a total 334 366) were shown as rural.

At the beginning of the 1970s, the area started to expand, with the building of small houses, co-operative housing and private lots. By the

37

end of the 1970s, the state gave an impetus to the urban development of the area, by means of the towns built by the Housing Corporation (CORVI), the 'Operation Site', or the construction of 'emergency housing' for sections of the poor. Many 'land occupations' by homeless people also took place, which were generally tolerated by the authorities.

In the 1970s, five large towns (including Nuevo Amanecer) were built for people displaced from other communities. The military coup of 1973 meant an end to the 'land occupations' and a tight control of the already occupied ones. In some cases, the settlers were moved to other communities of Santiago. From 1976, the state began to play a secondary role in the construction of homes, and the private sector became more active. Numerous residential towns for the middle-income population appeared.

Población Nuevo Amanecer

Nuevo Amanecer has its origins in a massive land occupation in July 1970. Most of the 1700 families that took part came from the southern part of Santiago. These land occupations, known as Ranquil, Magaly Honorato and Elmo Catalán, were the beginnings of the Encampment Nueva La Habana, as the settlers were moved to land assigned to them in an attempt to give a lasting solution to the problem of housing. The Encampment Nueva La Habana, now called Nuevo Amanecer, was situated in the Community of La Florida, in the eastern part of Santiago.

The settlers' organization

At the beginning of the occupation, the settlers organized themselves by blocks and by 'fronts' (meaning the specific activities carried out in the areas of health, housing and leisure).[7] The encampment's organizational structure also included the leadership, the directory and the governing body. 'The leadership was formed by seven people, universally elected by all the settlers over 10 years of age. To be a candidate for the leadership it was necessary to be legitimated and supported by some organization, especially the blocks.[7]

The government of the time (President Salvador Allende), began the construction of 1284 homes for the encampment's settlers, through the state Housing Corporation (CORVI). In this way, the objective which had been embodied in the origins of the occupation (decent, owned homes) was achieved.

It is important to emphasize the method used in the construction of the houses; the settlers took an active part in it, expressing their opinions about the planning of the area and the design of the houses. The plans were discussed and analysed in meetings with the settlers. They also took part in the construction. To facilitate this, some of them attended development courses, which gave them the opportunity to gain a vocational qualification. The entire process (the occupation, the organization, the construction of the houses) left an indelible mark on the settlers. It is an experience they will cherish all their lives.

The military coup

The military coup of September 1973 resulted in the termination of the settlers' organizations. In fact, it was one of the objectives of the military government to put an end to these popular organizations. As a result, the sole function of the encampment's new governing body was to collect the social and burial fees. The settlers lived with a permanent fear of being moved out to other areas of Santiago. This, and their terror of the military, resulted in the settlers' passivity. This attitude is understandable. 'We did nothing. How could we, when we were never sure if we were going to stay?'

The new popular organizations

Although the military government tried to put an end to popular organizations, it was only partly successful. Some disappeared while others grew stronger. In the course of the years, new organizations such as Labour Workshops, *Comprando Juntos* (buying co-operative), Popular Canteens and others were created, originating what was known as the Popular Economic Organizations.[8] One important characteristic of these organizations was the high participation of women. This broke the tradition prior to the coup, when the organizations in the encampment were led by men, with only a very limited participation by the women.

It is thanks to women that popular organizations were kept alive through the darkest years of the military regime, and their levels of participation remained essentially unchanged until the early 1980s.

Present characteristics

Nuevo Amanecer has 15 000 inhabitants who occupy a total of 3000 homes. The rate of inhabitants per home is therefore 4.5, higher than in the La Florida where it is 4.14. As for the age of the settlers, 64 per cent of the residents of Nuevo Amanecer are under 30.[6] Nuevo Amanecer has been growing fast in the past few years. The population density is very high (163.5 inhabitants per hectare). Almost all homes (95 per cent) have a meter-controlled electricity supply.

There are three neighbourhood committees with a total of 1656 members over 18, which is approximately 18 per cent of the adult population. There

39

are also seven neighbourhood groups, four *Comités de Allegados* (committees of relatives), a popular canteen and a children's refectory.

Development and domestic fuel

A Programme of Development in the Efficient use of Domestic Fuel was carried out in two stages: the first took place between November 1991 and January 1992, and the second, between October and December 1992. Twenty women from Nuevo Amanecer took part, of whom 10 were interviewed for this study. The main objective of the programme was to teach the participating women the necessary techniques and technologies for a more efficient use of domestic fuel, with a view to improving the social and economic conditions of their respective families. Together with learning how to make and use devices for a more efficient use of fuel, the participants were expected to change and/or improve certain patterns of behaviour which result in wasteful use of energy.

By bringing in this programme, the organizers wanted to show the possibilities that exist for an improvement of the living conditions of the families in Nuevo Amanecer. They also wanted to appraise the level of social acceptability of the programme's contents.

Contents of the programme

The programme consisted of 10 sessions of two and a half hours each. Approximately 60 per cent of the time allocated to each session was devoted to practice. The programme was structured in four parts:

o Food preparation;
o Electricity;
o Water;
o Thermal insulation of the homes.

These are some of the guidelines given in the course to do with food preparation and water heating.

o To use as little water as possible when cooking.
o To be aware that any cooker's oven consumes more energy than its hobs.
o To keep the cooker (both oven and hobs) clean always.
o When possible, to use a pressure cooker.
o To avoid pre-heating the oven.
o To defrost the food before cooking.
o To use ceramic and earthenware pots.
o To steam rather than boil the vegetables.
o To lower the heat once the water in which the food is cooked has boiled.

Women use the solar water heater and cocina bruja *to save fuel and time*

The women were also taught how to build and use a *cocina bruja* or witch's stove and a solar water heater. The *cocina bruja* consists of a box which can be made of cardboard and in which pots can be kept at relatively high temperatures for long periods of time. Between the pot and the box, chopped newspaper acts as thermal insulating material.

The solar water heater consists of a thermally insulated box, covered in polythene, in which black-painted bottles are placed.

Lighting was also covered by the programme. Practical advice given to the women in this subject included the recommendation of the use of fluorescent lighting in the kitchen and bathroom.

41

Refrigeration was another topic the programme included. The women were taught how to know whether the fridge is hermetically closed, how to defrost it and how to clean the condenser. They were also told why it is inadvisable to keep hot food or uncapped liquid containers in the fridge. Finally, among other recommendations, they were told about the benefits of emptying and defrosting the fridge if it is not going to be used for a long period of time.

The programme took an interest in the subject of water. The following aspects were considered:

o Why water should be conserved.
o The benefits of water for people.
o Ways to conserve water.

The first two points involved theoretical principles for a better comprehension of the usefulness of saving water. Suggestions for different ways to save water included:

o Eliminating water leaks through taps in bad condition (the women were taught how to repair taps).
o Avoiding running water unnecessarily while washing (for example, while brushing teeth).
o Putting bottles in the lavatory cistern to reduce its capacity.

The programme included pointers about thermal insulation. Again, the women were taught some theory of the subject and given some practical advice on how to deal with low temperatures in winter. The advice included:

o Plugging all the gaps which let the cold air in.
o Putting gutters on the roof and around the house, to avoid dampness on the walls when it rains.
o Not building rooms with high ceilings.
o Building the rooms with the windows to the north, and with adequate eaves, so that they are directly exposed to the sun in the winter and avoid it in the summer.
o Drawing the curtains to allow the sun to warm the rooms.
o Covering the windows well.

The women participating in the study

As previously mentioned, 10 women were interviewed for the purpose of this study. The aim was to discover the results of the Development Programme. Of the 10 women, six had already taken part in other development projects, implemented by different non-governmental organizations (NGOs). For the remaining four, this was the first time they had taken part in an activity of this nature. Other courses attended by the women ranged over a variety of subjects, such as macramé, pastry-making and vegetable gardening. Among the 10 women, seven had the support and encouragement of their families to continue taking part in territorial organizations, and in training courses.

The reasons why the women attended TEKHNE courses are considerably varied. One of them said that her neighbour invited her to come along. Two others were interested in learning how to use the *cocina bruja*, which they had seen on television and in a magazine (the name of which they could not specify). Another woman enrolled because she had learned how to make jam at a previous TEKHNE course. In general, it can be said the reasons for attending the courses were related to their usefulness, and their practical application in the home.

Housing, utilities and electrical appliances

The settlers' homes are built of brick and have all the appropriate utilities. They have an area of 100m², which is enough space for a family. The problem persists that, in some cases, the houses are occupied by more than one family, resulting in overcrowding. All the houses visited have electricity and running water. As for appliances, they all have a gas cooker and a kerosene stove for heating.

The 10 women participating in this study answered a questionnaire. This was followed by interviews in order to confirm the consistency of their answers. The purpose of this was to ascertain, as accurately as possible, which of the elements taught at the development course were being most effectively used by the women. It was also possible to verify the application of some of our suggestions, on the spot. They showed us their *cocinas brujas*, water heaters and bottles in the lavatory cisterns. The information gathered by means of on-the-spot observation, and the interviews with the 10 participants, led to the following conclusions.

Food preparation and water heating

It is not easy to appraise the effectiveness of the course's recommendations in relation to cooking, in contrast to those recommendations regarding the use of the refrigerator. This appliance is always installed in the kitchen and it is possible to check visually its good or bad usage. Therefore, we could not evaluate the aspects relating to the cleaning of the cooker or the state of the hobs, nor the cooking habits, use of the oven, amount of water used for cooking and so forth. However, we *were* able to gather enough information with regard to the *cocinas brujas* and the solar heaters.

One of the main objectives of the course was to promote the advantages of a *cocina bruja*. For this reason, at the end of the course, each participant was given one. The witch stove is used in six households to prepare food—which is a good take-up rate. Two people even told us that they took part in the course in order to learn how to use it. The other four households do not use it. The reasons for this were varied:

○ 'Because it is very slow.'
○ 'Because you can only heat one dish at a time.'
○ 'In this house, everyone heats their own food when they come in.'
○ 'I don't have enough room and I have to carry the pots all over the place. If only I could put it in the kitchen.'

On the other hand, the people who do use it, although acknowledging its flaws, are satisfied with the advantages of the *cocina bruja*.

The major advantage and the one the women value most is the stove's fuel efficiency. Three of the families (with four or five members) said that their gas bottles had lasted for three months in the summer. The bottles contain 15kg of gas and previously lasted only two months.

Women who used the *cocinas brujas* thought that they saved time and so made life easier for them. They do not have to 'worry about the pots', because there is no danger of the stove catching fire, or of the boiling water overflowing and putting the flame out (therefore allowing gas to keep running). In this way, they do not have to wait on the cooker. 'The witch stove takes care of itself.' The women used this extra time for other domestic tasks, or for resting. One of the participants proudly showed us about 20 jars of fruit jam, made 'thanks to the time I save with the *cocina bruja*'. Four women were using their spare time to work with popular organizations.

The solar heater is used by only four women. Its use is limited, because it needs the sun to heat the water. In Santiago, however, it could be used between September and March. The families use it mainly to heat the water for laundry, for washing and, to a lesser extent, for cooking. The solar water heater also saves fuel in domestic use.

Recommendations for the use of electricity

In general, it is not easy to check whether our recommendations with regard to the use of electricity are put into practice, particularly if the houses are visited in daylight. In four of the houses, however, we could see that the lights were on in unoccupied rooms. Second, in seven of the houses the TVs were on. Our visit coincided with children's programmes or soaps. In two of the houses, however, nobody was watching them; the TV was on, as if it was a radio. This is a relatively common habit among the poorer sectors.

Last, in only two households was fluorescent lighting used in the kitchen. One of them had already been using it prior to the course. This indicated that only one family had followed our recommendations. The other families said that they had not installed it because of the cost (a 40w fluorescent bulb plus installation costs about $10).

All the families said they were following the course's recommendations about refrigerators, but we noticed that three refrigerators did not close properly. The families' explanations were that they had not been able to buy the rubber seal. It is, however, normal to use the refrigerator as a piece of furniture on which to put decorative objects, such as vases or flowerpots.

One problem area was defrosting: a significant number of women carried this out (except for the three which did not close hermetically). Most of the women said they did this in order to save fuel, but some did not understand. Another problem area was what should not be put into the refrigerator. Although all the women said that they did not put hot food or uncorked liquid containers in the fridge, we saw that they kept liquids in open plastic jars.

The study also checked the implementation of the water conservation methods. Although five women said they used bottles in their lavatory cisterns, it has not been possible to determine whether there are significant water savings, because Chile has different winter water rates from the summer rates, in order to encourage people to save.

It was not possible to evaluate how much thermal insulation of houses had been done, since the study was carried out during the summer. Our impression is, however, that the course's recommendations in this respect were not followed by the participants. The main reason would have to be economic, because in some cases it is necessary to purchase door and window sealing materials, thicker curtains and other items.

The orientation of the development programme

One of the most important contributions of the development programme was that it addressed problems specific to the women. When our suggestions for domestic fuel saving implied changes for all the members of the family unit, they were not as successful as when these changes implied a direct benefit for the women (the witch stove, the solar water heater). The conclusion is that a development programme aimed at women or at the family must pay particular attention to the problems specific to women.

TEKHNE wanted the main orientation of the programme to concern the efficient use of domestic fuel. Many women, however, preferred to see it as a programme which sought to meet part of their specific needs regarding domestic tasks.

Women and technological innovations

Women have an enormous potential for acquiring knowledge applicable to the labour-intensive daily routines they have to carry out constantly. This

45

programme was oriented towards domestic fuel saving, and gave the women some recommendations on the matter. Of these, only the ones which implied direct benefits for the women were followed. It is difficult to imagine that women could make the whole family change certain habits with regard to energy saving. Certain recommendations were not followed by the women because they involved changing the family routines, something for which the rest of the members of the household were not prepared to do (for example, changing meal times). It must also be said that it often is the case that families do not care about the amount of work the women have to do, and do not try to alleviate their burden.

This proves that implementing technological innovations not only requires an intellectual effort, to change certain working habits or to understand the functioning of new tools, but also an effort to break down the barriers which society (and in many cases, the family) forces upon women. Applying innovative technology also has social and political dimensions. Women would be able to contribute much more to these innovations if their social environment recognized their technical and technological potential. Women are continually demonstrating their potential when carrying out their traditional domestic tasks. As well as showing their strength and their capacity to overcome extremely difficult conditions in caring for their families, Chilean women have played an important role in trying to confront the social and political crisis of their country over the last few decades.

Building hope: self-management and construction

MARCELA ARANCIBIA BALLESTER and ANA MARÍA SALINAS BRIONES

The *Bioclimática* Centre, a private consultancy specializing in development in the area of architecture, landscape design and geography, had the opportunity to find out about the experience of a group of poor urban women who built 40 homes in the framework of a self-managed project called 'Building Hope from Squalor'.

The location was the *población* (a marginal urban settlement) of La Chimba in the northern part of Santiago, Chile. The group, together with another 200 families, was living in an emergency camp in the area. The strength and perseverance of its leaders (mostly women) made it possible to transform the squalid area into an area of permanent housing.

In this specific case, we contacted the women (invisible technologists) of marginal urban areas. These women have, according to themselves, been able to prove to men that they were capable of building their own homes. When we invited them to take part in this investigation, some of the women felt the urgent need to be recognized, to publicize their unique experience and all the aspects of their work which were not apparent. For them, it was an opportunity to make the invisible visible.

The interest of this case goes well beyond the case itself. The object is to give an account of what women have achieved from sheer squalor. It is also to prompt a consideration of the importance for groups of joining together with regard to production and non-paternalist training, in order to share their gender perspectives and overcome their traditional inequality in education. By doing this, they can increase their real chances of success in the labour market. We are talking about a direct approach between women in positions of responsibility in the private sector and groups of ordinary women.

MARCELA ARANCIBIA BALLESTER and ANA MARÍA SALINAS BRIONES are architects who have set up *Bioclimatica*, a private consultancy with a special interest in design and construction from the perspective of women.

Framework

The framework of this investigation is that of gender, specifically women, who have fewer opportunities in our society. This investigation highlights the work of women in the area of housing. On the one hand, the experience of self-management and the building of 40 brick homes, the drive and hard work of a group of untrained women who managed to act, saying 'I can. I'll build it'; on the other hand, the initiative of the private sector (the *Bioclimática* Centre), which discovered and valued the women's project highly, and sought to open up ways of enabling women to access the labour market in the field of construction.

We identified a latent interest among low-income women in learning everything about construction; not so much because they felt that it could open up real work opportunities, but because they wanted to make improvements to their own homes.

For the purposes of this investigation, we understand 'technological innovation' as the process through which women are changing their traditional role, turning into self-managing and self-sufficient builders of their own environment. It is a process of opening themselves to the city and to the world, of taking advantage of contacts and available knowledge, and of managing resources and making projects more concrete. Finally, we want to include in our framework the motivation that prompts the private sector to act directly in conjunction with less-privileged women.

We think that one of the ways to release women from the bad living conditions in which they find themselves in this society, is by training them so that they can compete in the labour market, by valuing their contributions, by paying them for their efforts, and by doing creative and innovative work. As women, we have many experiences and views to contribute to the area of home design, construction and environment.

General objectives

This investigation emphasizes and defines the role of women as users and innovators of technology in the field of house construction and management in a poor urban area.

Specific objectives

The aim is to study the process of management, development and the actual building of housing, from the first stages of decision-making through to the course of action taken and the results achieved. We are interested in showing the impact of this experience of self-management and self-construction from the point of view of the women, non-governmental organizations and the media.

48

We sought to end this investigation with a few recommendations, aimed at widening the present scope of women's organizations and at encouraging outside organizations to form links with ordinary women in the area of technology, by means of a specific project: *Building Hope*.

History of the group

This consists of a brief historical outline of the group and of the course of its development from the very beginning. We revised the written documentation available from the organization itself and from the non-governmental organizations involved. The media was one of our sources of information, thanks to the register of the TV channel in which the women were interviewed about their experiences. We went through a number of documentary videotapes and other archive material (such as a video with Princess Anne of the United Kingdom). All of this constituted a valuable source of visual information on the subject of self-construction.

At the same time we had conversations with the women, interviewing both the leaders and the women who attended the practical workshop.

The practical experience

The second line of work was carried out in a practical workshop in which domestic refuse (Tetrabrik cartons used for long-life liquids) was recycled. This workshop was started with members of the group Women of the Future who had participated in the self-construction project, and with other women interested in the subject. This activity, which enables experimentation with the possibilities offered by domestic refuse for improving heating in the home, gave us the opportunity to establish a face-to-face relationship between the investigators and those being investigated.

In order to see the concrete results of the self-construction project, we visited the women's homes, in particular those of the women at the workshop. At the same time, we held interviews and had conversations with different people whose opinions we thought relevant to this investigation:

O local women who do not take part in organizations;
O relatives and husbands;
O the architect of the non-governmental organization JUNDEP;
O customers of the centre;
O women from other communities who saw the group on television.

As a support tool, a questionnaire was given to the leaders for them to review its contents.

In terms of method, this work was carried out horizontally, that is, in order to see the whole, we wanted to see the parts. We even became a part. This meant gathering the views of each of the parties involved (textual quotations) before we could get a combined vision. The testimonial way of compiling the information transforms this investigation into a story of La Chimba, the invisible story of women.

Historical outline

We wanted to trace the origins of this group of 40 women builders, what the 'seed' was, and where their story began.

What the group enjoys today as a result of its drive, capacity and perseverance, is owing to the story of one of its leaders, Señora Juana Manríquez. Her story has been the most invisible of all. It was she who, as the leader of the emergency camp in 1979, granted a space to the family of Señora Mary Rojas. This woman came with the recommendation of a political party, and her daughter would later be responsible for the project *Building Hope* in 1987.

At first she was living in another municipality in the south-west of the city, where she organized a Mothers' Centre (1960). In 1970 she organized the locals and they took occupation of lands in the municipality of Conchali. Some of her daughters went to live with their grandmother.

After the 1971 earthquake during the socialist administration, the municipality relocated those families affected and those in the occupied lands to a provisional site where the future Urmeneta Avenue would be. The result was an emergency camp: Guanaco. Here, 200 large (and mostly unemployed) families settled themselves in an L-shaped corridor. Conditions were inhuman: two cesspools, four water troughs and a central spotlight were shared by approximately 1000 people.

In 1973, the year that Salvador Allende's democratic government was toppled by a US-backed coup d'état led by General Pinochet, Señora Juana was elected leader in the municipality of Conchali. She managed to have a water trough and a cesspool installed on each lot—this was a definite step forward towards the proper layout of the area. For 16 years the residents lived in this provisional location, waiting to be moved to a permanent home in accordance with the official 'eradication' plans of the military government.

The social leaders, who remained active under the guise of a sports club, focused their demands to ensure that people stayed in the sites they were occupying. Fifty families had already been moved to a marginal municipality of Greater Santiago (Peñaflor). This social atomization was a plan of the military dictatorship to spread and control the poor, preventing their social and political organization.

After the emergencies brought about by the storms of 1987, and coinciding with the population movements ordered by the military government in their 'eradication' plan, about 100 families arrived in the camp. They occupied the back of the camp and some of its corners. This resulted in social stratification within the camp itself. Some of these families were

50

ones formed by people who had grown up there, and were products of the camp. The demand for space made this second occupation even more cramped, and the conditions worsened (physical and mental illnesses, problems with relationships, and so on): 350 families were living in 288 homes (*Renacer* union, 1990).

Later, towards the end of July 1988, the families were granted a definite place according to the official layout. This meant smaller lots so that there was space for more subdivisions. Before, the lots measured 9 by 18m; now they were only 7 by 14m.

Inside the site itself, there were various removals of the *mediaguas* (provisional plank houses). The first step consisted of occupying the empty lot. By means of the subsidies, they opted for 'serviced-lots', with a 'sanitary hut' (kitchen–toilet, 7m^2). The *mediagua* had to be moved aside in order to build the hut, and then moved again to attach it to the new building.

Some of the 40 women who undertook this challenging work started by building the perimeter walls, leaving the *mediagua* inside. In this case, once the roof of the permanent house was finished, they moved the provisional one over nearer the new building.

These women, who still have Juana Manríquez as their leader (a woman who has not stopped working for the improvement of the living conditions of the inhabitants of the former camp, now La Chimba Town), embody the drive and ability for achieving their objectives that the women from marginalized sectors often have. Their achievement—the construction of their own homes—is, to date, unique in Chile.

Renacer union

Renacer means 'to be reborn'. The union was a popular social organization, with 63 per cent of its members female. It started in 1979, at the height of the military dictatorship and was officially licensed in 1983. It is made up of a group of people from the Guanaco camp in the former municipality of Conchali (now Recoleta). Its members are peddlers, craftswomen, independent and unemployed workers, united by a basic survival need: the *olla común* or 'common pot'—a situation that highlights the cost in social terms for the poor of the economic policies of the military dictatorship.

> 'People organized themselves in order to face the problem of nourishment. They had the support of the Vicarage (*Solidarity*). They had a card made and went to the fair, to *La Vega* (Santiago's popular market) asking for food which they then cooked and distributed among the people who came to them with their pots. They paid a coin and their pots were filled. The groups took turns. This went on for three years.'

Due to the social and political conditions endured by the country through the years of dictatorship, specifically the restrictive policies imposed by the

51

government on popular organizations, the union defined itself as 'a socially responsible organization devoted to diverse activities which, if not solving the root of the problems, can make the grave situation slightly less painful' (*Renacer* union, 1990).

The union has the support of other sectors (such as professionals, students and non-governmental organizations), a support derived from the fact that they belong to the same political party. They recognize the permanent relationship with other similar organizations at community, regional and national levels, to be the most important characteristic of their organization.

The forming of the project (1987)

'This project was born when we started to realize that we had lots of sick kids, sick with diarrhoea and bronchial problems. We started to say to ourselves: "So much effort to give them penicillin, so many health campaigns, and every year the kids are down with the same thing". So, do you know what we began to think about? We began to think about changing the *mediagua* for a proper house. We can't do any better, we can't stuff the kids with penicillin when, at the end of the day, the problem is still going to be there. So it was then that this idea about the houses began to take shape.' (From an interview with the leaders.)

And so, 40 women got together, prepared to face this big challenge. Twenty of them belonged to the union from the beginning and they decided to bring along one more woman each, in order to increase the numbers and achieve their objectives (in spite of people's comments that '[they] were mad').

The group organized itself, choosing leaders and arranging work groups.

○ Leaders: Project co-ordinator
                 Activities co-ordinator
                 Co-ordinator of the building methods
                 Finance co-ordinator.
○ Work groups: Groups of 10 women who, as well as the construction work, worked in the community, doing additional fund-raising in the afternoons and evenings.

Once organized, they held discussion meetings in order to establish the type of houses they needed.

The materials

When choosing the materials, they 'wanted the best', what for them represented a solid home. 'It has to be cement, or we don't want it' (referring to plastered brick). 'We had this idea, whether because of our culture or our way of life, that this was the best; we wanted it to last for the rest of our lives, for the family to die in it. We wanted something done well. We hate planks, and mud smacks of poverty . . .'

Self-management of the project

And so they began going out into the public domain:

'We created the project and started to publicize it, to show it to different non-governmental organizations'.

The leaders showed the project to different organizations in order to get financing and technical advice regarding the plans. This was carried out through the support of other sectors. One of them is a non-governmental organization, JUNDEP (Youth for Development and Production), which says:

'The group of women, through their own initiative, contacted us, as we work in the area of social housing and self-construction. They came as an independent syndicate which had set up an initiative for solving the problem of housing. Their slogan was "Building Hope from Squalor". They contacted us, knowing the whole time that in the following year they were going to have "sanitary huts" built. We suggested to them that the best thing was to start with the design of the houses, taking into consideration the developed site and the "sanitary huts".

'In 1987, we could do nothing because of the storms. We were working on that problem even in other regions. In 1988 we started a process of participatory design. A group of young residents from Conchali, called *Amerindio* [American Indian], who were attending one of our schools for social leaders, offered to take part in the women's project. They belonged to the same political party.

'There were two groups in this same sector: that of the women and that of Urmeneta. We worked with both groups, giving them design proposals that they studied and returned to us with their amendments.

'When this stage was finished, we left La Chimba. We kept working with the Urmeneta group. They started building their houses following our design. They had better management ability. The group of La Chimba was more politicized, they wanted to follow other lines. It was the women who led this matter, because they were the most needy, the ones most motivated to face the problem of housing.'

And what was the interest in working with women?

'The fact is, it is not as if we had been planning to work with women. It was something purely circumstantial: most of the people in La Chimba were women.

53

'With all this work, in 1989 we presented a report (called Participatory Design and Progressive Building in an Eradication Camp of Conchali) to the Housing Institute of the University of Chile at their First Conference on Social Housing.'

With regard to the process of participatory design proposed by the non-governmental organizations, the women tell us:

'A limited solution was achieved for space. The house must relate to the family, and this was not understood because of a lack of participation in, and a relationship with, our organization. But we needed the plans in order to keep looking for finance. "Please do the plans for us!".'

At the end of participatory design work, the NGO 'kept' the project of La Chimba until 1990, when it saw the light again thanks to the convocation of a private competition by the College of Architects ('Improvement of Housing for Low-Resource Sectors'), sponsored by the European Community. The NGO saw the opportunity for proposing itself for this financing. The NGO said that, during the time elapsed between the design and the College proposal, the group remained inactive. 'Having the design, they were unable to start. They had the desire, they had the strength, but they lacked the impulse.'

The view of the women in this respect is: 'When the stage of participatory design was finished, the NGO told us: "This is as far as we go." But we knew that, at some stage, our project would be approved. Finally, in 1990, and through that same NGO, we were told: "The project has been approved".'

Beginning to build hope

The group assumed its functions, already defined and mentioned above: leaders and work groups (teams, activities). The first part of the money allocated after the College's competition was administered by the NGO, which allocated a share for materials to each family, and gave them more money as construction progressed, proportional to the lineal metres built. This was the first stage. Besides, the NGO proposed a contribution for each family. To be put in a rotating fund, 'in order not to give out money for the sake of it', as one of the women put it.

The NGO clarifies: 'What happened was that the College of Architects gave the money as a non-returnable donation, but we proposed to the women that this was not a donation—we talked about rotating credit.'

The construction of lineal metres of wall corresponded to 'the front of the house plus part of one of the sides, forming an L-shape. The ones who had already started by themselves, closed the square. Then the women, with their share of the money, other money raised through other activities, and other additional funds from the College of Architects, kept closing the perimeter of the houses.'

'As they already had the design, we supported this project by the College. But this ended. It lasted for eight months and, in 1990, we left La Chimba.'

We want to point out here that the women's labour in the construction work itself was not considered a monetary contribution by the families to the project.

The women tell us that construction was carried out in stages:

'In the first stage, nine lineal metres of wall were built, three here, three there and three here. This was the first stage. Some people already had the walls, so they only had to finish them.'

'The second stage consisted of "closing the box". This was made with other money, it was self-management. In order to be able to do it, we proposed using the accumulating rotating fund, plus another share [of money] from the College. That's how the second stage was financed. It was the only money that we, the women, administered.'

In order to get the rotating fund together, they promoted a series of supplementary activities which made 'the population live'. Fridays, Saturdays and Sundays became a fair. We called them supplementary because they were carried out at the same time as the construction of the houses. This was done until the end of the project. Through the sale of food (chips, fritters, fried fish) and used clothes, and through fairs, balls, lotteries and raffles they turned La Chimba into a market, a place in which the whole community could meet, socialize and unite.

At the end of the first stage, some of the families left, making place for exactly the same number of new ones. The reason for their leaving was that they didn't work at the building site or at the other activities.

'The others tried, they took the wheelbarrow and showed determination, even though they got tired. Many damaged their backs and fell ill. Construction is a very hard job, but there were people who did it, they accepted they simply had to do it. If any of us didn't want to work at the building site itself, either because of chronic illnesses or because they had jobs, some relative of theirs would do it, their partners, daughters, daughters-in-law . . . And in the evening, when they returned from work, they took part in the other activities, kneading, baking, etc.'

'There were also women who didn't pay or didn't want to pay, but they took part in the activities and in the construction itself. These women, at least, generated work for the project. They were supposed to pay, but really, if we were very strict in that respect, we would be behind time, we had to stick to our schedule. So these women stayed. They proved their determination, their interest for the project. If some people didn't have the money one month, they would have it the next month, they would catch up.'

The first and second stages lasted for about eight months. The houses reached a stage of semi-construction. There were still the roofs and the finishings to be done. This was 1990. The NGO which supported the women at the beginning tells us:

'The women of La Chimba started to work on their own and kept building. We left them alone even more than at the time of the College of Architects. They managed to get funds from another NGO: OCAC (Coordination Office for Assistance to Peasants), who were working with foreign financing. The women were very active, very political, and came back to us to ask for technical assistance on the matter of roofing, which was already on the plans. We advised them, and they themselves made and put up the roofs. They kept active.

'In 1991, when there was a woman mayor, María Antonieta Saa, President Aylwin, together with the Minister of Housing, came to Conchali to talk to the people. The women of La Chimba "nabbed" the Minister and took him to see their work, telling him: "Now, Mr. Minister, get going with the finishings".'

The Minister told them to apply for an existing subsidy for aid with second stage progressive buildings at the MINVU (the Department of Housing). They had to have the support of an executive organization. They could apply through the NGO with which they had already been working, or the NGO itself could apply on their behalf.

They were successful, and it was JUNDEP which, as a construction company, finished the houses of La Chimba. One of the conditions of the MINVU was that they provided guarantees, and that they had the municipality's approval at the end of the project, to show that they complied with the by-laws.

At the finishing stage, the NGO 'did not involve' the women in the work. They say: 'The women didn't work because it was the finishing stage (on walls, plastering, whitewashing, internal divisions, firebreaks, etc). However, they took an active part in the building work itself (excavating, filling pillars, doing the roofing, etc.).'

This is how the women remember the steps they took in order to be able to do the roofing and to finish their houses: 'It was like starting ant-work.' They started collecting existing material from each *mediagua*, anything that could be put to use. They chose, counted and cubed the materials they needed to finish the 40 houses. They valued them and began seeking new possibilities for financing.

They found these, in part, at the NGO, the OCAC and at the MINVU, through a national programme for improving housing. This helped them obtain the money to finish the houses. They also got financing from the

56

British Embassy, following the visit by Princess Anne to La Chimba. Another private company also made a donation. These resources were destined for projects which did not qualify for the MINVU programme. Finally, 'the women finished the houses'. The municipality, then run by a woman, also supported them by paying a mason to help them.

We think that this way of achieving things in stages, little by little, taking advantage of every opportunity and means of obtaining resources, is of the utmost importance for the final results of the project. Here, we would like to emphasize the women's perseverance, endurance and faith in the project, and the fact that they did not stop until the end.

Training

The relationship between the NGO (which ultimately became a fully-fledged construction company) and the group of women during the development of the buildings consisted only of the teaching of techniques. The NGO says:

> 'They didn't know about the subject. They only had the strength and the will-power. The training consisted of teaching them to do the layout, to square off the houses, you know, basic lessons in building. We taught them all this while working on the design with the commissions (formed by six people), which then passed the information down to the others.'

As the NGO points out, financing from the College of Architects did not take into account technical training. This does not detract from their promise of technical assistance, which, however, according to the women was not kept.

> 'At the moment of beginning the building work, teams of 10 women were formed. There was a mason for every 20 families. The College of Architects paid for the mason and the materials. This, together with free labour from the women, allowed them to build slowly.' (NGO, 1993)

With regard to the technical training, the women say:

> 'We didn't have any technical advice from anybody. The NGO had something very traditional in mind, they only wanted to say what they wanted to do with the organizations, instead of doing what the organization wanted. So we were never trained in building or carpentry. We learnt to build the houses by ourselves. We were self-taught. The only training we had came from a leaflet in which we read how to build the walls, about the quantities, etc. And what a technician once told Juana and me. So we told Iris and Señora Lucy this, so that they could do the work with the centrings. That was all our training. Nobody helped us. The masons came and just counted the metres of wall.'

57

Conclusions

The process of management, development and building in the sector of low-resource women took place step-by-step and with perseverance in their objectives. It was very important for this process that they knew, had access to, and made use of all the channels available during the project (for financing, technical advice, diffusion and contacts).

We have called this way of achieving things slowly the 'technology of resources management'. It was acquired by the political path of this women's organization after 14 years. A fundamental part was the work of promoting the project on the part of the leaders, who managed to gain international recognition. The formation of women in the social area was a determinant, in terms of local development, management and union facilitation, among other subjects. This was a consequence of belonging to a political party.

For the women the most important aspect of the project was their opening to the world. They realized that they were capable of doing what they intended, valuing themselves, knowing that they are not restricted only to the home, but that there are other alternatives which allow them to share, to develop and to participate. They could leave the home, enjoying a newly earned freedom.

The NGO thinks that, with initiatives aimed at the community, it is important to take into account the fact that the main protagonists are women (in the case of housing). This means that it has to be made sure that women are involved in a production process in which they are not treated as 'women with time to spare' just because they work in their homes. The women are given dignity when they are involved in a production process which solves the problem of housing and which allows them to have access to the labour market.

On the subject of how they are affected by a non-traditional role (carrying out a job which has traditionally been a male one, such as construction), two aspects should be mentioned:

o In the public sphere: being women, they said it was difficult to operate naturally on the same level as men (harsh deals, coldness, manipulation); on the other hand, being a woman brought with it a special sensitivity for 'grasping' situations.
o In the sphere of work itself: the job was physically difficult to accomplish, because the tools and equipment (their weight and size) are made with men in mind. Women had to struggle with them. As for the job itself, there was keen interest to learn, and some women even wanted to be trained in some specific aspects of it, according to their own personal interests. They did not feel that their feminity was affected by their work, physically or mentally. They also discovered that they already had some useful skills—for example, they were able to transfer the concepts

of measurement, which they used in making pastry, across to making cement.

Recommendations

The ordinary women say that in order to work with them the first step is the personal development and growth of women. This is the group's dynamic, the aim of which is to prepare them to face successfully the problems that construction work involves at the level of the family, labour and emotions.

On the subject of the NGOs, the women think that these put their own objectives first, instead of caring about what the social groups want as a development strategy. To this must be added an ignorance of the world of women. The methods and content of the work were not characterized by their gender perspectives and by an interest in the development of women. The women think that development must be experienced jointly so as not to restrict them or to impose the particular objectives of the NGOs.

Changing attitudes to health in the Dominican Republic

LOURDES PERDOMO DE GOMEZ, MARIA DOLORES MATEO MONTERO and RITA OTTE

Between 16 and 21 November 1992, a workshop was organized in Ecuador, at which representatives of different countries put forward ideas about the work being done with women in their respective countries. Each of them reported different experiences all of which were very interesting; and all related to the exciting work being done by women. This workshop stimulated a more detailed investigation of other projects being carried out by women which have so far gone unnoticed. One investigation studied the changes in La Zurza, in the Dominican Republic, since the arrival of health technology, and whether or not the women had accepted or rejected these changes.

We also looked at the situation of women 10 years ago. We looked at the organization of women, we studied the role it plays in the process of change, and what women in the district thought about the subject. We also studied how the women solved their problems and how they used their time.

The principal objective of the research was to emphasize the nature of women as versatile and productive social entities, capable of solving their own problems and of helping to solve the problems of others.

Geographical description of La Zurza

The district of La Zurza is situated in the northern part of the city of Santo Domingo (capital of the Dominican Republic). It is slightly more than half a square kilometre, with nearly 50 000 inhabitants (or 658 inhabitants per

LOURDES PERDOMO DE GOMEZ and RITA OTTE are project workers with IDDI—the Dominican Institute for Integrated Development.
MARÍA DOLORES MATEO MONTERO was a health worker in the La Zurza township in Santo Domingo.

hectare). La Zurza's topography is rugged, with sloping, uneven terrain. There are six large streams into which domestic refuse, human waste and liquid industrial waste from 54 nearby factories are discharged. There is also considerable air pollution from the cement factory situated in the western part of the district.

The drainage system is natural, which means that rainwater and human waste run in the open, down the slopes until it flows into the river. For most of its residents, refuse collection is non-existent. This is due to the lack of paved roads and to the rugged landscape, which prevent the refuse collecting lorries from entering the area. What is more, the district does not have any kind of state-run social services, which would satisfy the basic demand of the residents in the areas of health, education and leisure. The problems which most affect the residents are the unhealthy conditions; the lack of basic services such as drinking-water, electricity and refuse collection, and the shortage of jobs.

Objectives

Very generally, a main objective was to study the level of change produced in the community since the introduction of a community-based health programme. The plan was, first, to study how these changes took place and which characteristics influenced this. Second, to find out what importance women give to being organized and their knowledge of other women's organizations in the district.

Methods

In order to gather information, we used a questionnaire, interviews, meetings at the headquarters of the Mothers' Club and a workshop. In our conclusions, we brought together the results of the different activities, and emphasized certain points which we thought were more important.

The questionnaire was conducted at the centre where the health promoters provide a health programme service. It was conducted using 282 women, representing 10 per cent of the families who take part in this health programme. We interviewed 50 women, with a view to further clarifying some aspects. These included the situation of women in the home, and the participation of husbands in the project. We held the meetings at the headquarters of the Mothers' Club, where women from the health programme, women from the club, and women not involved in either, took part. Thirty-five women in total participated in the final workshop, most of them from the Mothers' Club.

61

The women's group organizes local health education in La Zurza

Existing variables

- The situation of women 10 years ago and the emergence of this situation.
- Background: how health technology came to La Zurza.
- How women accept or reject new ideas in relation to health issues and what they do with these ideas—whether they keep them to themselves or share and disseminate them.
- What the organization of women is like and what role they play in the adaptation of this process.
- Benefits derived from the introduction of technology.
- How women use their time and solve their problems.
- The role of women in the home.
- What changes in activities the women experienced and the consequences for the family.

The situation of women 10 years ago

One way of seeing how women have changed their attitudes is by getting them to think about their lives. We did this by means of a questionnaire.

We were interested in knowing where they had lived before and what their reasons were for coming to live in La Zurza. The most commonly cited motive was the desire for change. It was interesting to see that a large percentage of them had come from the city, both the capital itself and a number of other cities—often San Francisco de Macoris and also other smaller cities. Most of them liked the change, particularly in relation to the opportunity it afforded them for solving their economic problems. A large number of the women surveyed had already been living in La Zurza for a long time.

Tables 1 to 5 show more clearly the different motives for this change and the reasons for the subsequent well-being or discontent of the women.

These tables show the importance of the market, situated very near the district and providing many work opportunities, most of them casual. The other most frequent reason was the desire to own a house. It was the main motive for those who were already living in the capital. The existence of social organizations in the district was important for only two women. Of the reasons for not being happy with the change, the most frequently cited

Table 1. The place where you lived 10 years ago

	Number	Percentage
Urban area	117	41.49
Rural area	66	23.40
La Zurza	96	24.04
No response	3	1.06
Total	282	100.00

Table 2. Reasons for coming to live here

	Number	Percentage
Economic reasons	49	26.78
Looking for a change	83	45.36
Family problems	23	12.57
Other reasons	35	19.13
Total	190	103.83

Table 3. Did you like coming to live here?

	Number	Percentage
Yes	134	73.22
No	46	25.14
No response	3	1.64
Total	183	100.00

Table 4. Positive reasons for living in La Zurza

	Number	Percentage
Work/market	44	34.92
Own house	20	15.87
Peace and quiet	16	12.70
More opportunities	16	12.70
Family here	14	11.11
I like the district	8	6.35
Better than the country	6	4.76
Many organizations	2	1.59
Total	126	100.00

Table 5. Negative reasons

	Number	Percentage
Bad atmosphere	17	34.69
Too much crime	12	24.49
Too dirty	6	12.24
Too noisy	4	8.16
Too many problems	3	6.12
Discomfort	2	4.08
Insecurity	2	4.08
Problems with electricity/water	2	4.08
No schools	1	2.04
Total	49	100.00

were the rubbish in the streets and crime. The bad atmosphere also had influenced the women; for instance, not being able to go out at night and the close proximity of houses. Alternatives, however, were virtually non-existent, which is why the women were staying in the district.

Economic situation of the women and their families

As most people know, the economic situation of women is always a special subject. In Dominican society women normally depend on their husbands. This fact is very evident in La Zurza. Of the 282 women surveyed, only 54 (19.15 per cent) worked away from home, while in 212 cases (75.18 per cent) it was the husband who supported the family. It is interesting to see that in 110 cases, women were heads of the household (see Tables 6 to 8). They devoted most of their time to domestic work; very few women use their time for studying or participating in an organization. Later in this study we will see how women make use of their time.

Of the 54 women who worked away from home, 21 did what is known as *'chiripera'*, which involves occasional selling or odd jobs. Only 15 women

Table 6. Are you head of the household?

	Number	Percentage
Yes	110	39.01
No	119	42.20
Both	48	17.02
No response	5	1.77
Total	282	100.00

Table 7. What does it feel like to be responsible?

	Number	Percentage
Good	74	51.75
All right	41	28.67
Bad	9	6.29
Tiring	17	11.89
Other	2	1.40
Total	143	100.00

Table 8. If you work away from home, what do you do?

	Number	Percentage
Work in the market	6	11.11
At a relative's	2	3.70
Public sector work	5	9.26
Private sector work	10	18.52
Casual work	21	38.89
Other	6	11.11
No response	4	7.41
Total	54	100.00

Table 9. Can you read and write?

	Number	Percentage
Yes	220	78.01
No	53	18.79
No response	9	3.19
Total	282	100.00

(27.78 per cent) were employed in the public and private sectors. Their education accounts for this; although most women can read and write (see Table 9), a large percentage of them (61.68 per cent) have never gone beyond primary school, as shown in Table 10.

65

Table 10. What is your highest level of education?

	Number	Percentage
Primary	140	61.68
Secondary	62	27.31
University	5	2.20
Other	5	2.20
No response	15	6.61
Total	227	100.00

The Mothers' Club and the importance of women's organizations

We wanted to find out to what extent the Mothers' Club was fulfilling its objectives and how familiar with the club the women in the district were. To this end, we asked the women if they knew of any women's organization or were in one themselves. The results were interesting: only 58 women (20.57 per cent) were members of an organization, and more than half the women surveyed knew of a women's organization, in one way or another. Most of them had heard of the Mothers' Club. (See Tables 11 to 13.)

The objective of these organizations was to contribute to raise the social, economic and political standards of the women of La Zurza (see Table 14). The work of the club brought about different changes, beginning with the setting-up of nursery schools. In this way, the women took more interest in the education of their children.

As well as the nursery schools, the club was also fighting for a supply of clean drinking-water, organizing several protests with the women. The

Table 11. Do you belong to an organization?

	Number	Percentage
Yes	58	20.57
No	186	65.96
No response	38	13.48
Total	282	100.00

Table 12. Do you know any women's organizations in the district?

	Number	Percentage
Yes	152	53.90
No	126	44.68
No response	4	1.42
Total	282	100.00

Table 13. If so, which ones?

	Number	Percentage
Mothers' Club	134	82.21
'Sodizur'	14	8.59
Church	12	7.36
Health promoters	3	1.84
Total	163	100.00

Table 14. Activities

	Number	Percentage
Improving the district	49	30.43
Health	28	17.39
Women's training and advice	24	14.91
Clinic	14	8.70
Nursery school	13	8.07
Hygiene	11	6.83
Co-op shop	8	4.97
Technical school	7	4.35
Loans	7	4.35
Total	161	100.00

same happened with the refuse collection service; and they eventually managed to have a council truck come to the district twice a week to collect the rubbish. They also set up a co-operative store which facilitated the purchase of food; a clinic, with two paediatricians, a general practitioner and a gynaecologist, all of whom gave their services to the community at reasonable prices. They managed to achieve all this with the support of the Health Programme.

There was also the possibility of receiving vocational training, which enabled the women to increase the family income. Twenty-five women had already qualified as press-machinists, and 50 had done the same in dressmaking. Most of them were earning their own income, which also meant a change of role in the home.

In addition to providing vocational training, the Mothers' Club was fighting to make the women aware of the importance of organizing themselves. This made them aware that, through organization, it was possible to make sure the state fulfilled its responsibilities towards the community, such as drinking-water, health services, electricity, refuse collection and education.

One benefit that they can get through the health programme is a loan to help set up a small business which might earn them an income, enabling them to improve their diet, their living conditions, and, therefore, the health of their children. Of the 50 women surveyed, only 4 per cent (2 women) had applied for this loan.

The creation of the Mothers' Club

After having started doing their community work, the health promoters got to know the reality of the women of La Zurza in more depth; in particular, their interest in organizing themselves in order to face specific problems, and their desire to improve themselves and their community. This was the motivation which led to the creation of a Mothers' Club, representing the women of La Zurza.

The situation of women in the context of the home

Women are always responsible for the well-being of their families, especially in the area of health. In many cases, they are overburdened and need the help of their spouses. Through interviews, we wanted to see how this was working in the families.

From Table 15 we can see that 52 per cent of husbands had involved themselves in these changes, that 4 per cent took part in meetings, and that 2 per cent helped with the care of the children. Unfortunately, we do not have any further information on how they involved themselves. It was noted that some men took the children to the doctor as they felt a bit more responsible for their children's health, but they still had much to contribute, if they were to *feel* completely involved. This area continues to be the responsibility of women. What is more, the husbands expect to be taken care of by their wives.

Table 16 shows that in the past five years women in La Zurza have not experienced any changes favourable to them. Only 38 per cent said that they had experienced some kind of change. Most of them thought it was normal to stay at home, while their husbands earned the money or did something else. We have already seen this from the questions above, in that

Table 15. Is your husband involved in the changes you have experienced through the work of the health promoters?

	Number	Percentage
No	22	44
Yes	26	52
A little	1	2
He helps with the children	1	2
He takes part in meetings	2	4
Total	52	104

Table 16. Has your lifestyle changed in the past five years?

	Number	Percentage
No	28	56
Yes	19	38
No response	3	6
Total	50	100

only 54 women said they worked away from home, and only 58 women were involved in an organization.

As for domestic income, we cannot be sure of this. Of the 282 women, only 250 gave an answer, and, in 160 cases, the money was earned on a day-to-day basis, which meant that the monthly income was very variable. Many of the men who worked at the market did not do so every day, and as a consequence there was no guaranteed daily income. In this case, the women found it very difficult to plan their weekly budgets, because they never knew what resources they could rely on.

Analysing Table 17, it is easy to see that many families were living in very bad conditions. A great number of them were earning between DR$500 (US$40) and DR$2000 (US$160). If the current situation is this difficult for the women and their families, one wonders what it was like before.

Most of the women had some idea about the activities of the Mothers' Club, although it seemed that many still did not know the club well. This was an open-ended question which meant that the women had the opportunity to mention more than just one activity. Taking this into account, it was obvious that there was still much to be done to make the club and all its activities well known. When we asked the women about their interest in

Table 17. How much money does your household earn?

DR$	Month	Fortnight	Week	Day	No response	Total
>50				42		
>100				80		
>200			6	28		
>300				9		
>400						
>500	3	4	11	1		
>1000	14	11	13			
>1500	9	3	2			
>2000	6	3				
>2500	3					
>3000	2					
Total	37	21	32	160	32	282
%	13.12	7.45	11.35	56.74	11.35	100

organizing themselves, the response was quite strong (see Tables 18 to 21). We were keen to know more about this subject since the contradiction between reality and the results is quite clear. That is why we decided to organize a workshop to deal with this issue.

Table 22 shows how important it was for the women to improve the condition of their district. Sixteen per cent mentioned that they would like to see the development of women. In this case, development also meant vocational training in order to help improve their economic situation. Fifty-

Table 18. Do you think it is important to organize yourselves?

	Number	Percentage
Yes	265	93.97
No	6	2.13
No response	11	3.90
Total	282	100.00

Table 19. Would you like to organize yourselves?

	Number	Percentage
Yes	232	82.27
No	30	10.64
No response	20	7.09
Total	282	100.00

Table 20. Reasons given

	Number	Percentage
To learn	74	30.96
To improve the district	60	25.10
For training and advice	39	16.32
Strength in unity	26	10.88
We must organize ourselves	18	7.35
Organizing women is important	15	6.28
Refuse collection	7	2.93
Total	239	100.00

Table 21. Reasons against

	Number	Percentage
Do not like getting involved	12	40
Do not have the time	18	60
Total	30	100

Table 22. What would you like the organization to be about?

	Number	Percentage
The well-being of the district	77	27.30
Women's development	46	16.31
Benefits for children	23	8.16
Health	16	5.67
Men and women together	13	4.61
Craft work	13	4.61
To be directed by women	10	3.55
Youth issues	11	3.90
To be responsible and efficient	7	2.48
Cleaning	6	2.13
Literacy	4	1.42
Fieldwork	3	1.06
No response	53	18.79
Total	282	100.00

three women (18.79 per cent) had no ideas about what they would have liked a women's organization to be.

The attitude of women towards health issues

An important part of the investigation was about women's knowledge of health issues. To this end, we included a few relevant questions in the interviews. First of all we wanted to know which methods the women used to treat themselves and their families (see Tables 23 and 24).

Table 23. Which methods do you use to treat your family?

	Number	Percentage
Granny's methods	48	17.02
Modern methods	254	90.07
No response	4	1.42
Total	306	108.51

Table 24. Which remedies do you and your family use?

	Number	Percentage
Home-made remedies	49	17.38
Go to the doctor	221	78.37
Buy prescriptions	136	48.23
Self-treatment	16	5.67
Combination of Granny's remedies and modern medicine	68	24.11
Total	490	173.76

Most of the women (90.07 per cent) used modern methods (usually medicine) to cure themselves and their families. A minority still used traditional methods, that is, what their grannies used. It can be seen that women trust modern medicine, visiting a doctor when a member of the family is ill and buying the prescriptions. A minority prefer to treat themselves.

We do not wish to imply here that traditional methods are always bad, but it should be emphasized that many of the women did not know how to use them properly, and in many instances they did more harm than good to their children. After attending courses on medicinal plants, they learned what the advantages and disadvantages were and it now seems they do not have much faith in traditional medicine.

During the course of the interviews we found out that many women had been receiving advice on health issues for about four years. This service comes to their homes through the health promoters and, during the last year and a half, through radio and television.

The questionnaire and the interviews allowed us to discover that most of the women found out about the Health Programme for the first time when

Table 25. How long have you known about the health programme?

	Number	Percentage
One year	10	20
Two years	8	16
Three years	7	14
Four years	17	34
Five years	5	10
Two months	1	2
Three months	1	2
No response	1	2
Total	50	100

Table 26. How did the health promoters help you?

	Number	Percentage
With health problems	28	56
Children are ill less often	6	12
Curing diarrhoea	5	10
Food preparation	3	6
Spacing pregnancies	3	6
Hygiene measures	3	6
Taking liquids for flu	2	4
Helping with a loan	2	4
Teaching me how to make fruit juice	2	4
Total	54	108

Table 27. What do you do if your child is undernourished?

	Number	Percentage
Go to the doctor	95	33.69
Feed it well	95	33.69
Give it liquids	79	28.01
Never had undernourished children	29	10.28
Use a serum	26	9.22
Give them fruit/vegetable juice	7	2.48
Follow heath promoter's advice	7	2.48
Give them medicine	3	1.06
Give them vitamins	3	1.06
Don't know	2	0.71
Total	346	122.70

the health promoters visited them. A minority found out about it through one of the district's organizations (SODIZUR).

All the women questioned and interviewed were happy with the visits from the health promoters, because they often helped the women to solve specific health problems. A large percentage of the women knew what to do and what to give their children if they were undernourished. This used to be one of the main causes of child mortality.

Table 28. What do you give your children if they suffer from diarrhoea?

	Number	Percentage
A serum	166	58.87
A lot of liquids	149	52.84
Take them to doctor	40	14.18
Usual diet	20	7.09
Pills	25	8.87
Fruit/vegetable juice	15	5.32
Milk	8	2.84
Ensure good hygiene	2	0.71
Home-made remedy	10	3.55
They never have diarrhoea	2	0.71
Total	437	154.96

Many women used to think that when their children had diarrhoea they had to be given a cleansing remedy; many children died from dehydration as a result. The survey shows that women today know how important it is to make their children drink a lot of liquids and that very few women use pills and home-made remedies.

The women had learned that when their children had flu they had to take a lot of liquids, see a doctor, be given a lot of love and attention and kept

73

Table 29. How do you treat your children when they have flu?

	Number	Percentage
Lots of liquid	83	29.43
Doctor	81	28.72
Syrup	71	25.18
Keep them dry	43	15.25
Keep them warm	39	15.83
Remedy	20	7.09
A lot of care	19	6.74
Tea	15	5.32
Keep them well fed	13	4.61
Honey and onion	6	2.13
Total	390	138.30

Table 30. How important is hygiene at home and in the district?

	Number	Percentage
Very important	245	86.88
Quite important	29	10.28
Not very important	4	1.42
No response	4	1.42
Total	282	100.00

Table 31. What do you do with your rubbish?

	Number	Percentage
Throw it in the street or in the stream	131	46.45
Bury or burn it	1	0.35
Put it in sacks	144	51.06
Other	23	8.16
Total	299	106.02

well fed. Very few women said that they still gave their children home-made remedies for flu.

For many women, it was a great effort to adopt new habits with regard to health issues because most of the time their poverty prevented them from buying anything special for their children. An important aspect of health is hygiene, both in the home and in the district. We wanted to know whether the women were aware of this and what they did with their domestic refuse.

The interviews showed that most of the women considered hygiene important. However, nearly half of them throw rubbish in the streets or in the streams. Although it is true that the council does not fulfil its responsibility regarding refuse collection, many people do not even put

Table 32. How do you treat your water?

	Number	Percentage
Boil it	81	28.72
Add lemon	41	14.54
Add chlorine	52	18.44
Use it without taking any measures	125	44.33
Total	299	106.03

their rubbish in bags or sacks. In this way, the district becomes even dirtier and health hazards multiply. This contradiction between their supposed awareness of the importance of hygiene and the reality is worrying.

Water plays an important part in hygiene. Although La Zurza has had drinking-water for some time now, the danger of infection from the water is still high, because inevitably dirty water gets into the piping because of bad maintenance. Because of this, we wanted to know whether and how the women treated their water.

Most of the women used the water without any treatment. Some boiled the water but only if it was intended for the children. No information is available about pollution in the water supply in La Zurza. Sometimes the children can be seen washing themselves in heavily polluted water, their mothers saying nothing. They continue to use it in their laundry, washing-up, house cleaning and bathing.

Many women of La Zurza (96 per cent) had experienced changes in their lives and their health. They believed that these changes had been very beneficial to their families. These changes came in the shape of talks, advice, visits from the health promoters and examinations in the clinic. The condition of their families had improved, as the changes had helped them to learn more about health.

The women of La Zurza felt very satisfied that they had learned more about health issues. Most women preferred to use modern knowledge, while some preferred a combination of both. The important thing was that they did not keep this knowledge to themselves; they shared it with their neighbours and with women from other areas.

Today, many women in La Zurza know how to space pregnancies (that

Table 33. How have you benefited from these changes?

	Number	Percentage
Increased knowledge	127	45.04
Improved health of family	197	69.86
No benefit	8	2.84
Other	2	0.71
Total	334	118.44

Table 34. How do you rate the usefulness of what you have learned?

	Number	Percentage
Good	207	73.40
All right	63	22.34
Bad	6	2.13
Not useful	2	0.71
No response	4	1.42
Total	282	100.00

Table 35. Do you prefer old or modern methods?

	Number	Percentage
Granny's methods	13	4.61
Modern methods	190	67.38
Both	68	24.11
None	3	1.06
No response	8	2.84
Total	282	100.00

is, they know how often they can have children) and how to prepare food better, especially their children's. In this way, they manage to keep them in better health. It has to be emphasized that the women of La Zurza care greatly about the health of their children and their families.

Problems the women have and how they solve them

In order to find out what problems they had, we met with them at the headquarters of the Mothers' Club. We had six meetings with a total of 165 women. Participation was good and the women showed keen interest in solving their problems. We conducted group work in which we acted only as facilitators. The results showed that the women knew the problems affecting them, both as women and as a community.

Tables 36 and 37 show that one of the things they worried most about was the lifestyle of their children (crime, drug-abuse, prostitution) and the lack of schooling.

Health was another problem affecting women. They did not care about their own health—children and the family always came first. Only at the end did they remember that they also have a right to good health. Many women mentioned that they did not have time to go to the doctor, although this has changed a little in the last few years thanks to the Health Programme, which also advises women on issues relating to their own health.

When asked about the problems they faced as women, they found it

Table 36. Problems for individual women

Problems with the children	7
Health	6
Bad state of their homes	6
No employment	6
Problems with spouse	5
Financial problems	5
No homes	4
Being head of the household	3
Problems in the home	3
Too many responsibilities	3
Family problems	1
No time for themselves	1
Total	50

Table 37. Community-based problems affecting women

No schools	9
No hospital	7
Crime	7
No electricity	7
No telephones	6
Pollution	6
Rubbish	6
No recreation space	6
No water	5
No pharmacy	2
No drainage	1
No toilets	1
No churches	1
High cost of living	1
Problems with youth	1
No adequate transport	1
Roads in bad condition	1
No training centre	1
Total	69

(Figures show the results per group and not the number of women altogether)

difficult to give answers. It is obvious that they were not used to talking about themselves.

As for problems in the community, most found the issue of education very important. There is no secondary school in the district, and the primary school is not big enough for all the children.

Many women mentioned problems with their husbands, who, in many cases, were an obstacle preventing their development, forbidding them, for instance, from joining an organization. There were also cases of domestic violence. Of course, this was a very delicate issue and they were reluctant to talk about it in detail.

They were prepared to look for solutions. The problem was that not all of them were organized and that the ones who were had little support from their organization in their struggle for the services to which they were entitled by law, and for which they were prepared to fight. One thing that came across very forcefully was that the women had the ability and the strength to try and solve their problems by themselves. Using role-play, they showed ways of demanding their rights from the authorities. An example was the schooling problem.

o No school
o Get together, form groups, make lists
o Go to the education department
o Go to the council, demand a site

In the role-play exercises they acted out a conversation with the person in charge of the education department. This was a challenge from real life. When the women had to choose a subject to act out in the role-play exercises, none of them chose a problem which affected them as women.

How women use their time

During the final workshop we saw how the women allocated their time, since the most important thing for them was looking after their homes and their families. They allocate their time in such a way that they can best fulfil these responsibilities.

As we have seen from the results of the survey, nearly all the women use their time to work in the house. Some take part in afternoon social activities (for example, they are health promoters or belong to an organization or

Table 38. How the women use their time

Time	Activity
6.00–7.00 a.m.	Wake up
7.00–7.30 a.m.	Prepare breakfast, feed children, send them to school
7.30–8.30 a.m.	Collect water
8.30–9.00 a.m.	Buy food
9.00–11.00 a.m.	House-cleaning, laundry, chatting with neighbours
11.00–12.00 a.m.	Cook
12.30–1.30 p.m.	Clean the kitchen
1.30–6.00 p.m.	Play, study, iron, wash, read the Bible, watch soaps, run errands, personal hygiene, social activities
6.00–7.30 p.m.	Cook supper and eat
7.30–8.00 p.m.	Clean the kitchen
8.00–10.00 p.m.	Go to church, watch soaps, see friends, play with children
10.00–11.00 p.m.	Make the beds and go to sleep

church), but most of them spend most of their time in the home. None of the women who took part in the workshop had a job away from the home.

When we asked them how happy they were with this schedule, most said they were happy with it. But after a little more reflection, most wanted to change their routine. Many of them would have liked to have had more time for other activities, such as taking part in organizations or learning something which would help them find a job and earn an income.

Their solutions for the problem of time were as follows:

o Be organized in order to plan time and activities
o Try and be aware of social issues
o Think about the daily activities and keep a diary
o Get together and fight for running water
o Ask for planning permission and have taps in all the houses
o Set aside a day for recreation
o Learn to fight the authorities for our rights
o Publicize the problems of the district

These ideas took us into the second part of the workshop.

What prevents the women organizing themselves

Many of the reasons which prevented the women from joining an organization were personal. It was something of a vicious circle. Nearly all the reasons had to do with the women's sense of self-worth and yet the organization was supposed, among other things, to strengthen their self-esteem.

o Their husbands
o The number of children
o Lack of awareness and decisiveness
o The limited scope of the organization
o Fear of not being able to perform well

At this point, the organization should place more emphasis on motivating the women, consciousness-raising and assuaging their fears.

The women participating in the workshop mentioned that they needed to know more about the organization and especially what was being done at the headquarters. It is here that there is the best chance of reaching the women and recruiting them for work.

Finally, it should be emphasized that the women participating in the final workshop felt very good and they all participated well in the group work. Some of them felt more motivated to join the organization.

The role of an organization member

We wanted to know what was, according to them, the role of an organization member in the context of the community. To this end we asked a few women at the Mothers' Club and received these answers:

○ To learn about and value oneself as a woman.
○ To fight to solve the problems of the community.
○ Gain a greater capacity for achieving one's objectives.
○ To train all the women in La Zurza.
○ Not to fear to express one's feelings and ideas, as a woman facing society.
○ A deeper knowledge of oneself.

The health promoters

The health promoters' network originated from a survey carried out in different marginal districts of Santo Domingo. The results showed that La Zurza had the highest number of undernourished children (58 per cent).

The Dominican Institute for Integral Development decided to work with health issues in La Zurza. They began by co-ordinating the district's leaders and existing organizations, which recruited the most active people in the district in order to form the health promoters' network. After many meetings, the first group of 24 people was formed and trained in all aspects of child survival.

After training, each group of health promoters was allocated a number of families. From this moment on, changes began to take place in La Zurza with regard to health issues. At the beginning, the health promoters had problems with the families. They were not welcome, because the families expected direct help in the form of medicine, clothes, food and money. But the health promoters 'only' offered advice and practical help. As a consequence, they were insulted and asked to leave the houses. What is more, many health promoters were very young, which proved to be a problem with the families, since some women were jealous and some husbands behaved very abusively, using obscene language and so on. Now, however, the training of the health promoters and the results of their work has brought about a change of attitude in all parties concerned, and these problems no longer exist.

The work of the health promoters consists of paying twice-monthly visits to each of the families they are allocated, offering them affection and understanding, together with advice on health issues. A promoter may also become a friend, a personal counsellor. Often women confide in the health promoter, revealing personal problems, and the promoter in turn will offer support and help with seeking solutions to the problem. The health promoters said that they are very satisfied with their work, as they were able to help their fellow human beings by putting their skills into use with the families, in their homes and wherever the chance presented itself.

At the end of every month, the health promoters attend a meeting where they present a report and explain the good and difficult cases encountered in their area, as well as making any personal complaints. There are also health supervisors, whose responsibility it is to support and monitor the work of the health promoters.

Finally, it should be emphasized that the work of the health promoters has become so important that all the NGOs got together to conduct a health information campaign on radio and television. The objective was to target those people without access to the health promoters, and ensure that they received all the messages and advice they had missed.

General considerations

One of the objectives of this investigation was to study changes in the attitude of women towards health issues. The results show that women have indeed changed. This proves they are open to change as long as they can see the benefit from it. The following indicators demonstrates this: malnutrition down from 58 per cent to 20 per cent; lower child mortality; and fewer cases of diarrhoea, flu and other diseases in general.

A very important improvement has been the establishment of a clinic in the district. The tenacious fight to get this clinic proves that the women rightly regard health a very important matter, and are capable of innovating through organization.

Another objective of this investigation was to show that the women realize the importance of organizing themselves. They believe it to be the best way to solve problems, for the individual and the community. The work carried out by the Mothers' Club is very positive. As the only women's organization, they are trying to solve community problems, especially in health. There is still, however, a long way to go before women's achievements become visible. There have been many changes not only in the area of health, but also in other areas closely related to health, such as problems of water, hygiene and women's mental health.

There is one problem which aggravates the situation: the economic climate. Although for many women the move to La Zurza has been positive because of the market there, they still have very little money.

Recommendations

Although the women in the district have learned many things, they still find it difficult to put this new knowledge into practice. It is important that the health team creates strategies which the health promoters can use in order to help the women put existing knowledge and skills into practice.

Functional pottery in Nicaragua

FRANÇOISE ROMEO B.

When the idea of an investigation of La Paz Centro was first conceived, those involved had to consider that, during the 1980s, the state had implemented a strict policy of reclaiming 'National Craft Work'. This was a product of the nationalism implicit in the revolutionary planning and discourse, accentuated by the economic blockade and the lack of foreign currency for imports. Consequently, craft work was seen as a substitute for what could not be imported.

Based on this, and an awareness of the popularity of craftswomen with non-governmental organizations and international aid organizations (which were doing their utmost to bring foreign aid into the country), it was felt that an investigation into the technological changes and the impact of external support to the pottery work of La Paz Centro would be timely and useful.

The potters of La Paz Centro had had to compete for new projects with the two other pottery production centres in the country: San Juan de Oriente which specializes in high-quality reproductions of pre-columbian pieces for export; and Matagalpa which specializes in decorative articles. We knew that La Paz Centro could not compete with its functional pottery for the popular end of the market. The NGOs, with exportation in mind, chose to favour the other two centres.

For this reason, the investigation focused on the outcome of external support, examining two cases. At the same time, the research was further broadened by the study of a community of potters whose functional products were always intended for a national market.

What is presented in the following pages, therefore, is derived from potters' testimonies and opinions, collected in numerous interviews and after having lived together with them. We hope to have succeeded in conveying the reality of this 'recognized and popular' community of

FRANCOISE ROMEO B. is a social scientist working for ECOTEXTURA—the Centre for the Innovation and Development of Appropriate Technologies—in Nicaragua.

potters, which, in spite of its reputation, has had to do without significant external help because of the functional nature of its products. Their reality, with the development of traditional technology, is one of survival and their future is threatened. Their survival is desirable because it also means that an important part of the country's culture will endure as well. Is this possible? We hope that this study will help to answer that question.

La Paz Centro

La Paz Centro is a town 60km from Managua, the capital of Nicaragua, and 33km from León, the second most important city. Its location on the road that links these cities makes La Paz Centro a traditional stopover on the way. Although its main industry is farming, this is now in crisis, like its other small industries such as baking and tailoring, which have not been able to compete with imported products—a result of the policies of economic liberalism existing in the country since 1990.

In spite of its being located on Lake Managua and its volcanoes, the landscape of La Paz Centro is dry and desolate. Only during the six months of rain each year are there any signs of green. Indiscriminate stripping and non-conservation of the soil has progressively impoverished the farmers in the area, forcing the town to gradually move towards becoming a 'dormitory' city and forcing its people to look for employment in nearby towns.

Pottery provides work for approximately 270 people, making it a direct means of support for about 8 per cent of the 17 457 inhabitants. This section of the population is divided according to gender and type of production. The manufacture of bricks and tiles in 31 production centres is a source of work for men only. On the other hand, functional and decorative pottery is a source of work for women only.

Pottery has given the town a nationwide reputation, and its proximity to the capital has made it a privileged supplier: bricks and tiles for building materials; while functional pottery supplies a market with objects which, until a few decades ago, were essential for everyday living: griddles, water vessels, cooking pots and other objects which have progressively been substituted by plastic and imported aluminium. Nowadays, not even the potters themselves use earthen cooking pots.

> 'My mum still cooked in earthen pots. I don't like them, I think the food tastes of mud. I only keep water in earthen pots because they keep it cool.' (Carlota Joaquín)

In this sense, functional pottery is currently in crisis, as a result of a low demand and an inability to meet the requirements of present-day society. The potters' being 'updated' does not, however, depend exclusively on new designs or quality improvements, and even less so on a change in

83

mentality—as the organizations that have been involved with them have chosen to see it.

The potters are the first step in a structure that consists of middle-men, retailers and users. The potters are at the vulnerable end of this chain. So far, readjustments, in terms of design and quality, have been carried out cautiously, always having to bear in mind not to lose their poor and deficient traditional market. Their simple economy and their lack of financial resources do not allow them to be adventurous in the market-place.

Functional pottery: women's work

Working the clay for functional and decorative pottery has traditionally been seen as 'a women's job'. We know only of three men working in this field.

> 'At the beginning, only women did this job. Then another man and I began doing it and people started calling us "poofs". But I never gave up. I never paid any attention to anybody. Later I even got married and had children.' (Don Rosa Vaca, craftsman and middleman)

The 'world' of this study comprises about 100 women, some of whom devote part of their time to pottery, combining it with other jobs, such as domestic work and tailoring.

The women start their day at 6 a.m. cleaning the house and taking care of the children. At 8 a.m., they stand at their work tables and begin working, almost without interruption, on the pieces they left to dry the previous day. Only at midday do they go to their ovens, sending the children to buy the rice and beans and starting to cook. Then they all sit in front of the television to 'watch the soap'. This is their hour of rest and leisure. In the afternoon, at about 2 o'clock, they start their second shift which is when they shape the pieces that they will start working on the following day. At 5 p.m. they finish the pottery work and go back to their domestic duties. They water the trees, wash and cook supper.

The space

The space used by the potters for production is restricted to the house which is nearly always built from pumice and tiles, both cheap materials. The workshop is generally a wooden, thatched shed at the back of the house and, in most cases, serves as the family kitchen as well. The oven burns constantly, keeping up with both the domestic and the pottery work. The workshop and storeroom are virtually the same size as the house, since it is here that more time is spent during the day. In the case of the poorest craftswomen, the livingroom acts as a storeroom, and the workshop is a small extension at the back of the house.

During this study it was found that the commercial field of their work, contrary to expectation, has diminished over time. Previous generations used to go to the capital and nearby cities to sell their products. Progresss has limited that possibility, since they can no longer compete economically with the middlemen.

'The pieces were sent by train to Managua. Then you went there and picked them up at the station, spending a lot of money, according to my grandmother, because you had to pay for this and that. She had to pay for a cart to take them to the old eastern market.' (Amanda Guzmán)

The growth of new communication links favoured middlemen who changed from using the train (traditional means of transport both for them and the potters) to trucks and vans, thereby reducing their transport costs. In this way, they took from the potters the chance of competing in Managua. As a result, the potters' commerical field was reduced to their homes, which is now the place where they produce *and* sell to middlemen and directly to clients. Occasionally, they still travel to the capital and other nearby cities occasionally, but basically for other reasons not directly related to their work, such as shopping or to sort out bureaucratic matters.

'I used to take my pieces to León and Chinandega. We used to carry them on our heads from the station to the market. Eventually, it wasn't worth it, because we were making as much money by staying here.' (Matea Valle)

Pottery and domestic economy

A large number of potters are the backbone of the household economy. Many of them are single or divorced mothers, and yet even having a man in the house does not necessarily ensure a stable income. Women consider men to be only sporadic economic support. Men do not take direct responsibility for the household.

'When I went to the fair in Managua, I told him: "Look, Juan, you have to help me. You stay here and take care of the child, sweep the house and water the trees." He doesn't like it but, hey, if I don't go out to sell, how can we manage? He works making trousers, but that's three days a week at the most and it's not enough. He knows he has to help.' (Jazmina Guzmán)

Participation of men in pottery work is minimal. Occasionally, they mix the clay, chop the firewood and help with the firing. They do not take part in the making of pieces nor in any commercial aspects. The men's work is at the tile-works and the tailor's shop.

The women's work creates conflicts in marital relationships. They devote most of their time to the pottery. This way of using their time and their economic independence give them certain control over the decision-making which affects the relationship. The women can demand from the men some help with the domestic duties.

'I tell him he has to help me around the house. When I'm working I ask him to feed himself and the kids, because I don't like interrupting my work.'

On the other hand, it is the men who have more physical freedom as a result of two factors: their indirect responsibility for the household, and their search for occasional work. Since their jobs (as tile workers, tailors and builders) do not guarantee steady employment, they are obliged to travel to other cities.

Learning methods and the transfer of knowledge

Pottery skills are normally passed on from mother to daughter and between members of the same family. The family is the basic unit of organization for the potters. Even if family-ties are not close or immediate, they live in the same neighbourhood and tend to make the same types of products as well as adopting the same technical innovations.

The families

o Valle: 5 craftswomen who use a ploughing disc as a rudimentary potter's wheel.
o Zárate: 3 craftswomen who produce griddles.
o Guzmán: 4 craftswomen who have a base-fed square kiln.

'My mum wouldn't let me go to school until I'd finished my pottery. I had to make lots of little toys. She didn't like my going to school, she used to say that books wouldn't feed me. I only got to Grade Three.' (Jazmina Guzmán)

The arrival of the first child often signals the point at which the pottery must become a proper job. Until motherhood, the women do not work full-time; some of them help out, but only inasmuch as it is one more domestic chore imposed by their mothers. It is when they have to support their own children that pottery becomes a profession for them. This relatively late involvement is directly related to the way society and family value pottery as a profession. The potters' economic status is one of survival and their social prospects are limited by their level of income—the main determinant of which is the location of their houses in marginal areas of the city.

Most of the families now want their daughters to study or improve their economic prospects through marriage. This is why the women turn to pottery so late. Having other expectations, they show no interest in pottery until it is very clear that these expectations are never going to be fulfilled. Only then do they turn to pottery as a profession and as a means of survival.

'My mum and my sisters used to do pottery. I didn't like it. I worked as a servant in León. Only when I got married and came back here did I have to learn it. I started making little thingummybobs until I was able to make a flowerpot.' (Lourdes Zamora)

In spite of the fact that most daughters resist the idea of joining this profession, having done so they contribute changes and new styles.

'My mum did other kinds of work. She made water-pots, that's what she says she made when she was young; but not little decorative things. Then I taught her how and now she makes small vases and things like that.' (María Eugenia Mesa)

Although the social recognition of the potters, as in every society and with every profession, is directly related to their economic status, from their point of view, they enjoyed a sort of golden age during the 12 years of *Sandinismo* [the political movement of the Sandinistas]. During this period, the Ministry of Culture carried out an extensive campaign to revalue national craft work. The UNADI (*Unión Nacional de Artesanos Diriangen*—The National Union of Craft Workers, Diriangen) was created which organized the craft workers and promoted their work. This had an immediate effect on the people of La Paz Centro, dramatically improving the community's attitude towards the craftswomen. They stopped calling the women 'mud-eaters' and called them artisans.

'Before, the people used to call us "mud-eaters". I hadn't even heard of the word "artisan". It was with the Sandinistas that I learned the expression.' (Leonor Guzmán)

From the point of view of family and society, the main drawback of pottery work is the dirtiness. The children accept it even though they dislike it.

'I don't like pottery. It's dirty. I help because my mum asks me to, but I don't like it.' (Carla Valle)

Matea Valle is an artisan and this is how she rates pottery: 'Clay is dirty, but it has given me this house and it feeds me. I don't regret doing it.'

Most of the potters do not value their profession very highly. As with the example cited above, their estimation has defensive undertones.

The production process

The potters have several different methods and styles of working, depending on each area of specialization. Griddle-makers use two varieties of clay, white and black, whereas those making hens, flowerpots and money-boxes work only with white clay.

After kneading, the clay is kept in a moist place. Sand is spread on the work-table to mix with the clay. This also prevents the clay from sticking to the table. The clay is then kneaded into a thick 'pancake' and placed in an inverted mould, which varies depending on what it is intended for (a griddle, a flowerpot, a pot).

With one hand they shape the clay, while the other hand turns the mould which acts as a potter's wheel. When the desired shape is achieved, it is stretched and polished using a wet corncob. To seal any pores, a round stick, an insole or any other suitable tool is used. Many of the tools used are old pencils, insoles or old pieces of plastic. When the mould is ready, it is covered with plastic so that it does not crack. It is then left to dry in the sun for a length of time determined by each potter. Then it is kept in a cool, shady place on a bed of sand, earth or rags so that the base does not warp. There, the piece is left to dry until the following day, when it will be given its final shape.

The final part of the process is the scraping. This consists of removing any remaining sand from the inside of the piece with the aid of a wooden calabash spoon, and then smoothing the inside walls. The edges are finished off with a wet cloth called a '*baqueta*'. Simple drawings such as flowers are incised on the flowerpots and cooking pots. To give them colour, *tague* (a red volcanic soil dissolved in water) is used as a dye. Griddles are not patterned and only their edges are painted.

The only work then left to be done on the pieces is the 'sanding' which is done with a washing brush or a stone from the river. This work is often done by the daughters. The pieces are then kept out of the sun and the wind until firing day. The working day is divided in two. In the morning they finish the work from the previous day. In the afternoon they shape the pieces on which they will be working the following day. Depending on the size of the pieces, they work on an average of nine to 12 pieces a day.

At the end of the week they have about 60 pieces, although this number varies depending on the other activities they have had during the week (housework, visiting relatives, running errands) or if they have simply slowed production because the previous week had been quiet saleswise.

The firing is carried out according to the number of pieces they have. At least five dozen pieces are needed for a weekly firing. The traditional firing method referred to as '*al campo*' consists of stacking the pieces in a circle and covering them with layers of thick firewood. When the pile is ready, a fire is lit. The colour of the pieces is checked constantly. Because of the intensity of the fire, the women cover their heads and faces and control the fire using a long pole. This process lasts for three hours and the pieces must be left to cool until the afternoon. The next day the women do not work or bathe in case they 'get ill'. That is why firing is done on Saturdays.

The materials

Previously, obtaining the clay did not cost anything. The women got it from their own plots of land or grounds nearby. As the town ceased to be a rural zone to become an urban area, they were forced to buy the clay from quarries situated in the outskirts of the town. Nowadays, it is the people who own carts who extract the clay and transport it. Firewood is also obtained from the carters, who have to travel for three hours to get it. This distance is becoming progressively greater as a result of the indiscriminate soil stripping which makes it more and more difficult to find firewood. Consequently, the price also increases. This has a very negative effect on the pottery since firewood is the most expensive material in the production process. Firewood is an important material for many of the industries in La Paz Centro, such as tile workshops, *tortillerías* (shops selling *tortilla*, a kind of pancake made from boiled lime water and mashed corn which is cooked in a griddle and is a staple food in Central America) and bakeries. Firewood is also used by 70 per cent of the population for cooking.

The firing

Firing is the last step in the production process. The potters consider it to be the most exhausting part. Also, from a financial point of view, the cost of the firewood makes it their biggest investment. Straight after the firing, the potters count all the broken pieces and then they know exactly what the weekly production has been.

The method of firing is a decisive part of the production process and is determined by the technology used. Nowadays, only a minority (approximately 10 per cent) of the potters fire using the *al campo* method (described on p. 88). About 40 per cent of them fire in a stone or brick circle with a

Table 1. Pottery production costs

Production materials	Cost
Clay	$11.00
Tague (dye)	$0.80
Firewood (in summer)	$22.00
Firewood (in winter)	$33.00

diameter of 2m and similar in height to the one above. Firewood is put underneath and on top of the pieces, and it is not possible to feed the fire during the process. Only the firewood burning at the top can be controlled.

The third method of firing uses a stone square, 2m in diameter and similar in height to the others, but which can also be fed from below. This kiln, open at the top, has an iron grate 40cm from the ground, enabling it to be fed through either of the two openings. The top part is covered with leaves.

This kiln is obviously the one that uses least firewood and considerably reduces physical effort. The origins of the innovation are uncertain and different versions of the story contradict each other. It is significant, however, that all those who use it say that they have done for three years or less. Everything seems to indicate that, although the first one was built by locals and with local materials, the idea came from outsiders. The unsuccessful co-operative which we analyse later could very well have been responsible for popularizing it.

Construction techniques and technological changes

The main potting techniques are moulding (using an inverted mould) and coiling. Both are ancient techniques to which have been added new tools and some technical changes in order to improve the quality of the products. Changes are resisted, however, and their transfer is slow. The potters are conservative when it comes to introducing changes to their working methods, as much in design as in technology. This phenomenon is not the result of a conservative spirit (which may or may not exist) but has more complex reasons. Looking at their production methods, we could detect three new techniques which were found in instances of mass-production.

The first, new technique is a method of sieving the clay. This has been adapted from other artisans whose work is of better quality and more refined, and, therefore, more competitive. This technique has been adapted only by the potters who make decorative objects, and not by those making functional objects, for whom the extra time required would not be cost-effective. The potters who do use it, however, argue that this spares them the work of flattening the clay, making up for the time supposedly lost and avoiding that part of the process which they dislike most of all.

According to one of the potters, the time she spends sieving the clay for a flowerpot is not paid for by her middleman, since he only buys the pots for nurseries which do not require better quality.

The second new technique is the concave ploughing disc, on which the piece is shaped while being manually turned serves as a rudimentary potter's wheel. We found this adaptation in only one of the families studied. However, it is significant because it approximates a real potter's wheel. This is an essential instrument which does not exist in La Paz Centro. Their version would seem to be a substitute.

The third and most important technological innovation is the base-fed kiln because it allows them to economize on firewood and to minimize their own physical effort.

Even though this kiln has proved itself as a fuel-saver, the potters are slow and cautious in accepting it. As with every kiln, the first firing results in an increased number of broken pieces until the potter has learned how to use it. The necessary initial investment needed to cover the cost of these broken pieces has made many potters reluctant to use it. This is why they prefer to stick with the top-fed kiln, which has some advantages over the *al campo* method.

> 'With this kiln I don't risk getting burned. One of my brothers, a tile maker, built it for me so that I didn't spend too much on firewood. With the other one I feel like I'm going to lose a lot. I have tried the other one but I'm used to this kind of kiln. I have the knack for using it.' (Gregoria Cajín on her top-fed kiln)

When and how the base-fed kiln was introduced is not clear. Some potters tell us their tile-making husbands built them, based on the furnaces at the tile workshops. Others have copied the idea from their sisters and relatives. One of the artisans claimed that it was she who invented it after seeing the furnaces at the tile workshops. What is clear is the fact that the transfer of this technology took place at a family level and that all of them estimate that their kilns are, at most, two or three years old.

The results of our survey confirm this family transference: 11 base-fed kilns are found in only four families. Not only are they all close relatives, but seven of them were involved in the Juan Figueroa Co-operative (see page 92).

What we can say is that the main determinant for innovations is the market-place via the middlemen. It is the market-place which, according to its needs, dictates the kind of products the potters must make, and in doing so, forces them to introduce changes to their production methods.

On the other hand, economic factors make them reduce costs and the physical effort—although changes are adopted only when personal experience has proved their guaranteed profitability.

Table 2. Kiln ownership in La Paz Centro

Family	Kilns
Guzmán	4
Castillo	3
Valle	2
Mesa	1

'They used to come to La Paz Centro and bring me a model (a heat-resistant base) that I could try out, but I didn't really like it. Only when I realized they were successful did I start making them. They were sold in large numbers. I stopped doing other things because I didn't have enough time. I made them until the end, that is, until the change [of government]. We lived off them from 1988 till 1990. I remember at one stage that a batch of them fetched a price of one million [*cordoba*], and I used to make up to 500 pieces a week. My son used to help me. We worked hard, the two of us. We made a fortune.' (Amanda Guzmán)

Design and use of the pieces

The pieces produced have traditionally been mostly functional: cooking pots, jars, griddles and flowerpots, used for cooking, storing food and water, as animal dishes and other household uses. As for decorative pieces, these are money-boxes, small toys and whistles, made specially for *La Purísima*—a national day of celebration in December.

The animal figures, such as ducks and hens, which are not traditional, were apparently introduced during the last two decades, an influence from the pottery of Honduras. They were introduced into La Paz Centro by merchants and clients who took the design to the potters and asked for copies.

The introduction of new designs is more common these days. The potters are progressively increasing their production of decorative pieces, in response to new markets. In this way, one can see new designs which include, among others, churches, money-boxes, vases and Nativity scenes.

'Some ladies from León came and asked if I could make churches. I had never made them and told them so, but they insisted that I try, saying they'd be back in 15 days. The days passed and I didn't even want to try, it seemed so difficult. Juan used to say to me: "Make one, Jazmina. Look, those ladies are going to be back. You can do it, come on, try." He insisted so much, that I started making one, and it's not easy. I managed to make only one the whole day. When the ladies came they were very pleased and since then they always come to me with new orders.' (Jazmina Guzmán)

Case study 1: the Juan Figueroa Co-operative

The co-operative was formed in 1986 as an initiative of AMLAE (The National Luisa Armanda Espinoza Association for Women), an organization of the Sandinistas—then in power. It later included other organizations such as Swiss Caritas, *Ceramistas por la Paz* (Potters for Peace) and FACS (the A.C. Sandino Foundation) which managed donations. This co-operative was successor to a preliminary organization of potters promoted by UNADI and AMLAE.

92

The project took shape after the donation of a roadside site by the local council. A loan was secured for setting up the necessary infrastructure and for purchasing raw materials. Initially, 10 potters took part. The co-operative was established with 'the main objective of changing traditional commerical methods and liberating the artisans from the economic abuses of the middlemen'. The underlying belief was that the middlemen were exploiting the artisans by taking a disproportionate share of profits.

AMLAE took an active part in the internal organization, creating the rules and regulations. It was decided that the potters would all work together and that profits and cost would be shared accordingly. AMLAE also organized workshops on technical training and the theory of co-operatives through UNADI and DIGECOOP (the Co-operatives Authority). AMLAE appointed a team which gave the potters monthly support and guidance.

Initially, it was hoped that, following the example of the first 10 participants, other artisans would join the scheme. This did not happen. The main reason being that the initial group was largely comprised of members of the same family, making the co-operative exclusive for other artisans. This was so much the case that those members who were not members of the one family left the co-operative until its membership was reduced to a group of seven women.

The co-operative's infrastructure offered suitable physical working conditions: they had at their disposal the spacious roadside premises (which was, in fact, a good sales point); a kiln; work opportunities; and financing for materials.

The co-operative was dissolved in 1990, coinciding with the change of government. By then, there were no longer links between AMLAE and the co-op. According to former members, the co-op was dissolved for a number of reasons, one of the most decisive being the change of government. On the one hand, electioneering caused a rift between AMLAE and most of the co-op's members because of party political differences. On the other hand, the new government brought an end to the loans and to much of the support the co-op had received from organizations sympathizing with *Sandinismo*. In addition to this, the new liberal economic policies resulted in a fall in national spending, and the co-op's sales fell. The co-op's members were unable to see out this period on their own, not without 'parental' support from AMLAE and the state.

The co-op came to an end when its members sold off its assets and divided up the money. They went back to their traditional way of working, which did not differ markedly from the other potters' methods in terms of either technology or design.

In the interviews conducted with the co-op's organizers, we found a clear contradiction between what they and the artisans had to say on the subject of middlemen: on one hand, it was a basic objective of the co-op to sidestep the middlemen, which led to repeated efforts on the part of the organizers to turn the premises into a competitive sales point: on the other hand, the women tried, throughout the development of the co-op to avoid any conflict with the middlemen, with the negative outcome of their having to compete with the middlemen. The details of this conflict were never completely clear; however, what is evident is the difference in the way outsiders and the potters viewed the middlemen.

The co-op ended for a number of reasons, the most important of which may be summarized as follows:

○ The loss of 'parental' support from AMLAE, the state and other sympathetic groups, which had previously been constant.
○ The organization of the co-op, which, by concentrating the work in one spot, upset the natural environment of the potters, affecting their daily lives and the family balance.

'The main limitation of an artisan woman and of any working woman, peasant, whatever, is that she's alone. You're alone in your house, perhaps with a bunch of kids. Who takes care of them, then? In La Paz Centro there was no alternative but to leave the house and go to the co-op. Who was going to take care of my kids? That was the most annoying thing.' (Norma Guzmán)

The main catalysts for the dissolving of the co-op were low sales and economic crisis among its members. Nevertheless, this would not have happened had the decisive factors mentioned above not been present.

Case study 2: the training workshop

In October 1992, ERCAC (Regional Company for the Commercialization of Central American Artisans) organized a training workshop in which 10 women potters took part. The course lasted six weeks with two sessions per week, making a total of 38 hours. The main objectives of the course were to improve the quality of the potters' work and to promote new designs and decorations with the national market in mind. The potters were also offered the possibility of selling their products in ERCAC's shop in Managua.

The convener for the area was Amanda Guzmán, a local artisan, best known for the quality and design of her pottery which mainly consists of decorative pieces. The instructors were herself and another potter from Managua.

ERCAC's proposal was for the women to improve the quality of their products and to help the women commercialize their products by exhibiting them in the ERCAC shop in Managua. New designs were taught, but these were particular in that they were small decorations such as flowers, Nativity scenes and fruit, which went against the traditionally large designs of the potters.

94

The training was based on new moulding and decorating techniques, experimenting with different kinds of natural, local materials. They studied new techniques for preparing the raw materials, such as sieving the clay, and reducing the amount of sand used in the mixture. Demonstrations were given of firing in a base-fed kiln. Bit by bit, some of the women left the workshop; some through lack of time, others because of family problems. Only six women completed the course.

According to ERCAC, the problems they subsequently encountered were:

○ No habit of working as a team
○ Individualism
○ No self-discipline in terms of the quality of work
○ Poor quality—the clay was porous because too much sand was used, making a bad mixture.

ERCAC's intention was to organize a second workshop with the same group of women, but as yet this has not happened. The original idea of constant commercial links was also not put into practice.

We found that, of the six women who completed the course, only two had put into practice some of the designs and techniques they had learned.

Why did the women attend the course? The first reason, for most of the participants, was that they hoped to be able to sell their products through ERCAC. This did not happen. Second, they wanted to learn how to make the designs of Amanda Guzmán, such as churches and other decorations, which they thought would guarantee them similar economic success. Amanda did not teach them her most successful designs. As she herself explains: 'Clay has its secrets. I teach, but only to a certain point.'

As for ERCAC, its objectives in terms of teaching were achieved, but the commercial aspect could not be put into action. The company's excuse was that it did not have enough capital to purchase the potter's work. As for the potters, their budgets were too small to enable them to give the company pieces in consignments. The 'faults' of the potters notwithstanding, the company is planning new workshops for the future, to be implemented in the following stages: improving quality, improving design, and working towards commercialization.

With these objectives they are seeking to develop the crafts. However, in not setting out their priorities in relation to the priorities of the artisans, they risk becoming redundant, as was the case with a seminar about feedback for the women.

For the women, the first priority is commercialization, because their economic survival does not allow them to take risks with their sales. That is why (as was seen above) the adoption of new designs and, therefore, improvements in quality are determined by whether or not they have a specific demand for a new product. We cannot imagine that

The introduction of new designs has gradually become more common

a potter would change her griddles, which she is guaranteed to sell, for an object of improved quality which she may not be able to sell.

Commercialization

One constant throughout this study has been the desperate need of the women to have a merchant who buys their products. The traditional method of commercialization has been the sale of goods mainly to middlemen and dealers. The women do not go out selling their products, it is the buyer who comes to them with orders. Payment, although small, was guaranteed—it is made either at time of purchase or in advance, when an order is placed.

In the 1980s, during the administration of the Sandinistas, they sought to break this commercial chain. Although the intention was to defend the artisans' economy, it was not achieved because this structure gives the artisans financial security and direct feedback from the market which enables them to adjust their production to meet current demand.

This is how animal figure flowerpots were introduced in the 1970s:

'The Americans came with models for us to make, they came in huge trucks and took everything to Costa Rica. Everything ended up in a restaurant, *El Guru*. Lots of ashtrays were made. Hens and ducks, apparently, were first made in Honduras.' (Amanda Guzmán).

The influence of social and political changes

The artisans' economy, being one of survival and lacking in financial reserves which might enable them to absorb the effects of unforeseen changes in the market-place, makes them extremely vulnerable to economic vicissitudes brought about by the country's political changes. In the case of Nicaragua, where political changes have been dramatic in the last few decades, the lives and work of the artisans have also changed dramatically.

Before 1980, there was an increasing demand for large decorative pottery as well as the traditional functional pottery such as griddles, cooking pots and jars destined for domestic use. This decorative pottery was bought by the wealthy to decorate their gardens. The most popular objects were the animal-figure flowerpots (such as ducks and hens), and also jars and other decorated flowerpots.

The artisans did not get any governmental or institutional help. They did, however, enjoy the certainty of a commercial structure and a traditional market which, because of its stability, afforded them the security of something familiar. In a survival economy, the value of this security should not be underestimated.

During the time of the Government of the Sandinistas (1980–90) production and sales were affected dramatically. It was a time of great drama when war and the new economic policies of nationalization resulted in hyperinflation, changing the potters' traditional way of life. From the point of view of production and sales, however, it was one of the best periods the potters have ever had.

'The trucks came and bought up everything. Sometimes they wanted so much that we had to do two firings a week.' (Lula Zamora)

This huge demand, however, usually occurred only in December. The rest of the year the demand was for functional objects which did not always correspond with the traditional work of the artisans. Its greatest expression was in the demand for heat-resistant bases for use on electric cookers. This demand was so massive and profitable that practically all the artisans

97

doubled their efforts to produce them. Although this guaranteed relative prosperity, they paid the price by neglecting traditional craft work and regressing in terms of quality and creativity.

The potters regard the positive aspects of this period to have been the loans, strong demand, and more contact with the outside world through the large numbers of interested foreign visitors. They consider the negative aspects to have been, fundamentally, the compulsory military service. Besides the constant risk of death to their sons, military service also upset family life and brought about dramatic changes in the use of time, as it is usual to travel all over the country to visit a son in uniform.

The current regime

In 1990, with the change of government and the end of shortages, the electric cookers were forgotten, the merchants stopped coming; but the potters, not reacting to the change, kept making them. Today, they lie piled up in one corner of their workshops. What is more, the cooking pots, jars and griddles are being replaced by plastic and aluminium utensils.

Once more they have had to adapt to the market-place and change their designs in order to meet the new demand, which is characterized by decorativeness. Today they make hens, ducks, and free-standing and wall-mounted flowerpots. One particular group of women, more conscious of the need for change and more skilful in moving with it, have begun working on churches for a new kind of middleman who buys these pieces and paints and decorates them before selling them to tourist shops or, in some cases, exporting them. In short, we now live in times that are characterized by a crisis in pottery which is gradually losing the demand for traditional functional objects and has not yet adapted itself to this new unknown market.

Conclusions

The crisis in which pottery in La Paz Centro finds itself is evident. Its future will be determined by the ability of the potters to adapt themselves to the new market, which is reducing its consumption of traditional functional pottery. What is more, the potters lack the economic resources and the capacity to adapt to this new market without external contributions, both economic and technological, as well as in terms of design.

Both NGOs and international organizations, as well as government-linked organizations, have tended to give help to centres for decorative pottery, with exports and quick profits in mind. In the medium or long term, abandoning functional pottery designs jeopardizes the survival of this tradition, and, therefore, part of the country's culture. If this process is not reversed, the inherent risk is that it will be replaced by a culturally hybrid decorative pottery, whose designs and techniques will be dictated by foreign consumers.

All contributions, both in terms of design and new techniques, will not have the desired effect if there is not a concomitant, relatively constant, spending power. The equation, new clients equals new designs, is evident; and it will have to be given priority if the potters are to make the necessary leap forward in terms of quality.

Necessary outside contributions which help reduce production costs and improve quality (such as kilns and clay-kneading plants with sales service for the potters), must be made, respecting the existing social and economic organizations. Success is made more feasible by financing an artisan and making her an independent owner than by establishing a co-operative, which damages the family unit and which is therefore a source of conflicts that can lead all its members to failure. The basic social and production units of the potters are, first, the home, and second, the family. We believe that any external contribution which does not take this social structure into account will inevitably fail.

From this study it is evident that the problem is not to be found in changing from traditional functional pottery to merely decorative pottery. The demands of modern life are more sophisticated but just as utilitarian: lamps, trays, dinner services, ashtrays and tiles, all present an endless range of possibilities for this new 'modern functional pottery' and which, as well as allowing the potters in La Paz Centro to keep working, allows the country to preserve its cultural heritage.

Whether or not it is behind the times, the potters have a technology which is suited to the space they have, their gender and their family responsibilities. What one tries to do is not to let 'modern technologies' destroy the harmonious sequence. This sequence interweaves production with domestic life and the transfer of skills to the next generation of producers. The challenge is to achieve a technology suited to this sequence and to adapt production to the new conditions for development.

Pork processing in Peru

MERCEDES LÓPEZ PINEDO

This case study presents the experience of a group of women devoted to making *cecina*, an activity practised by an increasing number of people. [*Cecina* refers to any kind of cured meat but, in this case, only cured pork.] Their job, although very hard, is handed down from generation to generation, from mothers to daughters. Nowadays, a small number of men are also engaging in this activity, but the fact is that most of them are either relatives of the *cecina* makers or men who have worked with the women as their assistants.

It is also the intention to analyse the technological innovations adopted by another group of women from a rural area who devote themselves to the production of *embutidos* (pork products, such as ham and sausages). Although they know the traditional technique for making *cecina*, these women have opted for this new technology with a view to learning new methods and therefore improve their income and the quality of their lives.

Background and context

This study was carried out in the districts of Tarapoto and Cabo A. Leveau. Tarapoto is a city in the province of San Martin, in the San Martin region of Peru's Selva Alta. It is 333m above sea level, has a population of 53 514 and covers an area of 67.81km². Tarapoto is considered an up and coming area with very good prospects in terms of its continuing commerce, industry, crafts and tourism.

Cabo A. Leveau is also located in the province of San Martin, to the right of the river Huallaga. Its population growth rate was 1.48 per cent between 1972 and 1981. The estimated population for 1993 is 1422.

The preparation of *cecina* in Tarapoto dates back to ancient times. It is believed that humans, from the time they began to hunt wild animals,

MERCEDES LÓPEZ PINEDO works for CEPCO—the Centre for Community based study and Dissemination in Eastern Peru—based in Tarapoto.

practised food conservation of any kind of meat, using salt and smoke-drying as preservatives. In this way, the technique for processing pork in Tarapoto and its surrounding areas has been passed down from generation to generation, specifically from mother to daughter in some families which, at the beginning, numbered only a few (according to the oldest *cecina* makers).

Production of the raw material is sufficient to meet the local demand. Selva Industrial, one of the biggest pig breeders in Tarapoto, claimed to have 550 pigs in March 1993. On average, they sell between 90 and 100 pigs per month to either the municipal abattoir or private customers. Other big breeders in the area include the farms belonging to the Santilláns, Jorge Arévalo, Diómedes Paredes and the University of La Molina. It is important to note that pig breeding in the region is carried out using traditional methods. In the municipal abattoir, 25 to 30 pigs are slaughtered daily, some of which are sold as fresh meat and the rest used for *cecina*.

Successive migrations have not affected the methods for making *cecina*, since the preparation of *cecina* in Tarapoto has its own style and technique. Each maker is always trying to improve her technique and, with it, the quality of her product.

Forty years ago, the basic diet of the area consisted mainly of bananas, beans and rice, supplemented by meat from wild animals and farm animals, generally pork and beef. When the coast road was built, products from the coast became more obtainable and therefore cheaper. The inhabitants of the

Cecina *(cured pork) is a traditional product in Peru, but its preparation is consistently being improved*

101

region started changing their consumption habits. This, together with the economic situation, reduced the demand for *cecina*.

A traditional craft

The origins of the making of *cecina* (and of the technology employed) cannot be determined exactly, but it is known that it dates back to ancient times, from the moment when the hunting tribes of the area felt the need to preserve meat because of their nomadic habits. Later, with the introduction of domesticated animals (such as pigs and cattle), this technique continued to improve, but always using smoke-drying and salt as preservatives. Well-prepared *cecina* can last between two and 10 days without being refrigerated, and up to a month if refrigerated, but this does not taste terribly good.

The preparation of *cecina* started in this area because of three reasons: first, there were large numbers of pigs; second, people did not have access to foodstuffs other than those they themselves grew or bred; third, and most importantly, meat preserved this way has a very pleasant taste.

Nowadays, the preparation of *cecina* is being improved constantly. The *cecina* makers try to improve the quality of their products by themselves, since they have no way to learn about new techniques. Previously, for example, the *cecina* makers used wooden smoke-driers known as barbecues. Nowadays, they have switched these for iron ones. They have also tried to improve the *pishtado* (cutting) methods so that the *cecina* can be cut more uniformly which will allow better smoking on both sides and, therefore, a better end-product.

Daily life of the women who make *cecina*

The *cecina* makers start their day early, when they go to their market stalls to sell their product. They stay there until 11.00 a.m. when they go back home to start doing their housework. Some are helped by their husbands or a servant if they can afford one. Others do it on their own, alternating the housework with the preparation of *cecina*.

The preparation of *cecina* starts at midday. They work all afternoon until dusk, when the product is finished. After that many of them have to finish their domestic work. Once all the work is done, they rest, because they have to wake up early once again the following morning.

The sexual division of labour applies to the preparation of *cecina*. The men are normally responsible for slaughtering the pigs or buying the meat at the municipal abattoir and carrying it home. In some cases, the men have a fresh meat stall in the market, and any unsold meat is used for the preparation of *cecina*. The children (and, very occasionally, the husband) light the fire (using firewood) and stuff the *chorizos* [a local kind of sausage], another product prepared at the same time as the *cecina*.

102

As for the women, the job consists of the following:

○ Purchasing the fresh meat (for women who work on their own).
○ Cutting the meat and preparing it for the different products which are made at the same time as the *cecina*.
○ Preparing the seasoning used in the making of the *chorizo* and the stuffing.
○ Cleaning the tripe.
○ Preparing the following products (in addition to the *cecina*): *chorizo*, stuffing, lard, offal products, crackling and skins.

Preparation process

The preparation of *cecina* is a hard job, since the maker has to be present at every moment of every stage. The stages in the preparation of *cecina* are as follows:

1. The pieces of meat are selected depending on their intended use (whether for making pure *cecina* or boned *cecina*). For the pure *cecina*, slices are cut from the legs and shoulders of the pig; boned *cecina* uses the rest of the legs and shoulders and part of the ribs.
2. The slices are cut uniformly (in thickness, not in size).
3. The meat is salted and left to settle for about half an hour to an hour, so that the salt penetrates the pork.
4. The meat is washed once or twice at the discretion of the maker.
5. The meat is smoked for half an hour on each side so that it acquires colour and flavour. Some makers cover the meat in banana leaves, the idea being to 'keep' the smoke inside this 'wrapping' so that the meat acquires a better colour and a more pleasant taste.
6. Once the meat has acquired its colour, the fire is turned down in order to roast the meat evenly. The roasting takes approximately two hours, depending on the type of wood used. According to some makers, the meat must not be allowed to dry completely because its taste is considered to be less pleasant. On the other hand, the drier the meat, the longer its life.
7. The *cecina* is left to cool and then kept until its selling date.

Different opinions from the women who make *cecina* reveal the reality of their work:

'The quality of the *cecina* depends on the type of meat used. It is preferable to use meat from the big breeding farms because the pigs are fed balanced diets and therefore have more meat than fat. On the other hand, the meat from small farm pigs tastes better because their food is different (mostly corn). Big *cecina* eaters can tell the difference.' (Sra Clara Pinedo)

103

'When I have *cecina* left, I keep it in the fridge. The next day I have to heat it, but this is not convenient because it changes colour and loses weight. What we need is to sell it on the day. For instance, I kept 4500g in the fridge one day and the next day it weighed only 3750g.' (Sra Eloisa Paredes)

'Many people devote themselves to making *cecina* just for the hell of it. Apparently some people simply smoke the meat so that it doesn't lose weight. This damages our image as good *cecina* makers.' (Sra Delfina Pinchi)

'Some *cecina* makers are apparently using colouring, which they apply to the meat during the washing. The result is a not-so-natural *cecina*, which is not right.' (Sra Isabel Lozano)

'Nowadays, you don't make much with the sale of *cecina*, because the price of the meat and other materials has gone up a lot. For instance, the other day, after paying off the cost of the fresh meat, I was left with 1500g of *chorizo*. That was my profit. It's a very hard job. Sometimes we don't even have enough to pay the taxes to the authorities, the slaughterhouse, etc.' (Sra Eloisa Paredes)

'We do this work to feed our children and pay for their education.' (Sra Isabel Lozano)

'Nobody taught me how to make *cecina*. I've learned by myself. Necessity makes you learn.' (Sra Delfina Pinchi)

'The way to make *cecina* is the same way my mother taught me. Same methods. It's just that the cutting gets better as we go along. My mum only taught me her way.' (Sra Isabel Lozano)

Makers and consumers of *cecina*

Cecina is produced first and foremost in the Department of San Martin, and then throughout the Selva Peruana in general. Anyone can make *cecina*, always bearing in mind that it is a very demanding job that requires an entire day. The techniques used are all very similar, but each maker has her own style and is always trying to improve the quality of her product.

For most of the *cecina* makers surveyed, 80–90 per cent of the end-products are destined for sale, the rest is kept for family consumption. They say they have grown tired of eating it and now only do so when they really feel like it. The consumption of *cecina* depends on many factors:

○ Income: because it is expensive, the biggest consumers of *cecina* are those with high incomes.
○ Religion: a large number of people in the area do not eat *cecina* because of their religious beliefs.
○ Health: the low consumption of *cecina* is also related to health motives.

High levels of cholesterol and other ailments, the most usual being liver and heart diseases, are attributed to the consumption of *cecina*.

Profitability of the product

These women do not only make *cecina*; they also make other different products, mainly *chorizo*, stuffing, lard, offal products, crackling and skins. For this, they buy the meat '*al gancho*' (50kg) at 3.8 soles per kg (US$2), and the offal from the same pig (intestines, liver, lungs, tongue, kidneys, vessels and stomach) is bought separately at 15 soles per pig (US$8).

With the other preparation materials required, plus transport, slaughter-house tax and other taxes, the final cost adds up to the amounts shown in Table 1.

Table 1. Final cost totals

Description	Price (in soles)	Total costs (in soles)
50kg of fresh meat	3.8	190.0
Fees and taxes	8.5	8.5
Transport	2.5	2.5
Offal	15.0	15.0
Meat grinding	3.5	3.5
Seasonings	2.0	2.0
Salt	1.5	1.5
Firewood	8.0	8.0
Labour	15.0	15.0
		soles 246.0 (US$133.0)

Apparently, *cecina* is a profitable product. If the women sold everything they produced daily, they would obtain a net profit of $34. However, the facts prove to be different. Not everything they make is sold; of these, the least popular is lard. They keep the lard stored in large quantities, but usually have to throw it away when it goes off.

The influence of the market-place

The market-place is a measurable concept, both in terms of production and the consumption of any foodstuffs. *Cecina* and its by-products are sold at the local markets or in the women's homes. There are about 34 *cecina* makers in Tarapoto, who process between 15 and 50kg of fresh meat between Monday and Saturday. Each one of them makes between four and 13kg of *cecina* and a similar proportion of *chorizo*, which adds up to a total output of 130 to 300kg, the same amount that is sold in Tarapoto. Previously, when the economic situation was better, consumption of *cecina*

105

Table 2. Total production and subsequent profit (in soles)

Product	Price	Total
5kg pure *cecina*	13.0	65.0
10kg boned *cecina*	10.0	100.0
7kg *chorizo*	12.0	84.0
3kg skin	4.0	12.0
6kg lard	4.0	24.0
2kg crackling	3.0	6.0
1.5kg offal	8.0	12.0
2kg head	2.0	4.0
0.5kg trotters	4.0	2.0
		soles 309.0 (US$167.0)

was greater. The demand was apparently big in areas notorious for drug-trafficking, which made the preparation of *cecina* increase to up to three times the greatest amount produced in its peak period. Nowadays, tourists and traditional restaurants serving typical dishes are the biggest buyers.

Organization of the group of women

Before the organization of the women makers of *embutidos* (preserved pork products), in Cabo A. Leveau (Utcurarca) there was a women's group devoted to local maintenance and repair work (such as repairing the school roof, cleaning the town square, removing weeds in the port). They worked in co-ordination with groups of men. These women had a certain part in decision-making regarding improvements to the town, but were sometimes marginalized.

When a non-governmental organization approached the best-organized groups in Cabo A. Leveau, certain other groups felt an urge to work for the community. A number of small projects began to take shape, for example, vegetable growing and the breeding of poultry and small animals. The community generally welcomed these projects, the main purpose of which was to revalue the important role women play in the rural economy of the country.

As a first step, men organized themselves in what was called the Pig-breeding Project, in order to supply the community with fresh meat. The development of this project not only enabled its participants to improve their income, but has also revitalized the local economy and boosted the business activities of the farmers involved.

In an attempt to give further value to pig breeding, and to help lay the foundations of a developing agricultural industry in our department, the *Embutidos* Group was organized. At the beginning it was made up only of the wives of the pig breeders. Later it was declared an open group, but with disappointing results—in the end, only 16 women took part in the group.

Once the *embutidos* work team was organized, it was felt that there was a need to learn the relevant techniques in order to diversify production and give an added value to the preparation of pork. Support was sought from a pork *embutidos* specialist from Cuzco, who gave training to the women.

The training consisted of a series of talks, later supplemented by some practical training carried out in the field. Some women tried to change certain aspects of the project, arguing that the community was not used to eating *embutidos*. They proposed making greater amounts of high-quality *cecina*, as there was more demand for this and the women had, from time to time, already made it and sold it to the locals. In the end, the project remained unchanged because the will to learn new techniques was stronger, and, furthermore, the women eventually decided that consumer habits could in fact be changed. So the project was carried out as originally planned.

Preparation of *embutidos*

The meat was supplied by the pig breeders. Pigs were available once every month, every three months or even every six months, hence there was a lack of continuity in the preparation of *embutidos*.

Other materials were supplied by the non-governmental organization, which purchased them in Tarapoto. The women did not have to worry about supplies.

The infrastructure was not appropriate, so plans were made for the building of a slaughterhouse and a processing plant. Even so, there was neither drinking-water nor electricity for the fridges. The tools and equipment used were simple. They included: a scale, a table, a saw, knives of different shapes and sizes, vats, pails, brine tanks, a grinder, a manual mincer, a manual stuffing machine, semi-industrial shelving, boiling pans and a drying rack.

The men were responsible for slaughtering the pigs, cutting-up the animals, buying firewood and cleaning the grills. The women were in charge of the whole preparation process itself.

The group made the following products: 'English ham', smoked *chorizo*, paté, *pork cheese* and stuffing. Sometimes they also made *cecina*.

Profits cannot be determined in exact figures, since there is no recorded data detailing production or sales. The *embutido* makers, however, thought they earned very little. Most of the profits were used to pay off the loan the non-governmental organization had given them to start the project. At present, there is a company in Tarapoto that makes and markets meat products, including 'English ham' which sells at US$7.0 per kg.

The city of Tarapoto was the main market for the *embutidos*. Cabo A.

Leveau, the place where they were made, was also a market. *Embutidos* were always welcome, but they were made in small quantities to be bought by the middle and upper classes. They are more expensive than *cecina*. Besides, *embutidos* need to be kept in a refrigerator, something that most households cannot afford.

An analysis of craft technology

The craft technology used in making *cecina* is a traditional technique originating from the need of the first nomadic hunters to preserve food. Some aspects of it have obviously been improved, such as the substitution of wooden grills for iron grills in order to improve the quality of *cecina*, and also because it was difficult to get fresh wood near the manufacturing site. Small manual *chorizo* stuffing-machines were another innovation.

The most important thing about the application of this technology is the fact that it constitutes a way of life, in view of the difficult social and political situations faced by Peru today. Groups of women find it personally satisfying to be the users of this craft technology, with all its flaws and virtues.

The preparation of Andean products in Peru

MARÍA ESTRELLA CANTO SANABRIA

This case study summarizes the work of a group of women devoted to the preparation of food products. The range of confectionery products by the National Sweet Foods Industry merely provides Peruvians with hundreds of calories and nothing else. In order to break the food dependency and consuming habits, however, a group of women (called *La Asunción*) during the last few years has been preparing confectionery, baking and other foodstuffs made from Andean ingredients with high nutritional values.

Thanks to their perseverance and to the motivation gained from winning some competitions, the group has been able to specialize in the preparation and commercialization of Andean products, in spite of the economic crisis faced by the country. It is also worth mentioning the ability of these rural women to distribute their time between this activity, the housework and the care of their children, and to reconcile it with their social and family life.

Brief historical description of Huancayo

In pre-Incan times, the people settled in what is today the Department of Junín (the *Huancas*, the *Chinchaycocha* and the *Tarumas*) were characterized by their deep regionalism and by their strong differences, due to the influence of the large Chavín culture. The economy was based mainly on agriculture, carried out in the valleys and ravines; farming in the high zones or plateaus; and, less importantly, ceramics. Commerce was based on the exchange of products such as corn, potatoes, coca, salt and wool.

The Huancas took an active part in the consolidation of colonialism in the central mountainous area, the *Sierra Central*. In 1548 they helped Pedro de la Vasca (the 'Pacifier') against the insurrections of Diego de

MARÍA ESTRELLA CANTO SANABRIA is a food technologist from Huancayo in the Peruvian mountains, who has started up her own food processing business based on local, high altitude foodstuffs.

Almagro, Gonzalo Pizarro and Francisco Hernández. During the decades between independence and the war with Chile, a strong dominant regional class was established. This class promoted the modernization of agriculture and ranching by transferring capital earned from the mining industry.

The 'Irrefutable City of Huancayo', as it was officially named in 1882, is situated in the Mentaro Valley with the best conditions for economic and political development. This is why it has historically assimilated large numbers of people from its department. It is also the capital of the department and one of the commercial centres of the country with a population of 321 549 in 1981. Huancayo, a city of ancient lineage, is surrounded by peasant communities, districts and towns. These include Uñas and Palián, the two places where this investigation was made.

Description of the area

The group in question came from the Progreso District in Uñas, a dependent of the Huancayo province. The district, situated north-east of the city of Huancayo, is 5km away and 3271m above sea level. It is a rural area belonging to the Quechua region. It has a magnificent landscape, with an abundance of eucalyptus plantations and farm land; a temperate climate; and a population of 600 (estimated in 1992).

Its various cultural events include the Festival of Manners: the *Santiago* or *Tayta Shanti* day on August 1 (dedicated to animal fertility) and the festival of *Señor de Mayo* on May 30, with its typical dances, *Huaylash*, *Chonguinada* and *Shapis*.

Consumption habits in El Progreso and nearby communities are based exclusively on agricultural products. The summer diet is based on crop and tender-leaf products, such as *yuyo shacta*, *chuchu chupi*, *alwirhs shacta* and *likcha shacta* among others. In winter (the dry season), the diet is based on dry grain (cereals and legumes).

Migration is common, especially among young people—both male and female. They move to Lima, the capital, or nearer cities such as Huancayo, in search of work. Women migrate earlier than men. In 1988 there was a negative migratory balance of 7995 people in the Department of Junín.

Description of the group

The Women's Group for the Preparation of Andean Products was founded in May 1990. With the help and support of María E. Canto (a graduate from the College of Engineering in Food Technology at the National University of Central Peru), the group started making *panetones* (a baked product) in December 1989 for two mothers' clubs, which was a success with the community of Uñas. This motivated them to make toffee and *kiwicha*

110

turrón (nougat) during the school year, to sell in several schools in Palyán Hyo.

In order to consolidate this group, documentary proof of their work was sent to the local authority of Uñas in February 1990, so in May the group was formally founded with six active local members, calling themselves *La Asunción* in honour of the Virgin Mary, who is for the members an example of love, dedication and commitment.

The industrial and agricultural situation of Huancayo

Huancayo is considered nationally to be one of the most important cities in the Sierra region. Its mercantile spirit (a legacy of the Huancas) and its Sunday and district fairs make it a commercial 'emporium' in the centre of the country. These days, however, the national economic crisis is dramatically affecting this commercial activity.

With respect to the industrial sector, Huancayo has four food companies, which are Fongal Centro (dairy products); Lopesa Industrial (seasonings and dressings); Fábrica de Embutidos Huayachulo (a pork products factory); and Fábrica de Gaseosa Venus (a fizzy drinks factory). There are also semi-industrial plants such as ALCE (dairy products); Embutidos Vega; and Almonacid (dairy products).

Among the large mills, the following can be mentioned; ALGESA, Sansón, Insumos Mantaro and PROAL, plus 38 other mills for split grain, grain peel and flour, of which only 20 per cent are working. There are also 168 craft bakeries and a few semi-industrial ones in the whole province.

Main food products of Andean origin

Peru's most important Andean agricultural products are grown in the departments of Cajamarca, Junín, Ayacucho, Arequipa, Cuzco and Puno. This region is full of valleys situated very near the mountains, gorges and high plateaus at an altitude of approximately 2000m, which results in a very high density of plants. The plants have always been exchanged between the inhabitants of these areas, achieving different levels of domesticity. Table 1 shows the main food products of Andean origin produced in Peru.

Quinua

Quinua is the most important native grain of the Andes after corn, and constituted a quarter of the diet of the pre-Columbian population. Called variously *quinoa* or *quinua* in Ecuador, Peru, Bolivia, Argentina, Chile and

111

Table 1. Main edible species natural to the Andean region

Common name	Family	Altitude for optimal growth (m)
GRAINS		
Corn	Graminaceous	0–3000
Quinua, suba	Chenopodiaceous	0–3900
Cañihua, cañahua	Chenopodicaceus	3200–4200
Kiwicha, achis, achita, coimi	Amaranthaceous	0–3000
LEGUMES		
Tarwi, chocho	Leguminous	500–3800
Pallar, cachas	Leguminous	0–2500
Pajuro, balu	Leguminous	500–2700
Kidney beans	Leguminous	100–3500
ROOT VEGETABLES		
Maca	Cruciferous	3900–4100
Yacón, aricoma, jicama	Composite	1000–2500
Arracacha	Umbelliferous	1000–3000
White carrot		
Camote, Apichu	Convolvulaceous	0–2800
Achira	Cannaceous	1000–2000
TUBERS		
Potato	Solanum	1000–3900
Oca, Ibia	Oxalidaceous	1000–4000
Olluco, papa, *lisa, melloco*	Basalaceous	1000–4000
Mashua, isañu, añu, cubio	Tropaeolum	1000–4000
FRUITS		
Capuli, uchuba, uvilla	Solanum	500–2700
Sachatomate de Arbol Berenjena	Solanum	500–2700
Tumbo, curuba, tacso	Passifloraceous	2000–3000
Lúcuma	Sapotaceous	0–2500
Custard apple	Passifloraceous	2000–3000
Granadilla	Passifloraceous	800–3000
'Castilian berry'	Rosaceous	2000–3000
CUCURBITS		
Pumpkin	Cucurbitaceous	500–2800
Caygua, achokkcha	Cucurbitaceous	100–2500

Source: Mario Tapia, 1990.

suba in Colombia, it grows annually and can reach a height of between 1m and 3.5m, depending on the type and the ecosystem in which it is grown.

The fruit of the *quinua* is an achene; its perigynous layer covers only one seed and is easily rubbed off. The seed is covered in a four-layered adhered episperm. Saponin can be found in the first membrane and the grains contain it in variable amounts. It gives the grain a bitter taste, which is why different techniques have been tried in order to eliminate it.

Analyses appearing in several publications indicate that the protein content can range between 10 and 22 per cent, although in most cases it is in the region of 13–15 per cent. Dietary analysis and biological tests show that the quality of the proteins is higher in *quinua* than in cereals. Essential amino acids are found in 37 per cent of the proteins. It has double the amount of lysine and methionine than cereals; approximately the same tryptophane; and less phenylalanine and isoleucine. This is why *quinua* is, in this respect, considered to be superior to wheat, corn and barley (Jorge León, 1964).

Quinua is used in a variety of preparations, the most common being soups and sweets, or as *kispiña* (rustic bread) and *mashica* (crushed, dried and ground *quinua*). It can also be fermented to prepare refreshing hot beverages. Its leaves are eaten boiled or in salads in some regions of the Andes where vegetables are scarce.

Cañihua

Cañihua (*Chenopodium pallidicaule aellen*) is one of the least-studied agricultural species. Its cultivation seems to be related to the Tiahuanaco culture which is why it has traditionally been used in the borders of the high plateau in Peru and Bolivia, and in the vicinity of Cochabamba (Bolivia), Puno, Cuzco, Ayacucho and Junín (Peru).

Cañihua, *kañiwa* or *cañahua* (*aymara*) is a therophyte plant, erect or very branched from its base, and between 20cm and 70cm high. Both its leaves and the top of its stem are covered in white and rose vesicles. The main varieties cultivated nowadays are *cupi*, *ramis* and the local types *Cañihua lasta* (*chillihua*, *puca*, *morada* and *condorsaya*) and *saihua* (*acallapi*, *puca*, *morado* and *condorsaya*).

Cañihua produces a smaller grain than *quinua*, and is cultivated in smaller areas, particularly in the Department of Puno and in some very high lands (between 3200 and 4100m a.s.l.) of Cuzco, Arequipa, Ayachuco, Apurimac and Bolivia. It is a species resistant to pests and low temperatures ($-3°C$), which do not affect its production. *Cañihua*, in spite of being a close relative of *quinua*, does not have saponin. As well as its use for human consumption, its stems are good forage for animals.

Cañihua has an even higher protein content than *quinua* and cereals. Its content and balance of amino acids allow the classification of *cañihua* proteins to be of prime quality, due to the relation between those amino acids and the presence of essential amino acids (see Table 2). Analysis of the vitamins show a very satisfactory content, although it does lack vitamin C and carotene.

Very little investigation has been done into the way *cañihua* is prepared. The most common way to consume it is roasted and ground. *Cañihua* is highly valued among both the rural and urban population. Perhaps its high

Table 2. Amino acid content in *cañihua, quinua* and wheat (g.16gN)

	Cañihua	Quinua	Wheat
Arginine	7.9	7.4	4.3
Histidine	2.5	2.7	2.1
Lysine	6	6.6	2.7
Tryptophane	0.8	1.1	1.2
Phenylalanine	3.6	3.5	5.1
Methionine	1.8	2.4	2.5
Threonine	4.8	4.8	3.3
Leucine	5.8	7.1	7
Isoleucine	6.8	6.4	4
Valine	4.6	4	4.3

Source: Bolhius 6.6 Chenopodium quinua en Chenopodium cañihua, minder bekende voedingswassen, *Landbouekondig Tigdschrift*, 1993.

oil content would favour the creation of an industry dedicated to the extraction of vegetable oil for human consumption.

Tarwi

Tarwi (*Lupinus mutabilis*) is known as *tauri* in southern Peru and Bolivia, as *chocho* in northern Peru and Ecuador, and as *chuchus* in Cochabamba (Bolivia). It is an annual legume, related to the lupins grown in Mediterranean Europe.

The pre-Hispanic population, in order to eliminate the alkaloids (especially sparteine), used a leaching process which washed away most of the active elements and at the same time made the residual alkaloids insoluble. This process consisted of boiling the grains in order to coagulate the proteins, and then putting them in bags submerged in streams, so that the bitter substances, mostly alkaloids, were washed away.

The alkaloids in *tarwi* are not only toxic, but have a bitter flavour. Apart from alkaloids, legumes have other toxic or anti-nutritional elements (proteases, haemaglutens). These have not been found in significant amounts in *tarwi*. The maximum level considered safe for human consumption is 0.002 per cent after washing.

Sweetened *tarwi* has traditionally been used in Peru for human consumption in a variety of dishes. Recently, it has been incorporated in the preparation of bread, sauces (*huancana* and *ocopa*), savoury purées, beverages, *tamale*, spicy dressings, *cebiche serrano* (marinaded fish) and sweets. In Ecuador, Chavez and Peñaloza (1988) investigated, with excellent results, the possibility of obtaining *tewpeh* from *Rhizopus oligosporus*.

The innovative technology used for the preparation of *tarwi* can open interesting possibilities for the development of new agricultural industries, provided that agriculturists manage to achieve greater production at convenient prices, which would allow these industries to have a market. Possible products may include oil, protein flours, and unbittered *chocho*.

Tubers

The main members of this family include: *oca* (*Oxalis tuberosa*), *olluco* (*Ollocus tuberoso*) and *mashua* or *añu* (*Tropaeblum tuberoso*). The Andean region is the only place where humans began growing tubers domestically for human consumption. This includes the well-known species of the *solanum* genre (potatoes) and another group of species less studied and less valued in the world of agriculture.

The domestic growing of *oca*, *olluco* and *mashua* dates back to ancient times, as evidenced by painted pottery excavated in the area. These tubers adapt very well to terrain above 3800m and they are even associated with potatoes in the Peruvian and Bolivian Andes. *Oca*, *ocullo* and *mashua* are good sources of energy, thanks to their high carbohydrate content, although their protein and fat content is very low. The composition of their proteins is very varied (see Table 3) and their quality very good. They account for the daily intake of amino acids recommended for children of nursery-school age (Tapia, 1990).

Fruits

Previously, there were plantations of wild and cultivated fruit trees (see Table 1). The wild ones were called *sacha* and their fruits were of common use if they grew in *sapsi* or communal land, but belonged to the gods Inca and Sun if they grew in their lands. In Ante or Amazonia, fruit trees were not grown intensively; they grew in the margins of inhabited areas.

Fruit was, apparently, very important in the diet of the natives. The climate was favourable to the trees' habitat, and they grew near people's houses and on their way to work and to look after the animals. Wild fruits

Table 3. Chemical composition of Andean tubers (g/100g)

	Oca	Isaño	Olluco
Energy (Kcal)	61	50	62
Protein	1	1.5	1.1
Fat	0.6	0.7	0.1
Carbohydrate	13.3	9.8	14.3
Fibre	1	0.9	0.8
Ash	1	0.6	0.8
Moisture	84.1	87.4	83.7

Source: Collazos, 1975.

115

such as *capuli, lucuma, tumbo* and many others are rich in vitamins A and C. There is no doubt that the diet of earlier Peruvians was high in vitamins thanks to the high consumption of raw or partly cooked fruits and vegetables (Antunez de Mayolo, 1983).

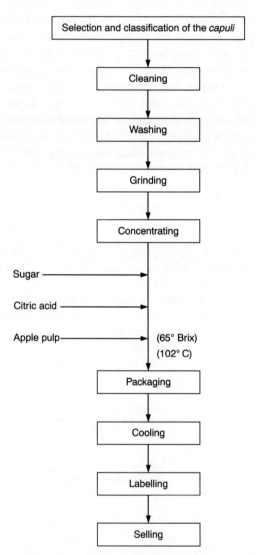

Figure 1. *Preparation of* capuli *jams (*Phiysalis peruana*)*

116

Background and description of *La Asunción*

The group of women, *La Asunción*, form a production project. They prepare different food products for selling in urban and regional markets. This is a project of individual initiative, not supported by any non-governmental organization. The aim of the group is to generate employment and income. The group prepares the products using ingredients from the Andean region, because of their nutritional value and the ease with which they may be grown. They also want to change consumption habits, and at the same time rescue the traditional technology of the ancient Peruvians.

The group works in three areas: confectionery (*turrones* or nougat, toffee, *cañihua* and *kiwicha* candy, *maca*, *capuli* and medlar jams); balanced flours (nutritious mixes of cereals and legumes such as T–Q–C, or *tarwi–quinua–barley*); and *chocomaca*, or *maca*, flour ready to eat; and baked products (bread and cakes made from the balanced flours).

Figures 1 and 2 show the stages of the work required for each product.

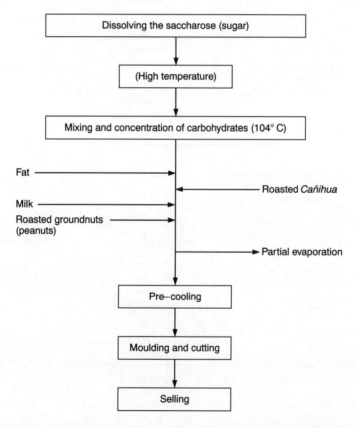

Figure 2. *Preparation of* cañihua *toffee (*Chenopodium pallidicaule*)*

117

The preparation of *kiwicha* nougat has the same stages; the only difference lies in the main ingredient and in the temperature of concentration (100°C).

Three rules apply to the preparation of balanced flours:

○ The primary role of proteins is their structural function at the level of cell, tissue and body.
○ For a protein to be considered 'high quality', amino acids not only have to be present, but there must be a balance of essential and non-essential amino acids, so that the synthesis requirements of tissues at an optimum and normal rhythm are met.
○ Legumes, as opposed to cereals, have high contents of lysine and other essential amino acids.

This makes legumes a good supplement for cereals, producing the desired 'amino-acid balance'.

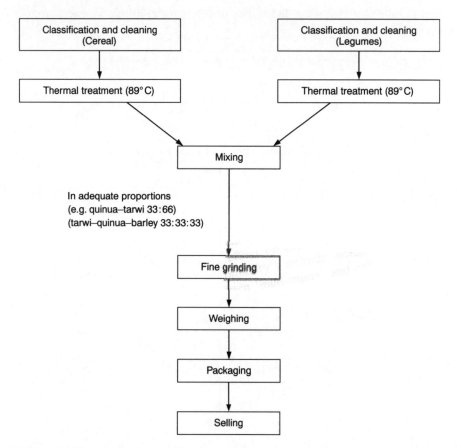

Figure 3. *The preparation of balanced flours*

Figure 3 shows the preparation of balanced flours. The mix of these flours is based on research and tests carried out at the Agricultural University of La Molina, the results of which prove that the flours have excellent 'protein quality' and are rich in minerals and vitamins, making them extremely suitable for human consumption.

Baked products are prepared periodically, when requested by schools and for the fairs in which the group takes part. They are also made from balanced flours.

Economic aspects

The products prepared by the group have both a local and an urban market. They are prepared according to the demand of both consumers and intermediaries. The production is small because of the group's lack of capital. The average monthly production is: 80 bags of 100 units of toffee, candy and *turrones*; 300 units of baked products; and 60 bottles of 300g and 200g of balanced flour.

Profits approximate the minimum salary per person for two months' work. Work is not done daily, but twice weekly for eight hours a day. Unsold products are shared out among the women for their own use.

The organization of the group

The atmosphere among the members of the group is one of co-operation, co-ordination and communication. The group's leader is responsible for management and co-ordination, for creating an atmosphere of trust and confidence, for supervising the women at every stage of production (classification, boiling, concentration, moulding, cutting and packaging), for quality control at each of these stages, and for checking the nutritional value of each product.

Regular meetings enable the women to co-ordinate their work, to find out about improvements and to hear opinions, all of which helps them achieve their objectives.

Techniques used for the preparation of Andean products

A sophisticated social structure, with excellent communications and a very active commerce, provided the Incas with a wide range of foodstuffs. When the Spanish arrived in Sausa, they found that approximately 100 000 people were trading in dehydrated and processed food.

Many rural and urban people told us that the following devices have existed since former times. The first is the firewood stove. Known as a *tullpa*, this consisted of three movable stones on which the firewood (*yanta*) from the local trees (alder, *quinua*, eucalyptus) was lit. *Mankas* (earthenware pots) were used on this rudimentary stove to cook the daily stews. Nowadays, it is called a *bicharra* and has changed its design and its material (bricks and cement with an iron plate). It is the one used by the group for roasting *kiwicha* and *cañihua*.

The second food-preparing device is a *batán*. This is a flat, oval stone with another smaller stone called *manizuela*. It is used to crush and grind grain and other products. It has been used since Incan times, and is also used by the group to crush groundnuts.

The third device is a *manual grain grinder*, used since the beginning of this century, when development and trade began in the Sierra Central. This consists of a worm gear propelled by a crank, with a set of tin teeth which crush and grind the food. The group uses this grinder. Other equipment used by the group include industrial grinders and a baking oven, which they hire in Huancayo. They also have an electric and a manual sealing machine for packaging.

Participation in fairs and competitions

The group took part in Expo '91, at the Fair in Yavis (Huancayo), with several of the products already mentioned. It won first prize in the category of Agricultural Industry with the trademark NUTRIVIT (in association with a private individual). In 1992 the group won third prize at the same fair and in the same category, for their produce, technical exhibition, stand display, information by means of brochures and bulletins, and the nutritional value of their products.

During the first few months of that same year, the group worked hard in preparation for the competition 'Women and Food Technology', organized by UNIFEM and the Women's Popular Educational Network. After presenting a written report, they won the regional and national prizes.

In April 1993, the group took part in a competition, 'Typical Eastern Dishes' and won first prize in the category 'Desserts and Sweets'.

Technological capability of women

The members of the group *La Asunción* have the following abilities and skills for preparing Andean products:

o Choosing and classifying the fruit (for jam) and the cereals, legumes and peanuts.
o Roasting *cañihua* and *kiwicha*, something they could not do before.
o Calculating the concentration point (both with the industrial thermometer and the 'gout test') of the dough for toffee and sweets.
o They are sensible and practise good hygiene, cleanliness and disinfection with regard to the raw materials, the preparation process and the

120

final products. They are concerned about the quality of the products. They have some knowledge of environmental and microbiological pollution.

o They are able to judge the hygroscopicity of roasted *kiwicha* and *cañihua* grains.

o They value the nutritional content and values of Andean products, something they did not think about before.

o The members of the group, and women in general, value their work in food preparation. They are proud that their products keep their physical, chemical and microbiological properties for a long time. This was proved after quality control of some products, months after their preparation, in the laboratories of the Agriculture Department in Huancayo in 1992.

Conclusion

Women from rural areas have the ability to leave the domestic world aside and confront the technological world. These women use traditional techniques and theoretical knowledge about the science and processing of food enables them to prepare long-life food products. The use of Andean ingredients in the preparation of confectionery and other products can improve the quality of nutrition, as well as change consumer habits and bring profitable results. Local women have the capacity to organize and manage a food-production company. The group contributes to the economic development of families.

Coping with a lack of electricity in marginal urban areas

LOURDES PALAO YTURREGUI

One of the most satisfactory experiences afforded us by our professional activities has been to witness the work of a group of women known as 'The Roses of America'. Based in one of the poorest marginalized urban areas of the city of Tacna, these women, largely Andean immigrants, have shown us their will-power, creativity and capacity for innovation while trying to solve their immediate problems.

The absence of electricity in the headquarters of their association (and obviously in their homes as well) underlined all the disadvantages these women face daily. What is important to emphasize here, however, is that, starting with a simple initiative, the women have mobilized themselves in an attempt to overcome the biggest obstacle affecting them both at work in their textile workshop and in their own homes. What is more, with their oil-lamp workshop, they have also been able to prove that good organization and participation in socially productive activities are powerful means of overcoming day-to-day difficulties.

What we hope to highlight here is the fact that, in spite of all the limitations which they face as a result of the sexual division of labour, women are not completely unused to either technology or innovation and creativity; and, furthermore, that collective strategic interests determine any plan of action to be followed.

In the three main sections of this study, we look first at some preliminary details of the project; second, we indicate certain economic and social factors relevant to Peru and Tacna in particular; and finally, we investigate the rationality of these women in their day-to-day living and also their ability to solve a basic problem at the oil-lamp workshop. For it is there that they combined their experience and new ideas in order to obtain definite results and very important possibilities for the future.

LOURDES PALAO YTURREGUI is a development worker with CEPROM—Centre for the Promotion of Women—an NGO in Tacna, Peru.

How the project was born

In about May 1992, ITDG contacted CEPROM (Centre for the Promotion of Women, Tacna) with a view to taking part in a project to be called 'Women: invisible technologists'. Its aim was to carry out a series of case studies in order to draw attention to women's technological achievements, since, due to their marginalization, it was almost impossible to gauge their contribution in this field, as users, disseminators or innovators of technology.

CEPROM took a deep interest in this project which it considered both relevant and valuable because of the possibilities it afforded for carrying out an immediate study from the perspective of gender and in a non-traditional area of investigation (that is, power supply): specifically, to study the women of Tacna who, in times of economic crisis, had been working together to solve the problem of the lack of electricity in their homes.

CEPROM was already working towards an alternative to the production workshops run by the Council (dressmaking, community refectories and municipal kitchens), as these had been showing signs of obsolescence on the part of women's organizations, which were facing difficulty selling their dresses and were therefore very demoralized. There was a good number of workshops, but no reasonable alternatives. For this reason, it was considered necessary that CEPROM commit itself to a new work option for women in the field of intermediate technology and ecology. The promotion of this alternative met with unconditional support from the women and the community.

Over the 1980s, Peru has experienced a dramatic deterioration in social conditions. Naturally, this has had an effect on the whole nation and in Tacna it has shown itself in a rise in immigration figures (12.2 per thousand in 1990—one of the highest in the country) which has generated a disproportionate growth of marginalized urban areas, where basic commodities and facilities are scarce or non-existent. People's expectations have sunk very low. It is the women who fully experience this reality, with their men going out to work as early as 4 a.m. and returning at 11 p.m. Perhaps this is the reason why it is the women who look for strategies to survive this grinding poverty and the deficient conditions under which they live in marginalized urban settlements.

One of the main problems for the women of Tacna was the absence of electricity in their homes, for several reasons: they wanted to make the most of the evening to speed up their textile work; they needed to feel secure in their homes; they needed to facilitate the task of caring for their children; they needed to make the night less dark; they needed to light the streets that they and their families used.

It was in the light of this that CEPROM suggested to a group of women

123

that they get together to participate in this project. Twenty-five women enrolled, calling the company's 'The Roses of America' because many of them (or some close relative) were called Rose and because most of them were living in the urban settlement known as *Las Américas*. The study was started in December 1992 and was completed in March 1993.

Objectives

o To identify and assess the technological contributions of the women, as users, disseminators and innovators, in order to solve the problem of the absence of a power supply in their homes.
o To analyse how these immigrant women changed their perception and use of time and space in relation to their families, their neighbourhood and their organizations.
o To analyse the women's rationality with respect to their gender-related subordination and dependence within their families, at work and in their everyday environments.
o To highlight the importance for women of self-organization as a mechanism for sharing practical, strategic and technological experiences, and thereby for revealing their contributions.

Method

The first stage of their method was the necessary field-work. This involved levels of observation and structured participation in order to obtain information and direct contact with The Roses of America through their three main workshops. They had an intermediate technology workshop; a workshop for artistic weaving with synthetic thread; and a discussion workshop on domestic violence.

This process required 30 work sessions, that is, 10 sessions per workshop, between January and February 1993.

The second stage was reflection by means of: two days of reflection; one video session on women and intermediate technology; two round-table discussions with The Roses of America; and one systematization of testimonies. This work was carried out in March.

Life in Tacna

Tacna is a province in southern Peru with a population of approximately 200 000. Tacna is situated in the Atacama desert, the most arid area in the country. There is a scarcity of hydro-energy resources, together with an agricultural industry of only 18 per cent. The manufacturing industry is equally small and of little significance. Mining carried out by the

American-owned Southern Peru Copper Corporation in the Toquepala mines pollutes the beaches and destroys hydro-biological resources, while the company's profits are not returned to the region or used to develop the area.

Tacna is one of the provinces with the highest rate of rural immigration from the Puno high plateau in Moquegua. The population growth rate was 9.2 per cent in 1981. In 1990 it was 12.2 per cent. Its attractiveness is based on the fact that it is considered a frontier point where smuggling, the main economic activity, enables immediate survival. As a consequence, settlements have grown in number from 26 to 96 in the last 10 years. In 1992 there were, among others, 16 communal organizations including municipal kitchens, neighbourhood committees, mothers' clubs, production workshops, and dressmaking and textile workshops. Nearly 40 000 women are thought to be earning a minimal income through small scale and informal work—peddling and hawking—because their lack of capital, illiteracy and ignorance of trading do not enable them to do anything else. It was within this context that the project investigated in this study was born: in the south-eastern part of the town, in the marginal settlement called *Las Américas*.

The area is seven kilometres from the city's main square and the journey takes about 20 minutes by public transport. It covers an area of 224 square metres and contains 26 blocks which house approximately 300 families. The settlement is the result of an immigration wave in 1988. In 1989 it was entered on the Public Register. Three-quarters of the population are immigrants from Punto, a town in the high sierra on Lake Titicaca. They are nuclear families, with the women staying at home most of the time. The women are young, between 20 and 35 years old. They have, on average, five children apiece, with maternity intervals of barely 18 months. Their education is poor: 65 per cent do not complete their primary studies. Bringing up children takes up most of their time. Due to the unsafe nature of their homes, they even have to take their children with them when going out peddling and hawking (selling bread, corn liquor known as *chicha*, refreshments, sweets or food). They face common diseases like diarrhoea (chronic in the children), respiratory and skin diseases due to the dust and scarcity of water (only septic tanks available). Most of them perform their bodily functions in the open. The houses are *quinchas* (huts made of rushes and mud) or stacks of blocks with roofs made of cardboard. There are six water troughs but no electricity. As a result of this lack of electricity, they must resort to various other means, depending on their economic situation, to light their homes at night if they are to carry out their textile work, or if the children are to be able to do their studies.

The organization of the neighbourhood consists of a committee fighting for basic utilities, a mothers' club (with 50 members), six '*Glass of Milk*' committees and a textile workshop.

Who The Roses are

The group of 25 women who decided to take part in this project were all working at the textile workshop, and felt, with a greater sense of urgency, the need somehow to solve the problem of the lack of power in their homes. This was particularly important because of their textile work, which they need to do at night, since their daily routine does not leave time for it to be done during the day.

These women organize their day-to-day lives around the care of their younger children, which takes up all their time and attention, leaving them no chance to pursue other interests. Any other activities must be of such a nature that they do not need to travel far from home. They even attend the textile workshop with all their offspring, which makes it more difficult for them to take in everything they are taught. The problem of non-existent family planning policies is self-evident.

Cultural patterns play a fundamental role, in that men want a male heir not only to continue the family name but also for reasons of masculine prestige. The situation reaches extremes when men will not allow their wives to use any contraceptives at all. Women dare not disobey their husbands. It is a very severe case of the dominance of men over women who, being economically dependent, cannot do anything but oblige.

This situation faced by The Roses of America is made worse by their limited education. Perhaps many of them went to school at some stage, but a lack of constant practice means they forget how to read and write. This backwardness and ignorance imposes many restrictions on them, making it even more difficult to expose the myth. They believe in obeying their husbands blindly and have learned to live normally with domestic violence. These values and norms of married relationships are transmitted from generation to generation.

'I wanted to separate from him, I couldn't stand it anymore, so I went to my parents. My mum made me come back here straight away. She told me: "He's your husband and you will have to get used to it." ' (35-year-old mother of three). Women are afraid of being abandoned because they feel too vulnerable to face poverty on their own.

Making this situation '*visible*' to the women themselves (in the sense that they learned to value the importance of their own responsibilities of maintaining the home, bringing up the children and doing other jobs) required strengthening their self-esteem. Socializing with the group The Roses of America was an option, and four workshops were arranged on subjects such as the importance of the right to family planning; how to minimize domestic violence through an awareness of rights; understanding that leaving the family is preferable to suffering excessive violence; and the awareness that economic dependence on the husband is not always necessary—which is what finally gives them the greatest power.

126

How group members see their conditions

The new urban experience confronted by immigrant women from rural areas requires a permanent process of change, so that they can ensure their family's survival. Since most of them come from rural environments, their perception of the world is limited to their small home, their orchard and the weekly *k'ato*. This is their space. The notion changes when migrating, since there is a multiplicity of complex relations operating in the city, a new socially productive environment. In the country, on the other hand, the position and usufruct of their plot of land is their main concern. Their attention is focused on the cycle of sowing, harvesting, consuming, and round to sowing again. This is the core of their lives—determining their organization of space and the use of their time. Both men and women are involved and the tasks are allocated as necessary. Bringing up children is one more job for the women, but not the focal point of their daily existence.

Coming to live as immigrants in marginalized urban areas forces them to adjust to a limited space and to different guidelines as far as nourishment, utilities, education, health, transport, work and leisure are concerned. This variation puts them in a disadvantaged position in terms of organizing their time, since they are permanently forced to change their activities in order to ensure their survival.

In this environment, women are perhaps more aware of poverty and of the sexual division of labour. Even if they take part in commercial pursuits like hawking and peddling, they take more risks, such as the possibility of suffering abuse, and they must demand even more of themselves if they are to fulfil their domestic duties as well. They also have to endure a permanent depreciation of their activities. It is as if they did nothing but 'execute their pre-assigned tasks'.

Women are in most cases heads of household; the ones who make the survival of the family possible, and it is they who are overburdened with more and more responsibilities always. For it is through them that the effects of the food crisis (brought about by the government's social and economic adjustments) must be alleviated. Because of their poverty, they are forced to organize mothers' clubs, '*Glass of Milk*' committees, and, in addition, they must submit to the rules of the 'institutional game' and accept certain conditions in order to receive help, which means they are even more tied to their domestic and maternal roles.

But what do they think? What is the rationality of The Roses of America in relation to this situation? One resident sums this up.

'Life here is very hard. Everything has to be bought and paid for. Even the air you breathe has to be paid for. You have to do all kinds of things in order to have something to throw in the pot' (says a woman who migrated four years ago).

The women are aware of the remarkable differences between town and country and recognize the need to take new courses of action. There is a practical rationality at work here; they accept reality and try to overcome the difficulties that the new environment imposes.

'If we don't take care of the water, the power, the draining, who is going to do it? It's us who live here. We are more and more concerned every day, that's why we agreed to learn how to make the lamps. We train each other. Someone knows something, someone else brings a new idea. At least we can learn what others already know. It's better together' (a woman who migrated six years ago).

'The best thing about the city, even in this hole, is that I have realized there are so many innovations. There are even devices that help you avoid having so many children. Kids start school from a very early age. I like television very much. I see other worlds on it. One day I'll manage to have all the things I see in the soaps' (a woman who migrated three years ago).

In the analysis of these and the rest of the testimonies, we can see that the rational answers of The Roses of America derive from their practical needs: trying to fulfil their domestic roles and their part in the survival strategies.

The oil-lamp workshop and The Roses

The absence of electric power in the homes of The Roses of America has been solved slowly through a variety of means which were improved as their usefulness was confirmed. A useful question to ask is: Where does the use of oil lamps originate?

In the case of this study, immigrant women from the high plateau use several devices for lighting which they have learned from their ancestors. There, the use of the 'mecha chua' is very common. This is a handmade candle crafted from local materials: sebum of alpaca, llama or sheep mixed with hot kerosene and strongly compacted and put on a small clay plate, with a twisted cayto in the middle. Smelly and smoky, it gives a good light for a couple of hours at least.

Due to the limitations of the mecha chua, they have gradually varied this type of lamp for another one which is based on the use of empty milk cans into which they put strips of braided rag or a twisted wick after fastening the can at both ends. Domestic kerosene is used as fuel. They normally put these lamps in the centre of their patios to surround the houses with a lit area when expecting a member of the family, usually the adult man. This lamp does not smoke or blacken too badly.

The lamps have undergone a number of variations by its users, who are always seeking to maximize its usefulness and trying to avoid the danger of

Parts for the oil lamp are cut from used milk cans

starting a fire. Among the women at the oil lamp workshop, only one of them had a different kind of lamp, made by her father, a tinsmith, who made what they called 'the gas lamp'. This was the one which stimulated the greatest interest. As they worked out its drawbacks, they added a few other elements to it, until they perfected a satisfactory model. During this process, they had to make up for the lack of some necessary tools, such as pliers or an electric soldering iron, and consequently have devised a few very imaginative instruments with which to make the process easier.

User . . . disseminator . . . innovator

One of the first technical relationships that the women had to acquire was the problem of power supply in Tacna and the lack of water necessary to generate electricity. They had not understood this relationship and it was necessary to learn about the different types of power, such as wind-generated energy and other types of intermediate technology.

They discussed whether a proposal by Gran Hidroeléctrica de San Gaban (located in Puno) was a real alternative for solving the problem of electricity supply in the region. They saw it as very uncertain and instead, applying their practical priorities, searched for more concrete and viable alternatives.

Their lack of financial resources made them study closely the expenses which they incurred in order to have electricity in their homes. They compared costs and expenses. At 0.50 centimos, a new candle every two days amounted to 15 soles per month which they could not afford. A second-hand car battery costs on average five soles, each charge lasts for five days if used sensibly for two hours each night and costs two or approximately 12 soles per month. There is also the additional expense of taking the batteries to the garage for recharging, so only television owners tend to use them.

Using a glass lamp is no good either; their homes are in such a precarious state that it is hard to keep the lamps intact. Glass lamps are fragile and do not give much light, illuminating a radius of 0.5 metre or less.

They tried mixing water and kerosene, but that did not change the combustion mechanism because these are unmixable substances. Since water is heavier, it only serves to keep the kerosene afloat and reach a higher level. Once the wick reaches the water, the flame extingushes itself. Combustion changes with the different substances used. It is simply not the same to mix alcohol with petroleum or with kerosene, since each substance performs differently. Temperature is of the utmost importance. If good heat conductors are used, the energy produced is greater and different levels of combustion take place.

As far as new skills are concerned, the women have manufactured their own tools to make the job of folding tin easier. Using a mechanism known as the 'metal window', they have developed a manual instrument made from metal scraps. In order to press the wick and to weld parts with a manual soldering iron, they have resorted to a variety of instruments, according to their needs: knitting needles and crochet needles to draw the patterns on the tin; pieces of iron with which to wrap circular parts; and also choosing tins which open more easily.

Making oil lamps: a craft process

Manufacturing an oil lamp requires the following tools and materials:

Two used milk cans	A pair of old scissors for cutting tin
A wick and Tocuyo fabric	Half-inch piece of iron
Paint (not essential)	A manual soldering iron
A 10cm piece of wire	A piece of wood
Pliers	A ruler
A knitting needle	

First step: using the heat of a stove, the cans are opened—one left with its base, and the other with both ends removed. The can open at both ends is

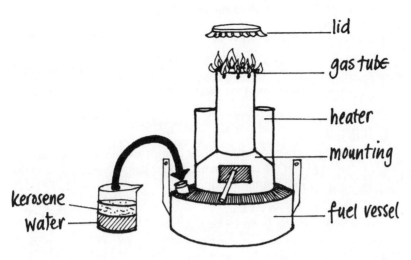

lid
gas tube
heater
mounting
kerosene
water
fuel vessel

The kerosene floats on the water within the fuel vessel and the lamp burns for up to eight hours before the wick reaches the water and extinguishes the flame

then cut along its seam, so that a sheet of tin is obtained from which to cut the patterned parts. The tin must be well cleaned and flattened to facilitate the task.

Second step: the parts previously patterned are cut from the sheet of tin which is large enough to cut the 11 parts needed.

Third step: the small parts are assembled by folding them along their creases and shaping them according to the patterns. Each of the parts requires careful precision to ensure successful burning. The main part is the gas tube and its heaters, which are mounted like this: holes are pierced around the tube by pressing with a knitting needle heated on a stove. The other parts are mounted using a soldering iron and tin. The wick, which has three guides, is mounted after securing the gas tube.

The rest of the parts are complementary accessories to the main mechanism.

Fourth step: the lamp is then lit to check that it is working well. For this, the vessel is filled half with water and half with kerosene (the wick is already wet with kerosene). The heaters are then lit and within three seconds kerosene gas is released, which escapes through the gas tube holes. It smokes a little at the beginning and then produces a steady flame.

131

Evaluating the results of the oil-lamp workshop

The Roses of America found that lamps manufactured this way from disposable materials, and with tools invariably found in the home, are very cheap. Fuel consumption is minimal. The lamp can be lit all night and lasts approximately two nights, a total of about eight hours. With a little practice, making them is simple. They are easy to maintain, requiring only a cleaning after use, especially the gas tube. It gives as much light as two candles and hardly smokes at all. It extinguishes itself when the fuel (kerosene) is finished. To keep it out of the reach of children, it can be hung on the wall by its handles.

One of the main drawbacks is the slight smell of kerosene that lingers in the house when the lamp is burning for a long time. It is more useful in closed environments with no air currents, since these extinguish the flame.

The women consider the lamp to be a marketable product, particularly when the areas of Tacna that do have electricity endure six-month periods of power restrictions between June and November every year. Its use may be extended to other marginal settlements of the city, and they are considering making it more presentable by painting it in attractive colours. They work on a kind of production line because some of them are more skilful at preparing the materials, others at cutting, others at assembling and others at finishing off.

It is obvious that the experience has opened new options for the women. They felt the need to train themselves in other areas. Further reflection led them to plan new processes such as fumigation, the cost of which is high. It is a service provided only by the municipality and which might just as easily provide the women with work since it is both necessary and urgent. They now consider it is important to have solutions at hand, understanding that high technology is hard to get in our country and that intermediate technology is a more feasible route.

How did The Roses of America feel throughout this process?

Here are a selection of statements made by some of the members.

'When I come to the workshop I forget all my problems. It keeps me busy and time flies. I like it very much.'

'Weaving is very tiring, all the ladies in the workshops weave, we want to earn something, but selling is very difficult, there is a lot of competition.'

'I like it very much. I learned lots of things, and we got to know each other. Now at least we look at each other when we meet in the street, we say hello and ask each other which stage of the work we're at. Before we didn't speak to each other, even though we lived so close.'

'We could study something different. We are skilful with our hands, we can understand things. We want to get better. My husband didn't like my coming to the workshop at the beginning, but I managed to convince him. I'll keep coming here to learn.'

Traditional techniques have undergone modifications to accommodate new conditions of living and changes in the women themselves. This has been a conscious process. In the case of the oil lamps it has meant an adaptation of combustion principles, changing from the gas used in stoves to kerosene gas. The knack for modifications might be particular to Puno, where the inhabitants are considered to be creative and clever. The women have rediscovered this ingenuity when perfecting their lamp, adding mechanisms for faster lighting; making the kerosene fumes safer; making better wicks; making it more stable on the wall; saving fuel by using water; preventing accidents from happening when the lamp is on; and even making it more artistic and attractive by means of colourful decoration.

The workshop, as a form of organization, has contributed by converting their day-to-day routine into a way of exchanging experiences and the knowledge of things such as the lamps. Also, with regard to their family life, they learned to realize the importance of self-esteem. The workshop was considered an ideal environment for their social and technical education.

Conclusions

o The practice of intermediate technology has important advocates in women, who play diverse roles as users, disseminators and innovators in the resolution of the immediate problems which affect their day-to-day lives, as in the case of the lamps.

o The movement of immigrant women from the country to the city puts them in a disadvantaged position as regards their use of time and space, due mainly to the new survival activities they must undertake and their new way of life in the context of poverty and the sexual division of labour.

o The interrelation between practical needs and gender-related interests at an organizational level facilitates participation, socializing and the option of looking for collective alternatives, where women are able to contribute, to re-create, to provide, to analyse, to reflect and to decide.

o The rationality of women is basically of a practical nature—trying to solve immediate problems. The critical poverty which they face inclines them to this approach in their social behaviour.

o The impact of the experience has made three substantial points evident: at a family level, the possibility of working in non-traditional domestic activities; at a neighbourhood level, the prestige and recognition which has strengthened their self-esteem; and, at a community level, the useful and significant example to other women's organizations.

Vegetable production units in Venezuela

LUIS MIGUEL ABAD, IGNACIO ALZURU, LOKMAN GONZÁLEZ, ROSENDO MORENO, and JAVIER VÁZQUEZ

The case study presented in the following pages brings together the experiences of a group of women who have been developing a project for growing vegetables with the aid of hydroponic technology in El Trompillo, a district of the city of Barquisimeto, Venezuela.

The project was formulated and co-ordinated by CETEP (The Centre for Popular Technological Management) between 1990 and 1992, and CETEP has also carried out the research for this case study. As a result, both the project and the case study are influenced by the stand-point adopted by CETEP when tackling the subject of technology, i.e. popular technological management. In this sense, the work presented here is not only the study of a specific case, but also an attempt to contribute a methodological analysis of the main principles that determine the management of technology in the case of popular production units.

Information was gathered by means of two different questionnaires. One was aimed at the individuals, the other at the whole group. Once all the information was compiled, it was summarized and presented to the group again, with a view to validating the first appraisals. This process of compiling information was carried out in such a way as to allow for reflection on the scope of the project and on its main strengths and weaknesses, in the hope that this material could be put to use in further consolidating the project.

The environment

The case analysed in the following pages is from Barquisimeto, the capital city of the state of Lara, in the west-central region of Venezuela. Lara, with

---

LUIS MIGUEL ABAD, IGNACIO ALZURU, LOKMAN GONZÁLEZ, ROSENDO MORENO and JAVIER VÁSQUEZ work with CETEP—the Centre for the Development of Technology for People—in Barquisimeto, Venezuela.

134

Six families were involved in the project to use hydroponic technology to grow vegetables in their gardens for additional income

nearly a million inhabitants, has historically been an important commercial centre, thanks to its strategic geographical position. It has enjoyed a long tradition of agriculture and livestock. In the last few years, it has become one of the cities targeted for alternative industrial development, following the policy of decentralizing the central region of the country.[4]

In spite of all these favourable features, Lara currently shows disturbing socio-economic indicators, particularly with regard to the levels of critical poverty, malnutrition, unemployment, access to health services, education and housing. Some of these have worsened notably in the last five years (even to the point of reaching the levels of 1960). Although these indicators are a reflection of the general situation in the country, they are even more significant in marginal districts, such as in the case of El Trompillo, where the project described in this case study is found.

El Trompillo is probably an unusual district. Situated in the north of the city, it is part of a group of working-class towns which sprang up in the 1970s. Nowadays, it can be seen to be a cohesive suburb. Most of its houses are finished buildings; there is electricity and (although irregular) running water; many of the streets are paved; there is a school and a nursery. About 2000 families (i.e. 12 000 people) are thought to be living in the district. What makes El Trompillo special is the degree of organization among its residents. In this regard, there follows a list of all the active organizations in the district and their related activities:

135

o Health committee: A group of women whose activities include preventive medicine, neo-natal care, vaccination campaigns and the use of medicinal plants.
o '*Tinaja*' group: A popular production unit devoted to the manufacturing of biscuits and '*ponqué*' (little cakes) for selling.
o Neighbourhood committee: This is an organization which represents all the residents of the district. They are responsible for lobbying for better services: water, home improvements, street surfacing, efficient public transport and related activities.
o '*El Trompillero*': A non-profit-making association responsible for cultural and educative activities such as a library, a newspaper and a cine-forum.
o '*Fraja*': A youth group devoted to social and religious activities: the instruction of Christian doctrine, reflection on social and human issues with adults from a Christian perspective.
o Family Consumers Fair: This is sales point or market linked to an essential food distribution system promoted by a national co-operative movement, and which, in Lara, finds its most dynamic expression.
o Popular hydroponics: A group of women devoted to the growing and selling of vegetables using hydroponic technology, i.e. a way of growing plants without soil and in a small space, achieving greater production in less time. The produce is primarily leaf vegetables, such as lettuce, coriander, chives, curled parsley and chard.

Main features of the project

After a phase of experimentation with hydroponic technology in just one house in El Trompillo, the Centre for Popular Technological Management (CETEP) decided to think about developing the project in the area. Since the idea was well received by residents, it was decided that a plan for increasing awareness be initiated and the first group of 'hydroponists' be chosen from the families interested.

In this case, the hydroponic technology used in El Trompillo, was adapted from that developed in Jerusalem, a district of Bogota in Colombia. Each of the six families involved in the project grew the vegetables on their own in their backyards. In this sense, each family was considered a Popular Production Unit (PPU). The rest of the activities were carried out as a group. Although it was never a condition for participation in the project, it was revealed that all of them had had some previous experience of growing vegetables, either the women themselves, their husbands, or their parents.

The most immediate goal to be realized by this project was the cost-effective growing of vegetables for selling, in order to improve the standard of living of the families by providing them with additional income. Particular to the project are its five main features.

○ It has an experimental nature. The project began with a first experimental stage, aimed at securing a basic grasp of hydroponic technology. Because it had been virtually unknown in Venezuela, it was almost impossible to rely on the help of specialist technicians for certain very specific questions. Most of the technical assistance came from the Colombian team involved in the experience of the Jerusalem District of Bogota. Consequently, this initial stage of experimentation lasted a whole year. Nevertheless, after having achieved a basic understanding of the technology, the experiment continues to the present day.

○ It has a pilot-scheme nature. In view of the fact that the project was new to Venezuela, it was necessary to maintain a constant attitude of flexibility, continuation and systematization, so that the experience might be repeated elsewhere.

○ The participation of the community and the strict observance of the rhythms and time-lapses which emerged during the development of the project. These were important for ensuring the adequate and effective involvement of the community.

○ The popular nature of hydroponics. This was based mainly on two facts: it is inexpensive and it is easy to manage.

○ The technological transfer. This was essentially a project for the transfer of technology from CETEP to the community involved, the different aspects of which it was hoped they would in future undertake independently. To achieve this it was vital that the transfer was carried out thoroughly.

It was decided that the study be oriented towards the analysis of the main elements that determine the management of technology in the case of women's PPUs. At this stage, two main subjects should be reviewed. First, the initial aims of the PPU. Second, the way to approach production.

The initial aims of the PPU

The work carried out by CETEP in giving technical assistance to a group of PPUs has enabled it to observe that there is a close relationship between the original aims of a production group (in this case, one formed by women) and its chances of consolidating itself as a production unit.

In this sense, it has been possible to identify, from among the existing production groups formed by women, two main types with very different initial objectives. These may be characterized as follows. The first type are those groups which are formed with the intention of reclaiming their dignity as women, of freeing themselves from their exclusively domestic work, of strengthening each other through reflection on shared issues (sex

137

and procreation, education of children, women and health, etc.) and which, in addition to all this, undertake a production activity as well. The second type are those groups which, from the beginning, were formed with the aim of producing goods or services. This kind of group might also take part in other activities such as reflection, community work, etc., but the main characteristic is that they are formed to pursue specific production activities. The experience afforded us by our work with the PPUs indicates that the second type of groups have a greater chance of becoming viable production units than the former, at least in the short term.

The information gathered from the women who founded the group studied here enables us to conclude that it constituted a production group from the very beginning. What is more, during the discussions and reflections which gave rise to the original information, the subject of how the participants saw the group as it was then and in the future was thoroughly debated. They all agreed that they wanted to remain oriented towards production.

'The group's objectives were to produce, to learn how to organize ourselves, to generate an income without having to leave the house.'

'Knowing about hydroponics, learning to live together, generating an income.'

'Growing vegetables, forming a production unit.'

The way to approach production

An analysis (however superficial) of all the existing PPUs in Lara, Venezuela, reveals that a great number of them begin with what they already know. Their basic aim is to produce what they know they can make. In CETEP's experience this way of approaching production seems limited since it neglects important variables, such as technology, organization and administration. It also pays very little attention to the market for particular products.

Some definitions

Technological capacity is the ability to use, adapt, improve or create technology.

The terms *technological capacity* and *production capacity* must not be confused, since the latter refers to installed capacity, that is, machinery and equipment. It is technological capacity that enables the efficient operation of production capacity and, above all, to maximize, adapt and re-create it. That is why a lack of technological capacity determines an inadequate and limited use of the production capacity, and an increasing dependence on the provider of technology.[1]

138

Having explained these terms, this chapter turns to an analysis of those areas directly related to the technological capacity of the case in point. That is:

○ Technical changes
○ Technical assistance
○ Attitudes towards the market-place
○ Organizational aspects

The women gave the following examples of technology that they use: sowing, transplanting, cultural activities/assembling cases, controlling pests and diseases, making seedbeds, harvesting, disinfecting the planting trays, making work plans, ways of organizing themselves.

As for *technical changes* in their strictest sense (that is, those changes generated in the area of production and which have to do with the use of certain raw materials, equipment, tools or machinery, and with the production process itself), CETEP has noticed through its work with the PPUs, that they occur slowly.

The information gathered from the women on this subject, is reflected in Table 1 showing the technical changes made. These changes were carried out by CETEP and the women working together. In many cases the improvements were based on the women's suggestions. In other cases the women dealt with problems themselves and did not report the changes.

The fact that the technical changes are made in order to solve specific problems arising in the work of the PPUs suggests that such changes should also be used as a way of approaching other questions which arise during the life of a PPU. For instance, taking advantage of new market opportunities, introducing new products, meeting a greater demand, and so on will all arise in turn.

The information compiled in this case study highlights a few interesting points which may be checked against the table of technical changes above. One example is when analysing the column showing the origin of the changes, it may be seen that all the changes were answers to specific problems. However, looking more deeply, some other interesting details emerge. For instance, in the case of the seedbeds, the change involved their moving their production from CETEP's experimental centre to the homes of the women involved. At first, this change would appear to correspond with the problem of lack of space, but it is also true that it originated from the need to increase production, in view of the rise in demand.

Another significant example is the decision to substitute the production of curled parsley for that of plain parsley. Where the former was not competitive enough, the latter turned out to be very much more so. In growing curled parsley, they were making the most of a new market opportunity, since this product was in limited supply and was therefore highly sought-after in certain markets.

139

Table 1. Technical changes implemented between 1991 and 1993

Initial situation and technical change	Time in months*	Reason for the change†	Methods used for achieving the change	Reasons for using these methods	Results attained	Time appraisal
Nurseries at experiment centre / Nurseries in each home	6	Problems with supply of trays / Lack of space / Problems with distribution	Modification in the process of making nurseries and in the raw materials / More responsibility on the part of the families	Information provided by technicians	Production fell at the beginning but increased later	Slow
Permanent fumigation as prevention / Fumigation in rainy season	18	Too much work perceived as unnecessary	Beter cleaning when servicing the nurseries / Use of ash	Women's experience	Less work and lower costs	Slow
Colombian 'nutrition solution' / Venezuelan 'nutrition solution'	11	Difficulties in bringing it from Colombia. Higher costs	Substitution of imported materials for national materials	Information provided by technicians	Production increased at the beginning but fell later	Fast
Hydroponic chives / Soil-grown chives	8	Low production did not compensate costs	Emptying of trays and planting of more profitable products	Women's experience	Increased production with lower costs	Slow
Plain parsley / Curled parsley	8	Plain not competitive / Curled had higher demand	Change of seeds and of cultivation methods	Information provided by women	Increased profits	Fast
Spacing between plants: from 17 to 20cm	3	Plants taking too long to grow	Modification in the transplanting methods	Information provided by women	Increased production	Fast

* This refers to the time elapsed between perceiving the problem and coming up with a solution.
† The situation which precipitates the change.

140

These examples prove that there can be other reasons for technical changes than the concrete problems arising from everyday work. They may, for example, arise from a close relationship between technology users and consumers.

As a result of the dynamic nature of the technical changes in the PPUs, results occurred at different levels:

○ An increase in productivity.
○ A reduction in costs.
○ An improvement in the quality of the products.
○ The development of new products.

Each of these results does not necessarily exclude the others. On the contrary, depending on the way a PPU is managed, good results can be achieved in several of these areas at the same time. This is closely related to what has been called the *technological capacity* of these units.

In the present case (as can be seen from Table 1), results were achieved at different levels, with a predominance of increased productivity together with a reduction in costs. But the most interesting aspect is that results have been achieved in the development of new products, as is the case of the so-called Venezuelan 'nutrition solution', which replaces the Colombian one. In order to accomplish this, CETEP had to carry out a series of consultations and exchanges of opinions with technicians and specialists in several areas of knowledge, both in Venezuela and in Colombia, as well as numerous tests before a definitive formulation could be made. This was then subjected to a trial period in order to establish whether it could be adapted to our context.

Results were also obtained regarding the improved quality of the products in two of the technical changes mentioned on the table; namely the introduction of curled parsley and modifications to the spacing between plants. In both cases, the products obtained were of a better quality. In the first technical change to curled parsley, it must be said that this meant the development of a product that they did not have before. It was a vegetable of improved quality that filled a gap in the market. In the second change, the sowing space between seeds was enlarged from 17 to 20cm in order to allow better growth of the plants—so that they could grow heavier and look better. With the 17cm spacing, some plants grew generally taller but lighter. The change brought about greater production and improved quality.

Technical assistance

'By technical assistance we mean those actions intended to advise, support, accompany and help sustain the PPUs with regards to the difficulties and opportunities which they face. The objective is to improve technological capacity.'[1] (i.e. a greater ability to use, adapt, improve or create technology.)

In the case being studied here, information was gathered about what technical assistance meant for the group of women. All of them associated it with the constant visits by technicians in order to solve production-related problems.

'Visits by the technicians to see what problems we have.'

'When we have problems and they come to see us.'

'The help given by those people who have helped us get ahead.'

'Suggestions the technicians give us for putting something into practice.'

'Indications of a specialized person in order to solve a problem.'

As a way of checking what has just been said, the group was asked to give examples of instances where they had received technical assistance.

○ Pest control;
○ Assembling and washing of (planting) trays;
○ How to make seedbeds;
○ How to harvest;
○ How to transplant;
○ How to disinfect the planting trays;
○ Problems in the plants' growth;
○ Production failures.

As can be seen, all the answers pointed to one thing: the group believed that they received technical assistance whenever there were problems with the production, or when they needed technical advice on how to produce something. If technical assistance is given with the objective of improving the technological capacity and therefore of achieving a greater command of technology (that is, the knowledge related to the production and commercialization of goods and services), then it should not be limited only to the technical aspects of production. It should also be present in other aspects related to the commercialization, organization and administration of the PPUs.

The women saw technical assistance as an opportunity to learn how to solve their own problems: they were sufficiently aware that the assistance was not going to last indefinitely. So when commenting on the technical assistance they received from CETEP, they said:

'They were with us the whole time. They told me how I should solve my problems.'

'They help us solve the problems and teach us how to solve them in future.'

'They have given us as much information as they could so that we were able to manage all this on our own.'

'When they come, they look at the problems and give us recommendations that then we have to put into practice. Or they explain to us how things should be done.'

With relation to the implementation of the recommendations given during the period of technical assistance, several points should be noted.

In general, the people who give technical assistance did not belong to the world of these women. They stood outside it and therefore also its values, customs and perceptions. In this sense, their recommendations were not only technical, but they were also loaded with their own values, perceptions, cultural patterns, and so forth. These recommendations may have been perceived in many different ways by the women, who might give different significance to the problems. CETEP has been in a position to monitor the speed at which recommendations by the technical assistants are implemented and to record the different concepts and values of time held by the women and the technicians.

It was very interesting to look at the answers given by the women in relation to the possible sluggishness or speed with which recommendations were implemented. Two-thirds of the group agreed by suggesting that it depended on the urgency of the problem. The other third said that they were always implemented quickly.

Finally, it is worth noting that, during the preparation of this study, it was mentioned that the recommendations were not always perceived as appropriate, which was often the reason behind apparent sluggishness in implementing the recommendations. Specifically, one woman remarked that her appreciation of the recommendations was based on previous experience in similar agricultural activities. Time proved the woman right; and so, the technicians learned something new and they altered their recommendation to suit the group as a whole.

Attitudes towards the market-place

Before starting this section, it is necessary to point out that commercialization is a fundamental part of technology, since it constitutes meeting a market demand or fulfilling a need.

In this sense, it can be said that: 'It is not knowledge by itself, or the product as such, that determines the value of technology, but its capacity for meeting the needs of consumers.'[1] Accordingly, production groups must monitor the market for which they are catering, study the needs and listen to consumers' opinions.

The information contributed by the group of women to this case study is very interesting. As well as discussing the concept of the market-place, the group was also asked if it knew what to do in order to find out about the opinions and expectations of consumers in relation to their products.

The answer was overwhelmingly positive. From the beginning, the group had been implementing activities in order to find out about consumers' opinions of their vegetables. With the technical assistance of the advisers, they developed a sales point advertising campaign from the start by naming their vegetables '*fresli*' (from *fresco* or fresh, and *limpio* or clean). In this way, consumers came to associate the group's produce (lettuces, chard, coriander, parsley and the like) with the adjectives 'fresh' and 'clean', attributing them with qualities not found in other products in the market-place.

During the marketing campaign, the women discovered that their vegetables had other attributes of which they had not been aware: their long life if frozen, and their suitability as food for small pets (birds) without the risk of poisoning. The women were also asked if they knew who were the main sorts of people buying their products. Their answers were rather specific: 'Most of the consumers are foreigners, vegetarians and people on diets.'

According to the group, these types of buyers were the main consumers of their products because it is part of their culture. They were people who knew the products already. The usual inhabitants of Barquisimeto, however, know only the creole and the cabbage-like varieties of lettuce, being unfamiliar with other varieties which are more easily produced by means of hydroponics.

As can be seen, this production group has some very clear ideas about the *fresli* vegetable market. Given this, no further problems are expected to arise when it comes time to set up new sales points. When asked their opinions on this topic, they gave clear answers about what they wanted:

○ To have a meeting to discuss the subject fully.
○ To establish possible new sales outlets.
○ To visit managers with samples of the produce and to discuss prices.
○ If in agreement, to introduce the produce slowly, increasing the stock gradually.
○ Initially, to introduce the produce at promotional prices.

Organizational aspects

'The quality of an organization can be measured more or less objectively by means of four fundamental criteria:

○ Democratic practice, whereby decisions are made consensually or by majority vote.
○ Autonomous decision-making, i.e. without external interference.

○ The capacity for self-management, i.e. the organization's capacity for accumulating and for negotiating with the outside world on equal terms.

○ The degree of internal decentralization in terms of authority and responsibility.'[3]

According to the experience gained by CETEP groups and organizations must have two important aims if they are to develop well. The first is the preparation of a programme of activities which includes all aspects of the production unit (production, commercialization, administration and organization). Also, the revision and evaluation of each of these areas should be by means of committees, so that none of them is neglected and in order to achieve better management of the PPU.

The second is the technical distribution of the production work. As far as possible, each member must specialize in one aspect of the production work, with the objective of attaining as good a command of it as he or she can, thereby increasing productivity. Logically, there must been an adequate rotation in order to involve all the participants in each area.

A few questions were devised in order to find out how the groups distributed the production work and how they planned it. With respect to the first point, the group said that they did not have an internal hierarchy. Decisions were made by the majority. Tasks were distributed by work committees (stock-taking, production and marketing, administration). When planning activities, they said that each committee planned its own work. In weekly meetings, things were constantly co-ordinated, agreements were revised, recommendations were evaluated and decided upon.

In short, this group considered itself to be an organization that allowed each and every one of its members to participate in all aspects of the production unit, with an atmosphere of mutual respect and understanding which enables them to consolidate themselves more every day.

'I like to see something growing in my garden.'—Angela

'We've grown up in the neighbourhood surrounded by groups.'—Migdalia

'I feel valued as a woman; because a woman, although she may do nothing, is worth a lot.'—Belkis

'To me it's like recreation and rest from my domestic work.'—Aliria

'I've now got involved in the neighbourhood committee. Before, I didn't involve myself in anything. I may even dare to participate in other things now.'—Yajaira

'It is very important because I work and produce, not a lot, but something significant. For me, work is a pleasure.'—Nelly

Main implications of the project

The participation of women in production work has brought about a series of changes at the levels of the individual, the family and the community. These changes were looked at in this case study. The results were significant.

Implications for individuals

Taking part in a production group brings with it a series of individual changes which are reflected in a person's personality and character, in their self-esteem, in their estimation of the production work and in their personal relationships.

Personality and character changes
The women in the group studied here identified positive changes in their behaviour. In some cases they changed from being slightly aggressive people to being more relaxed, more tolerant of criticism and more sensitive when it comes to giving criticism to others.

'Before I was a bit quick-tempered, but not so much now.'

'I used to say things without even thinking, but now I stop to think before saying anything.'

In other cases, they changed from being introverted and shy to being more assertive and confident about expressing their opinions.

'I was afraid to talk. Now I can express myself without fear.'

Sense of self-worth and being useful
One of the consequences of participating in some sort of production is that the women value themselves more. Their improved self-esteem and the knowledge that they are not just another burden make the project more and more important for them.

It was also noted that, in general, the women felt that they were useful because of two things. First, they felt useful because the project had allowed them to learn. This way of growing things was new, they had known nothing about hydroponics. Now they have mastered this technique.

'I am more useful because I have now learned many new things.'

Second, they also felt useful because what they were producing was being consumed by a large number of people.

'Now I feel more useful. Producing something for others gives me satisfaction.'

146

How they think other women see them
The researchers wanted to know how they thought other women saw them, because their production work can also influence the rest of the women in the community. The group felt that most of the other women in the neighbourhood valued their work highly and believed it to be very important, which, no doubt, encouraged them even more.

'Many women think that what I do is valuable, which makes me feel very good and encourages me to continue.'

'They think my work is very nice.'

In other cases, some women felt they were envied. Although relationships are good, some comments may make them think that there was a certain amount of envy surrounding their work and all the activities it involved.

'You have to grant us audience nowadays!'

'She's so important! She's never at home anymore, always going from meeting to meeting.'

Their estimation of the production work
Work is the only human activity capable of producing wealth. However, depending on the relationships that humans establish and on the way they distribute wealth, it can generate either pleasure or dissatisfaction. Production work turned out to be highly valued by the 'hydroponics' women. First, because it generated a much-needed source of income.

'It's good to see how important it is to produce something that enables one to buy things.'

Second, because they have a new way of looking at work, not as an obligation or as punishment, but as an activity which can help them regain their dignity and self-esteem. And so, the women in the group regarded their work with great respect and as something they enjoyed doing.

'I work but I enjoy myself. It is like a hobby.'

'Work is a pleasure to me.'

'To me it's like recreation and rest from the domestic work.'

Personal relationships
This project wanted to place special emphasis on personal relationships. Any group wanting to consolidate itself and to survive must not ignore the importance of establishing good relationships between its members. With this in mind, meetings between the women and their families were promoted and encouraged.

Although some women said they had always been on good terms with the

147

others, others admitted that it was the meetings which helped to create and strengthen good relationships.

'I have always got on well with the others.'

'At the beginning there were no relationships in the group. After some meetings, those relationships were established and the ice was broken.'

'There has been mutual respect. Some people may think you are stupid, but then you bring up the matter at the meetings.'

Implications for families

Very important changes have been observed in marital relationships, in the relationships with children, and with regards the domestic work and family budgeting. These are considered next.

In the marriage

When women begin participating in production work, they experience a series of changes in connection with their marital relationships. These changes can be positive and beneficial for both partners.

The changes witnessed in this case varied, depending on the way spouses viewed their partners' work. The majority of the women claimed that their production work had considerably improved their marital relationships, to the extent that, in many cases, their husbands took part in some of their activities and encouraged them to carry on.

It was also found that the husbands, whether or not they agreed with their working, respected the women's decision to carry on in the project.

'They have improved. He shares some activities with me. He doesn't really like my taking part in the project, but he respects my decision to carry on.'

'It has helped us to be closer, because we do a lot of work together. He encouraged me to stay in the group.'

In other cases, the woman's participation generated problems.

'It has brought me some trouble, because he feels I can now do certain things that I couldn't do before.'

In relationships with children

One of the main roles of the women is as carers and educators of their children. When the women join the production work, important changes occur in the relationships with their children. In this case, it was noted that these relations had changed for the better, inasmuch as the women treated their children considerably better.

'Now I am less strict with my children. Before I was too severe.'

148

'I have learnt to treat them better.'

This change in the way the women treat their children is closely related to the fact that most children help their mothers with some of the work, which improves communication between them.

'They help me with everything.'

'They're also very enthusiastic about hydroponics.'

'One of my sons helps me prepare and deliver the lettuces; I get on very well with him.'

It is significant how many of the children had joined the production work by having their own cultivated lots. They keep the profits and buy themselves books or sweets. It is an interesting example of educating children in the context of their own family.

'Several of them help me and get something out of what we produce.'

Domestic arrangements

The changes here have to do with the fact that the women must do both their production work and the domestic work in the same space of time. They have been forced to distribute some of these tasks among their children or to start their working day earlier. It is important to emphasize here that the reason why the women do not see this as something negative is because the production work is carried out in their own homes.

'Sometimes I have to wake up early to do everything, especially the cooking.'

'I share the housework with my daughter, so that it's not such hard work.'

'It hasn't done me any harm, because I organize my time and can manage all my activities.'

Family budgeting

When a woman joins a production unit, she plays a more active role in the home, because the family income increases as a result of her work. The money they earn helps to meet some of the family expenses, something their husbands approve of greatly.

'It's been vital, because when my husband's money runs short, I can contribute a little.'

'It has helped. Now I pay for the electricity and the kids' supper.'

'It is used to help with the expenses. I help my husband.'

The way this money earned from the production work is spent is decided exclusively by the women—their husbands respect their decisions. Invariably, they use it to cover family expenses.

149

'I decide how to spend what I earn.'

'It's my dosh.'

'I decide. It's my dough.'

'My husband acknowledges my work and encourages me.'

Another important implication on the family level is that, although the produce is not supposed to be for family consumption, all the families have admitted to consuming it. This is very positive, not only because they are eating healthy and highly nutritious produce, but also because they end up saving some of their income.

Implications for the community

As it was mentioned above, a woman joining a production group plays a much more active role, which facilitates her integration into other community activities.

The women in this group had undergone a training process with rather positive results; it led to their participating in other community activities and joining other groups in the neighbourhood (neighbourhood committee, health committee, vegetable fairs and the like).

It is also worth mentioning that many of them (who, before, dared not even talk) now take part in the active struggle for improvements in the neighbourhood (that is, problems with things such as water supply and street cleaning) and against things such as the recent attempt to evict the residents of a certain area. Some of them have even joined protest groups against the apathy of the government in their living conditions.

'I take part in the Family Consumers' Fair.'

'Now I'm in the neighbourhood committee.'

'I'm involved in the problems of the neighbourhood, you know, eviction.'

'It has helped me take a more active part in the community because now I'm more assertive in front of other people.'

'I'm involved in the problem of the water supply.'

'Before I wasn't in anything. Now I dare to get involved in other things.'

The way the project was handled and its positive results are believed to be why it has served as an example for the formation of other hydroponic groups. This influence has, to some extent, arisen because their work proved so inspiring for other groups. The study enabled confirmation that this was indeed the case. The women were an example for the organization of other groups both locally and nationally.

150

'In the district of "El Carmen" they are already sowing. In "La Peña" they want to sow too.'

'In Guyana as well.'

Obstacles the women encountered

The participation of women in production work forces them into a double working day, since, in addition to the production work itself, they have to do their housework. Their views on this subject were elicited. Some of them admitted to feeling that they were doing double work, but said that they felt good about it because of all the benefits it had brought them. There is enough compensation to encourage them to carry on.

'I feel constrained, but I like this.'

'I feel good because it's entertaining and I like seeing something growing in my yard.'

Others, however, do not feel the burden of double work because they have time enough for both, be it because they have only a few plants or because of the satisfaction they get from the work.

'I have time enough for both jobs.'

'I don't have many plants.'

'The plants are not work to me.'

Even though they take part in production work, women do not give up their housework, which in fact, to some extent limits their involvement in the production work. In this regard, some women agreed that it did, and some maintained that it did not. What they all agreed on was that doing the laundry was the activity that limited their involvement in production work the most. This is the one job that, according to them, takes the most time. They proposed three possible solutions:

o Having a washing machine.
o Having enough water to control the washing.
o Having someone to help with the job.

Naturally, if they could have any one of these they would be able to be more active in the production work, which not only involves producing, but also marketing and selling and attending work committees.

Towards consolidation

If a production group does not manage to consolidate itself as a production unit, this may lead to discontent among the participants and a refusal to

151

repeat the experience. A production group is consolidated insofar as its participants assume all the activities specific to the production unit and have the ability to find solutions to any problems which may arise. One of the fundamental conditions for the stability and consolidation of a group is the spirit of its participants. Work can be kept in hand, but spirit is essential.

The women were asked about the consolidation and stability of the group. Some of them felt that the group was already well-consolidated, because they had assumed all the activities of their production unit, they had a clear idea of what they wanted, and because they had confidence in their own ability which enabled them to solve any problems which arose.

'It is consolidated. We know the basics, so we can manage the group on our own.'

'Yes, we are [consolidated], because we manage the administration and marketing and selling, and control the production and the technical aspects.'

'We know what we want and what we have to do.'

Other participants felt that the group had not stabilized itself. This perception was based on the dismay they felt with the often sharp falls in production which necessarily affected their income.

'I sometimes think the group might be dissolved. The drops in production make us lose heart.'

They were also asked about the relationship between stability and spirit. They all agreed that a relationship does exist, but they were also clear about their willingness to accept responsibility and the need to compromise in order to carry on.

'There is a close relationship between stability and spirit. When it's not stable that's because one's not sure of what one's doing.'

'There is a relationship, but when despair spreads we encourage one another.'

'There is a relationship, but there is also the responsibility to carry on; having something of one's own, of not having to account to anyone for one's actions.'

Finally, they were asked about the possibility of repeating the experience—setbacks and all. In this respect, the whole group showed its willingness to continue their involvement in similar projects, even if they have nothing to do with hydroponics. A possible explanation for this positive attitude lies in the fact that there are plenty of people's organizations in the neighbourhood.

'Yes, I would not give up what I am doing.'

'Yes, but it would have to be well thought about.'

'Yes, I would [repeat the experience], because we have grown up in the neighbourhood surrounded by groups.'

'Yes, that wouldn't be enough to discourage me. There's always something to be learned from failure.'

'Taking part in groups is very good.'

'I have worked in groups before. I wouldn't mind if we failed. We have to carry on.'

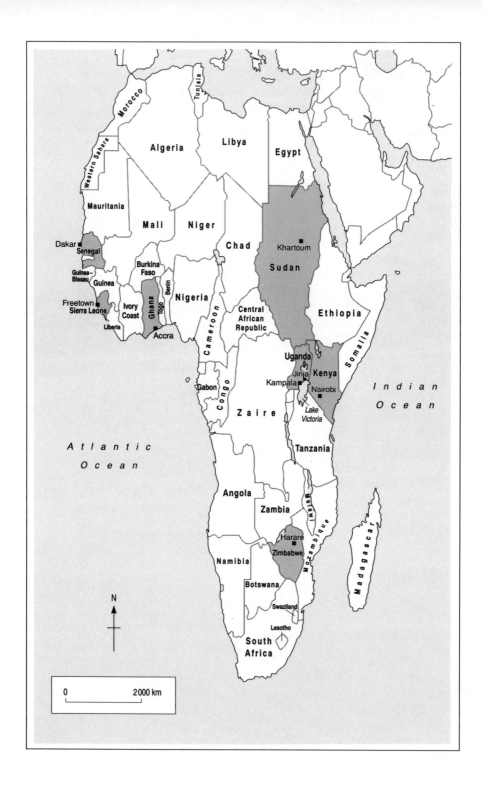

PART II

Africa

Shea butter extraction in Ghana

YVONNE WALLACE-BRUCE

Shea butter is widely used in Ghana as the only traditional cooking oil, as well as an ointment and cosmetic. It is also exported to industrialized countries where the butter is used as a substitute for cocoa butter, and in the pharmaceutical and cosmetic industries. The shea-nut tree (*Butyrosperum parkii*) grows wild in the savannah of western and central Africa in a belt about 5000km long and 600km wide, stretching from Gambia to southern Sudan. Women in these areas use variations of a traditional extraction technology, which achieves a very high oil extraction rate. In Ghana, women from the Dagomba tribe in the northern region are said to have the most advanced traditional technology, which provides an efficiency rate of around 83 per cent to produce shea butter of high quality. The process is nevertheless very time-consuming and labour-intensive. The collection of the shea fruits and their processing into butter is exclusively a woman's job in northern Ghana and one of the main sources of income for women.

Uses of shea butter

It is estimated that the average daily consumption of shea butter in Mali and northern Ghana as cooking fat is 20 to 30g per person. Shea butter is also used as a pomade for hair and skin, for the treatment of boils, wounds and other skin diseases. Additionally it is used for the manufacture of soap and as fuel for lamps.

The medical properties of shea butter are believed to be due to the presence of allantoin, a substance that has been used to stimulate the growth of new, healthy tissue in ulcerous wounds.

YVONNE WALLACE-BRUCE is an engineer working with the Konrad Adeneur foundation in Accra, Ghana. She was previously with GRATIS, Ghana Regional Appropriate Technology Industrial Service.

The traditional process

The traditional process of shea butter production involves the following stages: collection of fruit; boiling of fruit to remove the flesh; drying of fruit; deshelling of nuts; drying and storage of kernels; crushing of kernels; roasting of crushed kernels; grinding of paste; kneading of paste and creaming; clarification and crystallization.

Kneading is the most crucial step in determining the quality of the final product. Its successful execution depends on the recognition of changes in appearance, colour, viscosity and temperature of the kneaded mass, possible only for the well-trained and experienced eye to see.

In the clarification and crystallization phase, the washed cream is heated in a big pot. The clear oil that is formed is ladled into a smaller pot. Scum floating on top of the oil is discarded. After clarification, a black, oily residue remains in the pot. This residue can be used as a replacement for kerosene when kindling the firewood. It is also used for waterproofing the mud houses.

The clarified oil is poured into clean enamelled basins and left to cool overnight. In the morning the oil starts to crystallize, sometimes after 'seeding' with a small lump of shea butter from a previous batch. The mass is stirred at hourly intervals with a wooden spoon until the oil has been transformed into semi-solid state. The shea butter is then transferred into the round bottom part of a calabash and built up to a round, white to yellowish white lump. This is covered with a piece of cloth and stored until brought to market.

Modifications to the traditional processing technology

The first attempt to mechanize the shea butter production process came from the women themselves. They adapted the corn mill, which was introduced to Ghana 32 years ago at the time of independence, for the grinding of roasted shea-nut granules. The crushing, removing of kernels and kneading activities were still done by hand. The second attempt, supported by the National Council of Women in Development (NCWD), was the introduction of the Mali oil extractor to the Dagomba women who abandoned it after a few trials. They felt that this extractor did not give them enough oil as compared to the traditional method, and the quality of the final product was poor.

The NCWD, this time together with two international development agencies, intervened using a different approach. Instead of attempting to import a machine designed elsewhere, like the Mali oil extractor, they employed a local engineering enterprise to produce machines to substitute the traditional manual processes. Machines to mill, crack and crush the nuts were developed and proved acceptable, but the kneader was abandoned by

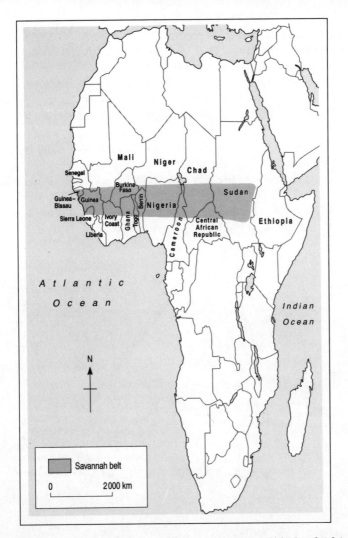

The shea nut tree grows throughout the savannah belt of Africa

most women after a few trials. The women had not been consulted over the design of these machines.

Technology development: women and technologists work together

The next attempt to produce a kneading machine was based on full co-operation with the women shea butter producers. The extension workers from a local technology centre acted as communicators between the engineers and the women producers. The project team initially studied in depth the traditional method of production, particularly the kneading stage, in the village. Initial trials with the women shea butter producers have shown that the traditional extraction method has an efficiency of around 83 per cent which compares favourably with current industrial technology. This convinced the project team further that the traditional technology which the women had developed over centuries through mere trial and error was an efficient one that produced high quality butter. Further improvements were needed to make the process less time- and energy-consuming for women.

The traditional method of kneading involves dipping your hand into the paste and stirring vigorously. While stirring with the hand, women can tell what to do next by the temperature and feel of the mass on their skin. When the paste is thick and difficult to stir, hot water needs to be added. When the paste is slippery, it means that the fat is melting, so cold water needs to be added. The addition of hot or cold water at particular times is an important

The mill was modified and improved in response to the women users' comments and demands

component of the production process, which determines the quality of the final product and the efficiency of the extraction rate.

When the project staff had gone into the village and worked with the women, they learned that the first mechanized kneader had been rejected because it simply stirred rather than kneaded. Acting as communicators between the women producers and the technologists, the project staff recommended the contracted engineer to design a more efficient baffle–impeller arrangement in the kneader along the guidelines provided by the women.

The best results obtained from the nine trials to establish the best possible performance of the kneader gave an extraction rate slightly lower than the manual process, but a reduction of about 66 per cent in the working time. There are still some shortcomings of the mechanical knea-der, but the established dialogue between the women and the designers, where the latter are instructed by the former, is expected eventually to lead to an acceptable kneader.

Two technologists with different attitudes: two rates of success

Throughout the course of several attempts at the mechanization of shea butter production under different schemes, the producers in pilot villages have been exposed to different technologists using different methods, and achieving different rates of success with oil extraction. Women producers in one of the pilot villages tell the following story to illustrate how the attitude of an outsider can make all the difference in women's willingness to co-operate, and consequently the success of the project.

'First, the technologist from town X arrived to study our traditional method of shea butter production and explore the potential for achiev-ing better efficiency rates. As we were going through the various stages, he would time the processes such as kneading, when to add water, and so on, look at his watch, tell us to stop, or to continue on without listening to whether we thought it was the right time to do these things. The few times we tried to express our opinions, he would not hear them. So eventually, we just gave up, and got on with what he instructed us to do just for his own satisfaction. We knew that the amount of oil extracted at the end was going to be low because he was making us do all sorts of wrong things.

After a few months, a second technologist came into the village. The way he worked with us was very different from the first one. At every stage of production, he would enquire why we were doing things the way we were, and really listen. Once we felt that he had an ear to lend us, we started listening to him as well. Eventually we got a much larger amount of oil from that trial. So if you want to get our message across to the people who are involved in such work, it is simple: just tell them to listen!'

161

Pottery technology in Kenya

JOSEPHINE A. MUTAGAYWA

In western Kenya, pottery has traditionally been the woman's domain. Women would produce various types of pots and pans mainly for household use in food processing, preparation, and storage. In the Luo area, for instance, the traditional repertoire of pottery forms consisted of 12 different types.

The distribution of surplus pottery production was originally limited to a small geographic area only. Due to the increasing economic significance of pottery in recent times, however, pottery has become a major means to a livelihood for the women in the area.

The process of production

Women potters, who mostly live in the western provinces of Kenya covering the Kakamega, Kisumu, Siaya and Nyanza Districts, collect the clay from communal lands along the rivers, free of charge. The top layer of earth is removed to expose and dig up the good clay. Different clay sources provide different types of clay, and the women potters can tell the various properties of certain types of clay by colour and where it came from.

In the Kisumu District, women use the clay immediately after they have dug it out from the source. In Nyanza, Siaya and Kakamega Districts, it is stored in a cool place out of direct sunlight for a week or two before use. Ageing helps break up the particles of clay which may cause cracking during drying or firing. Women know by experience the proportions by which the various colour clays are to be mixed for different purposes. The Umba Women Group in Siaya, for instance, collects three different types of clay at the foot of Got Ramogi (the Ramogi Hill) which they dry and then grind into a fine powder to be mixed with water before use. The potters carefully knead the clay either using their feet or hands, adding a little

JOSEPHINE MUTAGAYWA is a businesswoman; formerly she worked for IT Kenya.

The different traditional forms of pot have different uses; those in the foreground are for cooking fish, for example, while those with a neck are for water and other liquids

water at a time while kneading. When ready, the mixture is sorted for any stones which must be removed before starting the shaping process.

Women use pot bottoms on which a little dry soil from the homestead is sprinkled. The clay is shaped into the bottom for a new pot. Coils of approximately six to seven centimetres in diameter are prepared by the potter by hand and placed one at a time to form an integral part of the new pot. Shaping is done at the end of this process and excess clay is scraped off. The pot is then sprinkled with water and smoothed by hand. Some parts of the pot are roughened on the surface by using braided papyrus.

Using her hand, the potter rolls the braid on to the smooth, damp clay. Other decorations are made while the clay is still damp. The finished pot is left to dry indoors for one to three weeks depending on its size. Slow drying is essential, and therefore the pot is kept in a cool place. Pots that need colouring and polishing are worked on inside a hut or at night when it is cool, a day before firing. Women use hematite powder, a small bowl of water and a smooth stone to polish the surface of a pot. Cooking pots and beer pots are polished without the powder.

Once they have completed all the above stages, the pots are now ready for firing. This takes place on a dry day at a time when the direction of the wind is fairly constant, usually in the afternoon. On the firing day, dry pots are put out in the sun in the morning. Stones or old potsherds are placed in a ring on the ground where the pots are to be fired. Within this ring, dry twigs and grass, pots, firewood, wet twigs and dry leaves are placed in

163

alternate layers. The pyre is thatched carefully with layers of dry grass. Wet grass cut on the same day is finally placed on the top and the pyre is ready for lighting. Two people kindle the fire in several places around the bottom running in opposite directions. Whenever an opening is noticed during the firing, it is immediately covered with fresh wet grass. A constant watch is required while firing, and more grass is used as required until the potters feel that their pots are ready. Smoke blackens the inside of the pots, helping to seal the surface. As the fire burns out, the red hot pots are left standing on the stones and potsherds.

Cooking pots are exposed to traditional proofing using extracts of plants. Bark from special trees, such as the acacia tree, are soaked in water for about a week and boiled on the day of firing. The extract is a reddish-brown liquid. The liquid is sprinkled immediately on the hot pots as they are removed from the burned-out fire.

Transfer of skills and knowledge

Although pottery is the major income source for many women in western Kenya, it is not a full-time occupation. The skills and knowledge are passed through generations as well as among the different regions and tribes, through informal channels of communication. Older and more experienced women tend to teach younger ones—mother to daughter, mother-in-law to daughter-in-law, aunt to niece, and so on—mainly through observation and working together. As the older women reach the point when they can no longer see well, the younger generation takes over and keeps the skills and knowledge alive. The two main tribes who live in the area are the Luo and the Luhya. The Luo are the Nilotics who are the traditional potters. Intermarriage between the Luo and Luhya has been the main channel for the transfer of pottery skills from the former to the latter. Today, young women moving to other regions via marriage still take their skills with them and continue this transfer of knowledge.

Traditional pottery forms in Kenya

o Simple open form: For processing and serving meat and vegetables (such as okra); or large sizes which are used for brewing and serving beer, or fermenting and serving porridge of millet/maize (such as *nyalora*).
o Simple restricted form: For cooking and preparing fish (*haiga*); cooking and storing grains and starchy foods (*kabange* or *dakuon*).
o Forms with a neck: To brew and store beer (*mbiru*); to carry and store water (*dapi*); for odd jobs (*agulu*).

164

Innovations to meet new markets

The appearance of modern aluminium pots for cooking, and jerrycans for fetching water, and the gradual abandonment of traditional practices in food preparation have threatened markets for the traditional potters. Women have responded to these changes by inventing a wider range of products in order to safeguard their only source of cash income. In response to changing eating habits, women have started producing ceramic casseroles for oven cooking, non-stick frying pans for cooking newly popular foods like chapatis, and shallower, flat-bottomed pots for cooking meat and vegetables on the stoves used in cities. They have also started producing decorative flower and plant pots, used in tourist hotels and big buildings in the cities, as well as lampshades, candlesticks, ashtrays and other ornamental pottery.

National policies have not helped the women. For example, the Lake Basin Development Authority's decision to clear the vegetation in the area, including papyrus, in order to make space for large-scale farming of irrigated high-value cash crops, has worked to the disadvantage of women potters. As a woman cannot own land or cut down trees in her own garden, the potters are dependent on the papyrus in these communal areas to use as firewood. In addition, the basket weavers and mat makers in the area who are also dependent on papyrus as their raw material have been made poorer. Although, in fact, the women are going over to plastic instead of papyrus because it lasts longer.

Due to increasing economic hardship, women have also adapted the organization of their productive activities. While traditionally women potters used to work individually, now they are forming pottery groups through which they attempt to maximize their resources, as well as minimizing the risks associated with individual small-scale enterprise. There are also environmental factors, such as the severe shortage of fuelwood, that have led women to reorganize their productive activities in groups. For instance, now women use communal fires rather than individual ones to reduce fuelwood consumption.

Innovations in the type and range of pottery products have resulted in a competitive market for the women. Women living close to urban areas have often been able to improve their businesses. For women who live in remote rural areas, however, lack of transport is a major constraint in marketing.

Some women's groups are now beginning to apply their skills to new activities, such as the production of ceramic liners for charcoal-burning stoves, and fuel-efficient wood-burning stoves. Some technical assistance NGOs have collaborated with women potters to support them in the innovative use of their traditional knowledge and skills. The demand for fuel-efficient stoves and liners is growing due to the general shortage of fuelwood, which means that their production is a potentially lucrative business. Women using the new stoves maintain that they save time, money and energy, and also are safer when small children are around.

Indigenous vegetables in Kenya

WINNIE OGANA

When Mary Owe, a 23-year-old member of the Okando Women's Group in Utonga, is asked to name all the indigenous vegetables that she knows, she has no problems remembering the first five: '*boo, mito, akeyo, apoth* and *osuga*'. She and the other women of the Utonga sub-location in Kenya's Siaya District (south-west of Kisumu) prepare these for their families, having either grown or bought the vegetables. Mary has more problems remembering the names of the next four indigenous vegetables she knows from her grandmother: '*nyasigumba, odielo, piupiou* and *amondi*'. These are among the local delicacies whose use is rapidly declining due to dietary and socio-economic trends which in recent years have swept through the country. Sylvia Odero, aged 56, of Mary's grandmother's generation, on the other hand, is able to draw up a list of 50 indigenous vegetable items without much difficulty. Traditionally, the cultivation and marketing of indigenous food plants have been carried out mostly by women on a nationwide basis, until the colonial administration insisted that local farmers grow cash crops, mostly exotic species, for the international market, rather than subsistence crops, which were dismissed as 'primitive and inferior in quality'.

Advantages of women's use of indigenous plants

'Kenya's food economy is now heavily dependent on wheat and rice. We produce enough of both grains during bumper years, but during lean years we face shortages and are forced to import. Such over-reliance on a few particular foods is dangerous because when a crop fails it is like having a famine. People who have not acquired the knowledge of how to gather, cultivate and make use of indigenous foods become desperate and are often rendered helpless.' So says a nutritionist, in explaining the disadvantages of the exotic species. Unlike the exotics, indigenous plants are disease- and

WINNIE OGANA is a journalist working in Kenya

drought-resistant, are not as prone to major pests, and are cheaper to grow since they can do without expensive fertilizers and pesticides. Many also have a nitrogen-fixing capacity. Crop management of indigenous plants is relatively easy and makes fewer demands on women's time and energy. Indigenous crops often grow faster than exotics, and can be harvested in weeks, rather than months. Moreover the preservation of diets rich in indigenous food plants means better nutrition. Indigenous food plants also tend to be environmentally more appropriate.

Low status of indigenous food plants

Women's farming, food processing and marketing in Kenya, as in many other countries, is perceived as haphazard and small scale. Women, who grow indigenous plants, are not credited with any value as producers. When a woman is seen cultivating or gathering indigenous food plants, it is assumed that she is doing so because she cannot afford better food. Agricultural policies and extension services often deny the importance of women's knowledge of local food plants by targeting male commercial farmers. Even when women do get involved in agricultural schemes, they have received little support for growing indigenous plants. One woman farmer in the Siaya District, when asked where she got her indigenous food plants from, pointed outside of her vegetable garden towards the forest. She explained that she had a small plot hidden away there where she planted a few indigenous varieties that she liked to use. As one of the farmers involved in the agricultural extension scheme operational in the area, she was expected to grow only the 'marketable' exotic species, rather than indigenous food crops.

The trend is reversing—women combine indigenous and modern practices

Despite negative opinions about indigenous foods, many rural Kenyan women still believe that indigenous food species are crucial for the livelihood of their families. They communicate as much of their knowledge of indigenous food plants as possible down to the younger generations through informal channels. Recently, some women's groups in the Siaya District have also taken the initiative to grow indigenous vegetables on a commercial basis, and in doing so have upgraded production and processing technologies. For instance, the Okando Women's Group, experimenting in production increases, has proved that indigenous vegetables do very well without fertilizer. Instead, women use cattle manure and compost to enrich the soil. Learning from this experience, the group members plan to use the same technologies to grow exotic crops.

Two national NGOs (Kenya Freedom from Hunger Council and Kenya

National Museums Council) are now collaborating with an international NGO to support the women in their efforts. They have started a joint programme called the Indigenous Food Plant Programme (IFPP). The implementing agencies maintain that programmes which help to create a positive and encouraging environment for women to make the best of their knowledge of food technologies is the only way to devise sustainable solutions to the problems of malnutrition and food shortages. The IFPP aims to support women's production, processing and marketing activities of these food plants, as well as document and disseminate information on a widespread basis for the re-introduction and promotion of indigenous food plants in sub-Saharan Africa.

This support has greatly facilitated women's efforts to upgrade their productive activities and enabled them to make use of modern technologies, anywhere they saw appropriate, to improve their local practices. The council provided the groups with water pumps which they used both for domestic consumption and irrigation. Growing indigenous species by irrigation was unheard of in the past. Traditionally women depended on rain to grow indigenous crops or simply collected edible plants in the forest. Facing a quite different situation than that which confronted the older generations, now that indigenous food plants are threatened by extinction, women found that with a constant water supply the indigenous vegetables fared better.

Through the extension services provided by IFPP in conjunction with the Ministry of Agriculture, women are learning new horticultural management practices. They have started to add their own improvements. One of these is intercropping local varieties with those from outside sources, which overcomes some of the disadvantages of monocropping (such as vulnerability to disease, weather and soil erosion) and extends the period of time over which women can take different crops to sell at the market.

The group has also started collecting seeds of indigenous plants in a move towards self-sufficiency in future. So far, most of their seeds have been provided by IFPP. Recently they have started collecting, drying and packaging their own indigenous seeds for sale. By increasing their own seed stocks, they hope to retain control and avoid dependence on multinational seed-producing companies, which have begun to take an interest in this potentially lucrative market.

Information dissemination

One of IFPP's activities is the preservation of women's knowledge and practices of indigenous food plant species through the documentation and widespread dissemination of this information. The species inventory includes the various local names of the plant, its traditional and present use, methods for gathering and propagating, seasonal aspects, local hand-

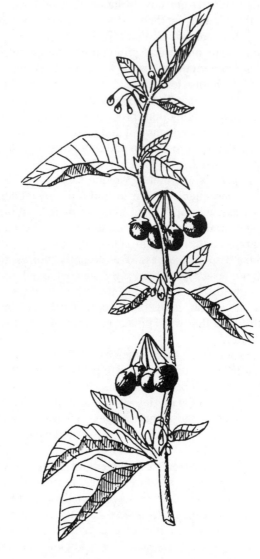

Solanum mnavu, also known as Osuga *(Luo),* Mathungu *(Meru),* Ksoiya *(Pokot), and* Esuja *(Turkana), is indigenous to Kenya*

ling, storage and preparation techniques, nutritional value and other specific properties of the plant. Already the programme has established a data base which lists details about more than 800 varieties; most of this information is supplied by the women. The findings are discussed within academic and scientific circles, and are occasionally disseminated in conferences. The IFPP therefore aims to channel this information back to the younger generation, as well as to the old who are often unaware of its importance. The information is repackaged for the needs of three main categories: for schools, adult readers and the general public (this latter includes local and international NGOs, institutions, government ministries and individuals). The information material is being developed not only in English, but also in some of the local languages. A network of NGOs involved in similar work is being built through workshops and newsletters.

Salt extraction in Sierra Leone

BERNADETTE LAHAI

A common joke in Sierra Leone explains the significant place that salt holds in the country. The joke says that the Konos (an ethnic group occupying the eastern part of the country) sold their birthright for salt to the Mendes (a neighbouring ethnic group) and since then have become the slaves of the Mendes. Indeed salt is an indispensable item for Sierra Leoneans, not only in food preparation, but also in fish, meat and oil preservation, as well as in the treatment of wounds and injuries.

Sierra Leone has no organized salt-processing industry and relies mostly on imported salt from Senegal and on small-scale producers in the informal sector, who are all women. It is estimated that only about 35 per cent of the salt consumed in Sierra Leone is of local origin despite its long coastline which could amply supply large-scale salt production. The foreign-exchange crisis that the country is now facing is bound to result in an increasing demand for locally produced salt.

Most women living in the coastal lowlands practise salt processing as their primary occupation and the main source of income for their families during the dry season. Women join this informal industry as soon as they are of age and they have usually mastered the difficult skills involved in producing a marketable product by their early 20s.

Women's innovations in salt processing

Originally Sierra Leonean women processed salt simply by boiling sea water in earthenware pots over traditional three-stone fires. Boiling was followed by sun-drying, and the operations took place in temporary huts built on beaches. However, the salt concentration of the sea water is low and therefore very large quantities of brine had to be evaporated to

BERNADETTE LAHAI is a lecturer at the Institute of Agricultural Research in Njala in Sierra Leone. She is carrying out research on women agricultural extension workers at the University of Reading in the UK.

The long coastline of Sierra Leone could supply much more of the country's salt consumption if local production were supported

produce a small amount of salt. Fuelwood consumption was correspondingly high.

These problems led women to the idea of collecting brine from ponds. To facilitate this, boreholes were dug along the tidal paths, which filled with brine during high tide. At low tide the brine was collected and evaporated until the salt crystallized. The salinity of the brine in the boreholes increased through seepage and solar evaporation leading to a shorter boiling time. The use of boreholes also overcame the problem of long and repeated journeys to the sea. Eventually women went on to develop a technique of extracting salt-from-silt, probably through the accidental discovery of salt crystals on the leaves and stems of the *bu-lei*

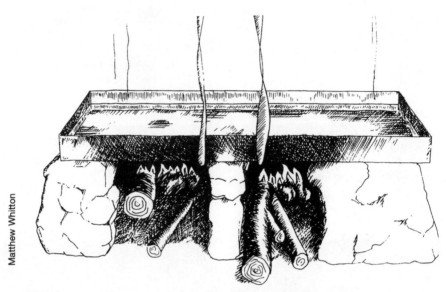

The women introduced a wall-protected fire for greater efficiency

tree (*Avicennia africana*) in the months of February and March. This observation led women to the discovery that the silt at the base of these trees was laden with salt. This in turn led to the clearing of the vegetation to facilitate the collection of silt, and the subsequent extraction of salt from the silt.

In order to leach salt from the silt, women adapted the perforated baskets that are traditionally used by women soap-makers. The salt-laden silt is collected from creek bottoms, mixed with sea water and left to separate in these baskets which serve as a percolation funnel when placed over wooden troughs in which the filtrate collects. The filtrate is then boiled on a protected three-stone fire in evaporating dishes until the salt crystallizes. The salt then is dried either in the sun or by heat from the fire.

In time, then women have changed the design of the perforated basket to a conical shape in response to technical difficulties. The perforated basket did not give very clear brine which resulted in poor-quality salt. The conical funnel on the other hand improved on the brine colour, but compared to the basket, had a low silt-holding capacity, which slowed down the rate of filtration. Building a larger conical funnel in order to increase the silt-holding capacity posed some problems for the women. While men build the wooden frame for the funnel, women plaster it with mud in preparation for the filtration. Larger conical frames required women to assume physical positions that were almost impossible for them. Also, the women found that a larger funnel was less firm and therefore less

174

efficient. Hence they suggested a rectangular design for the funnel which enabled faster and more productive filtration.

The stoves used during the evaporation stage have also changed. The first adaptation was from the traditional three-stone open fire to the more efficient wall-protected fire which was designed by the women themselves. The second adaptation was a two-burner stove introduced by the Fourah Bay College. While this stove was a 50 per cent improvement over the open fire and a 35 per cent improvement over the wall-protected fire with respect to efficiency in fuelwood consumption, its adoption has been very low. This was partly due to the fact that it needed a blacksmith for maintenance and partly because it could not accommodate all types of cooking pots. The wall-protected fire, developed by the women themselves, is the most common method used by most processors. Apart from needing less fuel, it can accommodate any size or shaped evaporating dish.

Evaporating dishes have also changed. Women found that enamel basins gave much whiter salt than the traditional earthenware pots. The only disadvantage is the cost and sometimes the availability. Presently all salt processors use rectangular-shaped evaporating dishes made from scrap metal and drums. These are fabricated locally and always available.

Technological skills involved in salt-from-silt extraction

The skill level of the operators of the salt-from-silt extraction technology is the most crucial element in determining the quality of the salt. Constructing an efficient funnel requires a very careful process of lining and plastering. The boiling operation on the other hand involves the skilful regulation of the fire, in order to facilitate the crystallization of pure salt (sodium chloride), while preventing the crystallization of bitter magnesium salts and the burning of the final product. The more experience a salt producer has, or the more skilled she is, the whiter and purer her salt.

The acquisition of skills and knowledge in salt processing takes place within an informal context of information transfer from older to younger women, mostly within a family. Born in a salt-processing community, most women master the various skills and procedures in salt processing through observation and practice. The sharing of information about new ideas, practices and technologies, similarly takes place at a personal level among the women producers. Inter-village marriages, visits between kin and migration are some of the factors that facilitate information sharing.

Salt processing as a woman's enterprise in Sierra Leone

The relatively low cost and year-round availability of locally produced salt has attracted a lot of traders to the processing areas. As the foreign-exchange deficit in Sierra Leone continues to rise, the local production of salt will continue to become more important. Relying mainly on local sources and expertise this industry already supplies 35 per cent of the nation's salt. At the same time it provides employment to 1152 households in the area (excluding temporary processors) with thousands more involved in salt trading. The government's only attempt so far at local salt production has been a short-lived attempt at large-scale solar salt works at Suen. It failed mainly due to environmental and technical problems. People's, and in this case, women's technology has survived through the years, however, adapting to changing circumstances and becoming more efficient.

Fermented foods in Sudan

HAMID A. DIRAR

Sudan has about 60 different kinds of fermented food products of which at least half are made from sorghum or millet, grains which have been an important part of Sudan's food culture for thousands of years. A sorghum sample, found buried in a pit alongside the White Nile, dates back to the year AD 245.

The most complicated sorghum fermentation process that the women carry out is the preparation of a clear sorghum beer called *assaliya*. The 40-step process produces a malt syrup from germinated sorghum grain and takes two days or longer to complete. It is thought that the West African clear beers, *otika* and *amgba*, developed from the *assaliya* process. If this theory is true, it leads to the conclusion that the transfer of knowledge has been practised horizontally across the continent. This must have been as a consequence of women's movements through the generations, as men could not transfer such a long and detailed process.

Among the most common sorghum foods in Sudan are a fermented stiff porridge called *aceda*, a fermented bread called *kissra*, and a drink called *abreh*. While women's preparation of each product entails a complicated and multi-step process, given the limitation of space, we will describe only the fermentation of *abreh* here.

The processing technique of *abreh*

Sudanese women prepare *abreh*, a traditional and popular non-alcoholic fermented sorghum drink, usually for the holy month of Ramadan. *Abreh* is in the form of fine flakes which are added to cold water, sweetened to taste and then swallowed whole while drinking.

The grains are first washed and hulled using the wooden pestle and mortar. The peeled grains are then washed again. Then the grains are

HAMID DIRAR, formerly Professor of Microbiology at the University of Khartoum, now works at the Omar Mukhtar University, Libya

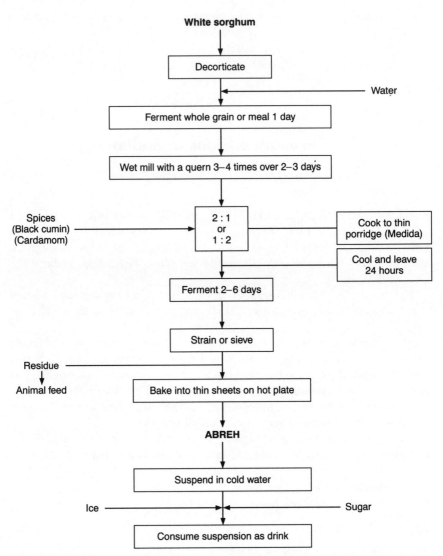

Abreh *production process*

wet milled on the *murhaka* (traditional milling stone) to give *derish* which is allowed to ferment. After 24 hours of fermentation, wet milling continues for one to three days until a very fine paste results. When all the *abreh ajin* (dough) has been wet milled, part of it is cooked into a thin porridge and the porridge is left to cool for 24 hours again before adding back to the remaining *ajin* bulk with some spices, such as *negila sativa* (black cumin).

The second stage of fermentation continues for about three to six days until the stiff dough becomes liquid. About 50ml of the dough is poured on to a *doka* (ceramic pan), covering the whole surface. The dough is spread flat and think, baked and swept into a container. Because the sheet is so very thin it breaks into flakes when it is swept off the hot plate.

The advantages of *abreh* and other fermented foods

The *abreh* drink, which has a fresh sour taste, fills the role of a nutritious thirst-quencher in the hot climate of Sudan. The Sudanese believe that a drink of *abreh* is a more nutritious way of satisfying thirst than plain water. In addition to being filled with an easily digestible sugar, the acidity of fermented sorghum decreases the risks involved in drinking contaminated water. Moreover, the flakes are lightweight and easily transportable by travellers.

Fermentation is a valuable method of preserving food for times of scarcity, and *abreh*, like other fermented food products, can be stored for a long time. Looking at the selection of fermented foods used in Sudan shows that the majority are famine foods: wild grass seeds, tree fruits and swollen roots. When food shortage is a chronic state, women develop techniques to make the most of any available organic material. Fermentation also improves the digestibility of a food, enabling women to produce high-value additions to the diet from substances such as bones, leaves, caterpillars, frogs and cow urine. Recent laboratory tests show that up to 86 per cent of the protein present in *kissra* and *abreh* samples is digestible. In the Sudanese context, women's knowledge of fermented foodstuffs has played an important role in coping with periods of famine, but a lack of understanding of this capacity has led to international aid agencies organizing relief operations around imported foodstuffs.

When mechanization takes over . . .

Abdul Wahab Musa's *kissra* and *abreh* factory in Khartoum is one of the first examples of the mechanized processing of traditional foods in Sudan. The roller-drier machine that Musa has designed can produce a variety of sorghum products simply by adjusting the speed of the conveyor belt and the temperature of the heating system beneath it.

In order to develop this machine, Musa consulted closely with women producers of sorghum foods. 'Women are the ones who have been processing sorghum to make these traditional foods for hundreds of years in Sudan, and are therefore the experts. Their feedback and inputs were crucial.'

While Musa's machine has the potential for relieving Sudanese women from a laborious task that they have been performing for years, it also carries the threat of pushing the many rural and peri-urban women

179

producers and marketers of fermented sorghum products out of the market. The factory-produced foods are sold directly to urban consumers for lower prices. Some people, however, still prefer to buy sorghum products from women producers, who make them using traditional technology, since the taste of the factory products do not achieve the traditional standards. Nevertheless, the price difference of five Sudanese pounds (approx. US$0.6) per sheet of *kissra* bread has serious implications for women's production.

Having first proved the capacity of his machine, Musa applied to two famine relief agencies for support in disseminating the product. He reasons that women's sorghum production and processing activities have been crucial in the survival of rural communities and that upgrading of local techniques can further improve the existing capacity for food security. One of the agencies was initially interested, but no conclusion was reached owing to disagreement over the price of the machine. The other agency wrote back saying they were not interested.

Cassava processing in Uganda

ERIOTH SIMWOGERERE

Ugandan women use the whole cassava plant not only as a food crop, but also for firewood, cooking oil, medicine and building material, and as a source of cash income.

Certain properties of cassava—such as its tolerance to drought, poor soil and neglect, and the fact that it can be stored underground for several months after maturation—makes this crop an important food source for rural populations in semi-subsistence economies in sub-Saharan Africa, particularly in times of food shortage. It is an excellent source of dietary energy and is traditionally prepared by women with protein-rich foods. However, although cassava constitutes one-third of the total production of cereals, roots and plantains in the region, it is often perceived as a low-status or poverty food.

Cassava was not a popular food in Uganda, but by the mid-1980s, when years of civil war had wiped out most other crops in the country, it was one of the few available foodstuffs. When people, mainly widows and orphans, returned to their villages at the end of the war, they found that the only crop available was cassava, which had remained in the ground. Women have since developed ways of using every bit of this plant for a whole range of needs.

Cassava roots normally cannot be stored for more than a few days after digging. They are usually dug up, peeled and then cooked, mostly with beans or meat, and eaten immediately. For longer-term preservation women usually slice and dry the cassava into tablets, which they store in sacks and pots, or mill into flour to keep it in this form. Women use the processed cassava for home consumption particularly during the dry season when fresh food is not readily available, or too expensive to buy.

The dried cassava tablets do not last longer than four months after which they will require further drying. A new product that women in Luwero have

ERIOTH SIMWOGERERE trained as a primary school teacher and now works as Women in Development trainer and a businesswoman.

181

developed recently is *mawogo nkyenka*—cassava pellets—which keep for longer periods if packed. These pellets made out of grated, dried and fried cassava, are ready-to-use all year round. They are often used as a breakfast food with boiled milk and sugar added; as a snack when mixed with roasted groundnuts (peanuts), *simsim* (sesame), or soybeans; and finally as a proper meal by moistening the pellets with clean water to be added to other foods like minced meat, fish or bean sauce. The simplest meal made out of *mawogo* mixed with cooked beans is called *katogo*. The mixture is boiled until it is quite tender. Cow's ghee can be added to improve the taste. Village women resort to this meal periodically because it saves firewood and does not require any other sauce.

The production of these dried cassava pellets is limited, however, due to poor grating facilities. There is room for improvement of the grating technology for increased production and also for upgrading the techniques for even longer preservation of cassava food products.

Marketing of cassava products

Women use pure cassava flour made from the sweet variety as a much cheaper and more available alternative to wheat flour, to prepare cakes and cookies, and to develop other new products for the market. They have succeeded in popularizing some of these, such as '*kabalagala*,' a kind of pancake made out of a mixture of cassava flour, sweet bananas, pepper and oil, which is then fried. Women in the countryside who live near schools can earn their living by selling *kabalagala* at breaks. Some women, either individually or in co-operatives, bake cakes for parties, or biscuits which can be packed and stored for long-term use.

Enguli—a new product and cash source

After the war, women adapted their traditional brewing technology for the production of the local alcoholic drink, *enguli*, from cassava, the only raw product in abundance at the time. In its processed form *enguli* is a colour-less liquid that is a mixture of different alcohols. Women sell it to breweries which further process it into a more refined drink, Uganda gin or Uganda *waragi*.

Cassava tubers are dug out of the soil, peeled, chopped into pieces and dried. The dried product is pounded by women who may be assisted by their daughters. Water is added and the mixture is kept in a pit to ferment. Meanwhile maize seeds are allowed to germinate, dried and then pounded. The fermented cassava is fried in a pan to brown colour, and water and the pounded maize seeds are added to the mixture, which is then left to ferment further.

The fermented mixture is squeezed and filtered, giving a brown liquid

Original drawing provided by Simwogerere

Ugandan women use the whole cassava plant, not only as a food crop but also for firewood, cooking oil, medicine, and building material

and a sticky yellowish residue. This residue constitutes an important animal feed in Luwero (see below). Women distil the brown liquid by heating it in drums over wood fires. The vapour is led through tubes cooled in water and finally condensed in a container. This condensed colourless liquid is *enguli*.

Marketing and further processing of *enguli*

The village women sell the *enguli* to men in the local markets. Despite the small scale of most women's production, the income generated is enough so that even single mothers can afford basic expenses such as school fees. The importance of the cash income from *enguli* sales can be understood better within the context of low-income areas such as the Luwero District, where 70 per cent of the population are widows and orphans. Some women manage to operate on a larger scale for marketing the locally prepared gin to some national distilleries. Quality is an important factor in selling to the larger distilleries. The local brew, which is simply stored in sealed cans for transportation to towns, is bought by the distilleries if it is at least 40 per cent alcohol. Distillers do the final refinement by eliminating impurities and adding flavours.

Use of *enguli* by-products

Women also can make use of many of the *enguli* by-products in the following ways:

○ Animal feed: The yellow residue that remains after the initial squeezing and filtration of the cassava during *enguli* production, as mentioned earlier, is the main source of animal feed in the area. Indeed, the village women in Luwero report that all the pigs and chickens that they rear flourish on this feed.
○ *Amuna*: Another useful by-product of *enguli* production is called *amuna*, a viscous liquid that remains in the distillation tank as a residue. Women have found that this residue, which can be easily drained out of the drums, is an efficient and cheap substitute for cement. Now most women in Luwero have reduced the dependence on cement and lime by in some cases completely replacing them with *amuna* for brickmaking, plastering, joining bricks during construction, and floor-making.
○ Preservative: Women who use cassava flour to produce cakes, biscuits, pancakes and other such products for sale in the market, use *enguli* as a preservative in these foods. Because of its high alcohol content, *enguli* preserves effectively.

Other uses of cassava

The rural women can use every bit of the cassava to meet other important needs as well. The cassava leaves, for instance, when washed in salty water, dried and pounded to powder can be kept for over two years. This powder, called *gobe*, is mixed with vaseline and used as a cure for skin rashes. The leaves also provide a good alternative to iodine or spirits in case of fresh wounds. They are washed, chopped, mixed with a little salt, and the paste is tied around the wound with a bandage. *Gobe* is also used as a condiment with groundnut soup.

Dried and pounded cassava makes a strong glue when heated. Another technique for making glue is using pieces of cloth or perforated sacks to press the white starchy liquid out of cassava. The glue is formed by heating the starch. Women use some starch residue for cooking or selling to laboratories, for use in the textile industry or village tailoring projects. The glue, on the other hand, is sold to local shopkeepers, who use it for making paper bags, or to distilleries which use it to attach labels to the *Waragi* bottles.

Nkejje fish in Lake Victoria

IRENE FLORENCE WEKIYA

For the people living along the shores of Lake Victoria, the Jinja District of Uganda, fishing has traditionally had a very important role in the economic, social and cultural aspects of their lives. Women make use of the many species of fish which exist in this huge area of fresh water to ensure the livelihood of their families.

The *nkejje* (pronounced en-kedge-ee) fish is of particular importance to those who live in the area for preventing malnutrition and related childhood diseases. This small fish, with an average size of three inches, contains 56.4 per cent protein, 11 per cent calcium and 8 per cent fat.

Traditionally women of Jinja have been involved not only in the processing of fish products, but also in fishing itself. Traditional fishing gear consisted of lift baskets, swim traps or scooping baskets. Women would weave this equipment out of papyrus, treebark, banana fibres and creepers and use them in shallow waters for fishing. To catch the *nkejje* fish, women use rectangular floats to which they would attach a special thorny shrub whose ash would attract the *nkejje* as it fell in the water.

As modern fishing technology has replaced traditional equipment, women's sphere of activity has become limited to the processing of the fish. Women prepare and preserve most of the local fish by smoking it covered in banana leaves, peels or grass. The low fat content of the *nkejje*, however, makes it suitable for sun-drying. Women prepare a clean rock on which they place the *nkejje* for sun-drying, cover with grass to preserve the flavour and also to protect it against direct exposure to sunlight. The drying process continues at night due to the heat radiating from the rock surface.

Traditionally the *nkejje* fish is believed to have medicinal value. The fish is believed to be preventive against measles and kwashiorkor. For a child who already has measles: 'There is no better treatment,' says an old woman from Jinja, 'the *nkejje* is boiled and the child can drink the water and get

---

IRENE FLORENCE WEKIYA is a Member of Parliament in Uganda.

better.' However, the women of the Jinja District are now faced with a severe shortage of the *nkejje* fish.

The introduction, in 1965, of Nile perch and tilapia into Lake Victoria, under a scheme supported by the Ugandan Government and two international development agencies, has led to serious social, economic and ecological changes. There was little local participation in this programme, and a foreign fishery expert had advised the the *nkejje* fish should be left to die of old age, and instead the production of the 'more profitable' Nile perch promoted. The Nile fish fed on the *nkejje* almost to the point of making it extinct. While the commercial catch of the Nile fish increased from 0.42 per cent in 1981 to 55 per cent in 1985, that of *nkejje* fell from 96 per cent in 1981 to none at all in 1985.

Increased algal activity is among the most alarming ecological imbalances occurring in the lake. The planktons, which were normally fed on by the *nkejje*, are now free to grow with no check. Due to changes in the distribution of these plankton, an algal bloom may flourish, causing the lake to look green and therefore less palatable. It is also common to see dead fish on the surface of the water, asphyxiated by the algae. The big Nile perch processing plants that have been set up around the lake are another pollution threat in the area.

Being dependent on the high-protein *nkejje* to combat malnutrition in their children, low-income mothers particularly have suffered from the scarcity of the fish. The higher fat content of the Nile perch makes it less easy for children to digest and, furthermore, local people do not like the taste.

Women respond to change

In the midst of the changes following the introduction of the Nile fish into Lake Victoria, the Jinja women have developed innovative ways of dealing with the new circumstances. In order to make the now-scarce *nkejje* last, women, after drying the fish, pound it into a powder using a mortar and pestle or a grinding stone, and sieve it. The *nkejje*, once dried and powdered, needs no preservatives and can be stored for long periods, and will last much longer as it is added in small amounts to baby and other foods.

The *nkejje* needs to be very dry in order to allow for easy pounding, which means that women cannot wash it after the drying process is complete. Hence the *nkejje* laid outside for sun-drying needs greater care to keep it clean. In order to assure the hygiene of the product women now have started washing the fish thoroughly immediately after catching, stacking them on sticks passed through their gills to be laid out on papyrus mats made especially for the clean drying of the *nkejje*. Seeing the demand for the ever-decreasing *nkejje* fish, various entrepeneurs have taken up the local women's idea of powdering the fish. Some small production firms using locally fabricated driers and hammer mills have been set up in the area. Today it is possible to walk into any grocery store and buy *nkejje* powder.

Women lose ownership of their knowledge

The traditional importance that women attach to the *nkejje* recently prompted some research into the fish, which resulted in the discovery of its high protein and calcium content. Protein supports the immune system and hence improves a child's resistance to potentially dangerous diseases such as measles. The discovery led to national nutrition clinics using *nkejje* in the treatment of various childhood diseases, and ironically to a strong government campaign to encourage mothers to feed their children with *nkejje*. The knowledge of the health uses of the *nkejje* fish for children which the women have been using for many years is now being offered back to them as 'scientific' knowledge.

There is growing recognition by the policymakers that decreasing *nkejje* supplies might lead to significant problems for many poor households in the area. Recently the Minister of Agriculture, Animal Industry and Fisheries, one of the woman ministers in the cabinet, appealed to the public to save the *nkejje* and banned the use of fishing nets with small holes on the lakes. Such measures are intended to reverse the adverse effects of the introduction of the Nile perch, exacerbated by advanced fishing technologies such as power boats and large nylon nets which allowed indiscriminate fishing. Despite such compensatory policies, however, the government continues to support the Nile fish-processing and export companies.

To ensure lasting supplies of the *nkejje*, the women of the Jinja Municipality have recently requested the Uganda Fresh Fisheries Research Organization (UFFRO) for assistance to grow the fish in artificial ponds that would be controlled by a woman's co-operative. UFFRO has promised technical assistance to the women on the condition that the pond would be within the reach of the research station. Following this response the women have applied to the Jinja Municipal Council for land, only to receive the response: 'You get fish from the lake, why make your own pond?'

Survival skills of Tonga Women in Zimbabwe

RODGER MPANDE and NOMA MPOFU

The silos are full, but the stomachs are empty: this is Zimbabwe's food security paradox. Year after year there are reports that people are dying of starvation in some parts of Zimbabwe. One such area is the Binga District, which is characterized by poor soils, erratic rainfall, and the presence of wild animals. The Tonga people, who are inhabitants of this area, originally lived along the Zambezi River and its tributaries, farming the rich alluvial soils which were annually flooded by the river. In 1957, however, the tribe was forcibly moved from the Zambezi River area to the escarpment to make space for construction of the Kariba Lake Dam and hydroelectric scheme.

When the Tonga were moved, their whole farming system was disrupted, to the extent that their survival was threatened. Binga District in Matabeleland North Province, where most the Tonga resettled, is considered to be the poorest in Zimbabwe in terms of soil conditions and rainfall; there are no lakes for fishing, while because of the Natural Conservation Areas law, hunting is prohibited. The levels of agricultural production are not adequate to sustain food security for average households of seven members throughout the year, and the district is classified as a food-deficit area. The drought relief which the government issues year after year is inadequate, and does not always get to the area because of poor communications infrastructure.

Tonga women innovate and adapt for food security

The Tonga people have through the years devised methods of coping with the harsh environmental conditions. Tonga women, who are responsible for

RODGER MPANDE worked for a Zimbabwe environmental research organization and is now a partner in Commutech; Noma Mpofu worked for IT Zimbabwe and now works for the Dutch NGO, NOVIB.

The Tonga women were relocated from the Zambezi valley to Matabeleland when the Kariba dam was built

providing food for the family and the community, innovated and adapted food production and processing technologies, and identified new sources of food. While the attempts by expatriates and development agencies to promote drought-tolerant crops have not yielded any significant results, Tonga women have managed to identify, collect and process 47 indigenous plants whose leaves are used for relish, and over 100 tree species with a variety of edible parts. Some examples are:

o In January, February and March, when food, especially the traditional cereals, are in short supply, the women collect cereals from certain types of indigenous grasses and process these to produce a meal which is used in place of sorghum, millet or maize meals.

o Women have substituted the traditional morning meal of tea and bread with a porridge and a drink made from the fruit of the baobab tree. The oval shell of the baobab fruit is cracked open and seeds which are embedded in a whitish powdery pulp are either soaked or boiled and a porridge prepared in the usual way. The pulp is also nutritious. Likewise the fruit of the baobab can be eaten on its own or used to prepare a refreshing drink which is also used to treat fevers and strobic complaints. Women can also extract oil from the seeds of the baobab. The bark of the baobab is soft and can be pounded and burned to ash which

189

women use as a form of caustic soda in the preparation of other green vegetables. Women also use the bark to weave rope or mats, and sell them for cash income.

○ In times of drought, which are frequent, plants not normally consumed because they are poisonous can be used provided skilled time-consuming preparation methods are followed.

○ Women use a wide variety of green vegetables as relish to accompany a thick maize, millet or sorghum porridge, called *sadza*. They also collect rainy season vegetables, sun-dry them on metal sheets, and store them in jute bags for consumption during the dry season.

The example of Tamarind

One of the wild plants that the Tonga women started using for a variety of purposes is tamarind *(Tamarindus indica)*. Tamarind is a tropical evergreen tree with a low, rounded crown, which may grow up to 24m in height and bears large quantities of pale brown pods, 10cm or longer. Although tamarind grows and is cultivated throughout the tropical and sub-tropical parts of the world and used for a variety of purposes, from medicine to fish preservation, it is hardly recognized at all as a useful plant in Zimbabwe. It

Although tamarind is cultivated and used for a variety of purposes around the world, it is hardly recognized at all as a useful plant in Zimbabwe

is due to the Tonga women's knowledge and skills that the fruit has started being used in the Binga District.

Women climb trees to collect the fruit, which they store in jute bags for a period of 12 months up to the next harvest period. The fruit is of high nutritional value and does not rot, which renders it especially valuable in drought-stricken areas, and women like to store large quantities of fruit for use in times of food shortage and when fruit is unavailable. The fruit is stored in traditional units which women make out of mud, raised slightly above ground level.

Women process tamarind in a number of ways for the following purposes:

o As a flavouring agent: its pleasant, sour taste enlivens porridge made out of millet, sorghum or maize. Either the fruit or, in times of food shortage, its leaves are soaked and boiled.
o As a substitute for commercially produced beverages such as tea and coffee, which are frequently not available due to lack of money or distance from retail outlets. Usually the ripe fruits are used, but when there are none, women also collect the unripe fruits, soak and boil them and finally add ash to help neutralize their acidity, to make a pleasant drink which can be either drunk alone or added to porridge.
o As a snack food: the seeds, which have a high protein content, can be fried and eaten as snack.
o As a substitute for, or addition to, scarce maize, sorghum or millet meals. Women collect the unripe fruit, soak and boil the seeds, pound them, and add them to cereals.
o As a medicine: concentrations of tamarind liquid may be used to cure gastro-intestinal disorders in humans, or even added to animals' drinking-water as a cure for sleeping sickness caused by the tsetse fly (it is not known how effective this is).
o As a coagulant: the acidic liquid from tamarind and other wild fruits, is used to curdle fresh milk, in the same way that other acids, such as acetic or citric acid, are used in laboratories.

Marketing initiatives by the Tonga women

The Tonga women have also realized the commercial potential of tamarind and other wild fruits, and have started marketing the fresh fruit by the roadside and at bus stops. They use this case to buy equipment, like metal pots and plates, needed in food preparation and processing. There is a so far unquantified market for tamarind in the urban areas in the Asian communities. The Asians are said to use agents who come into the area to barter for the fruit with the women in exchange for clothing rather than paying cash, which makes it difficult to assess the money value of tamarind.

The Tonga women have identified more than 100 tree species with a variety of edible parts

Women are aware of the existence of this market but have not identified the strategies for exploiting it. Their concern is that once large-scale commercialization of tamarind catches on they will lose control over the source of the fruit, and that this subsistence crop, an important part of their diet, will move into the control of others.

Extension services and the policy environment act as obstacles

As part of the community development programme, the extension services encourage women in Binga to grow non-indigenous commercial varieties of fruit and vegetables, which have a high market value. Such varieties usually are not very tolerant of the high temperatures prevailing in most areas of Binga. Some women were observed planting local vegetables outside the gardens along the fences. Asked why they planted the wild vegetables outside, the women said:

> 'the extension services want us to use the available land, water and labour for the high breed, exotic varieties that they have given us. Therefore we think that they would not like us to cultivate wild plants inside the gardens. They do not see the local plants as of any importance, although they are the ones that survive the high temperatures from

September to November. By planting them alongside the fence we are able to water them at the same time as we are planting the garden without getting ourselves into trouble with the extension workers'.

Despite the wide availability of tamarind in many rural areas of Zimbabwe, and its prime importance in the diets of many rural families living in areas of poor fertility, there is no recognition of the fruit by governmental or non-governmental organizations working in these places. On the contrary, in many cases they are actively promoting cash crops. Given the enormous range of uses for tamarind in Asia, Latin America and other parts of Africa, and the availability of processing technologies, there is potential for further development of tamarind use in Zimbabwe. Such development would be encouraged by the sharing of information between countries of the South.

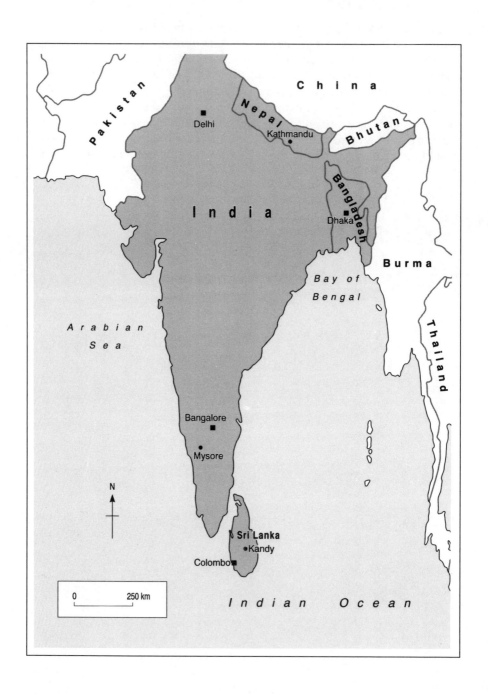

PART III

Asia

Land reclamation in Bangladesh

AYESHA SHAHJAHAN

In the area of Char Baggardona, Noakhali, in coastal Bangladesh most of the people (roughly 95 per cent) are landless. They are mostly migrant people who lost all their land and property either through river erosion or through some other reason. Their main sources of income are:

o Growing paddy in a less-fertile, saline newly accreted land by share-cropping (50 per cent basis) in the monsoon season.
o Working as day labourers in government or private development activities (mainly earth cutting) for construction or repairs of roads, canals and ponds.
o Seasonally migrating as day labourers to other areas and getting work in agricultural activities, brickmaking, construction, or rickshaw pulling.

The Land Reclamation Project (LRP) is a joint collaboration between Bangladesh and The Netherlands for developing new lands in the coastal area of Bangladesh. The development process involves the following steps:

o Accretion of new lands by tapping the silts coming through the rivers in the coastal areas.
o Poldering the new land with the objective of initially raising land level, sealing the polder to prevent saline water intrusion, draining the polder for quicker desalinization.
o Developing the polder land for settlement with landless farm families on a co-operative basis.
o Research and extension for agriculture development of the polder.
o Social and infrastructural development on the polder.

The Bangladeshi policy is that the government-owned, newly accreted land is to be distributed among the landless farmers only. But in reality very often new land is illegally taken by big landowners using fraud and force.

AYESHA SHAHAJAN is a women in development trainer.

In the Land Reclamation Project, women wear the burka to do the weeding, which is traditionally men's work in Bangladesh

These big landowners subsequently allow the landless poor peasants on the land to sharecrop.

The Dutch government provides development finance and technical assistance, while the Bangladesh government begins and carries out the project. The agents acting for the Dutch government are Euroconsult and Delft Hydraulic Laboratory while the Bangladesh Water Development Board acts for its government and is responsible for executing the project.

To attract the landless farmers into the project and then to enable them to use the land most efficiently the project adopted the following criteria.

o Land ownership should be vested in the co-operative and the farmer will be a member (shareholder) of the co-operative. Since the farmer is not the title holder of the land, he cannot transfer the title.

- The land has to be cultivated on co-op basis which means no farmer owns any piece of land. It is easier for a group to collect agricultural inputs, and perform the agricultural work most efficiently.
- The members of the co-operative must live near one another in a cluster to encourage close relationships, easy communication, easy supervision and better development of co-op adherence.

The pilot polder

1100ha of newly accreted land was newly poldered in Char Baggardona, Noakhali. The polder comprises 30 clusters to accommodate 895 landless farm families, adequate drains for better drainage and desalinization, roads for communication, a central marketing area for community development and infrastructural facilities, a sluice to control the water-management system in the polder and a research plot for developing agricultural technology for crop and seed growing, poultry, livestock and fisheries development and undertaking various research programmes on collective cultivation and landless settlement.

Each cluster comprising about 30 landless farm families has the following provisions:

- 24ha cultivable land
- One pond × 0.2ha.
- Housing area on the three sides of the pond × 0.08ha.
- An open yard at one side of the pond for after harvest work, meetings, ceremonies and a playground.

For each five or six clusters there is a cyclone shelter which also could be used as a school, central storage area and a community centre.

Women in agriculture

91 per cent of the agriculture labourers are male. A few women work in the field in the northern districts but in the south-east where the project is located women are not allowed to work in the field. The do some agricultural activities in the homestead such as threshing, clearing, boiling and storing. Therefore the women's role in the project area is strictly confined to the post-harvest operation. Women even are not allowed to go outside the home without wearing a burka.

The reasons for becoming destitute are as follows:

- The main earning member, or the male head of the family dies, leaving no land or cash property and while most of the family members are too young to earn.
- The male head deserts his family.

199

o The wife is divorced and takes a few children with her. Neither she nor her parents have much property.

In June 1986, 895 landless farm families were given physical possession of land. Since then cultivation and polder development activities according to the LRP concept have started.

Simultaneously the LRP authorities in the field at Noakhali started to plan some development with poor women in the area. Obviously the destitute female-headed farm families needed early consideration. Noakhali is regarded as a very conservative Islamic area where women must remain in strict 'pardah'. 'Pardah' is the veiled seclusion of women within the four walls of their home and veiling of women when they move outside their homesteads. Under extreme need when they are to go out they move either at night or early morning before sunrise by wearing a 'burka' to protect against glances of men.

For these reasons and because women are believed to be weaker, women are not made full co-op members in their own right. Destitute women in and around the pilot polder are either divorced, abandoned or widows with a number of children. Some live with a disabled father or mother or both, and lead a miserable life. These families entirely depend on the mercy of the neighbours and there are not many people to help them because the neighbours are also poor.

The Dutch Field Engineer, LRP Agronomist and Executive Engineer, Nijera Kori (an NGO) discussed the issue and resolved that a research programme would be undertaken to see the feasibility of rehabilitating these destitute women in the field of agriculture. If this proved feasible, in future polders, some land will be reserved for settlement by women-headed landless families.

Selection criteria

The following selection criteria were determined:

o The women must be widowed/divorced/abandoned.
o The women should not possess more than 0.2ha land.
o There should not be any male member in the family over 16 years of age.
o The family should not possess any business, property or enterprise which generates an annual income of more than $30.

Keeping the above conditions in mind, Nijera Kori, a local NGO which is engaged in organizing the farmers for the project, was asked to nominate 10 women for the first year and did so. During the second year one member was excluded from the group because she got married. By the end of the second year, 10 members were found to be too few to manage all the crop production activities in the peak work period. Ten members were also too few to form an officially registered co-operative for which at least 16 members are required.

Crop cultivation

A meeting with the selected women discussed the prospects and problems of crop cultivation. The women listed the problems of shortage of funds, lack of experience, social constraints, logistics and input collection problems. It was decided that all the problems should be solved jointly. The women got very interested and the experiment started in July 1986.

The soil of the Charbaggadona pilot polder is silt/loam in texture. The structure has not yet formed. The pH varies between 6 and 7.2 with organic content very low. The soil is very saline. Salinity is low (+4 mS/cm) during the monsoon season and up to 20mS/cm during April. There is no irrigation facility in the area. There is one rainy season when 3000mm falls.

Due to the above soil and environmental conditions the area is mostly single cropped, a monsoon rice crop of local variety giving a low yield (0.8t/ha). In a few small patches a pulse (*kheshari*) crop is grown during winter. In a year when there is some winter rainfall this crop yields 0.3t/ha. If there is no rainfall during the winter there will be no appreciable pulse yield but it will provide wild grazing for the cattle together with extra organic matter to incorporate naturally with the soil. This natural fertilizer improves soil structure helping it to conserve moisture and reduce resalinization.

Financial arrangements

During the first year the project donors provided an interest-free loan of Tk8000 (in small instalments as and when required to cover all the expenses of cultivation such as seeds, a plough, fertilizer, insecticide and labour). During this year the women could not provide any financial support for cultivation.

The total paddy yield was 3860kg, out of which they sold 1400kg to repay the entire amount of loan. They kept 650kg of paddy as savings and seed for the next year. Each of the participating members got 181kg of paddy for their own family consumption.

In the second year the total cost of cultivation was Tk24 800. They provided Tk3800 from their savings and took an interest-free loan of Tk21 000 from the project. After harvest they repaid the entire amount of project loan by selling 3740kg of paddy. They kept 1374kg of paddy as savings and seeds and each member received 374kg of paddy for family consumption.

In the third year total cost of cultivation was Tk39 060 for which they

201

received an interest-free loan of Tk31 760 and provided Tk8180 from their own savings. They repaid the entire amount of the loan by selling 8200kg of paddy. Each family received 460kg of paddy for family consumption and they kept 2760kg of paddy as savings and seed for the next year.

In the fourth year the total cultivation cost came to Tk52 000 for which they took an interest-free loan from the project of Tk40 000 and provided Tk12 000 from their savings. Again they repaid the entire amount of loan by selling 6757kg of paddy. Each family received 574kg paddy for family consumption and they kept 914kg of paddy as savings and seed for next year. It should be mentioned here that during the fourth year the paddy yield was very low. The reason for this was a combination of factors. First, paddy yield in the whole zone was low due to alternating flood and drought. Second, there was a severe insect pest attack. Third, the group switched over to local variety dominance which has a lower potential yield.

Training

Since the women are not acquainted with crop cultivation activities the LRP agronomist conducted on-farm training from the beginning of the growing season. The practical training covered preparing the seedbed, sowing seeds in the bed, fertilization, irrigation, insect pest control in the seedbed, raising seedlings, land preparation, water management and fertilization in the field, transplanting seedlings, weeding, insect pest control, harvesting and post-harvest operations for rice. Since the women had never done such activities before, during the first year most of these activities were done by hired labourers. In the first years the women did not attempt to plough or ladder, apply insecticide, harvest or carry. But with time, gradually they took over most of the production activities and by the fourth year they were able to do all the activities except ploughing and laddering.

The LRP field staff help the women buy seed, fertilizer and insecticide. With advice from the LRP agronomist, the women decide how much seed, fertilizer or insecticide must be purchased and request LRP staff or Nijera Kori staff to buy it for them. Every day at the end of work the female organizer explains the account to the women, who are illiterate. From time to time the account is checked by the agronomist, the field engineer and the Nijera Kori co-ordinator.

Marketing and management

The Nijera Kori co-ordinator, organizer and LRP field staff help the women group in selling their produce. Since there is no storage facility available the group must sell the produce immediately after harvest. The role of project staff in marketing is to inform and bring the buyers to the group. The group decides to whom and at what price the product is sold.

An attendance register is maintained for the women. Every day attendance is recorded in this register. At the end of the season attendance is counted and average attendance is calculated. Anyone who has managed less than the average attendance must pay for the days she is short to those members who have worked over the average. The rate at which she has to pay is decided by the group. All members must abide by the decision of the group.

Monitoring the women's group

Interest in the women's activity in the Land Reclamation Project, Noakhali, prompted further research. The focus of the study was on how the poor adapt to the agricultural activities. The problems faced by the group and the way they solved them were also examined. Information was gathered using group discussions, individual interviews and questionnaires.

Out of the 18 destitute women, 10 are widows, four are divorced and two have been left by their husbands. Two women have elderly and disabled husbands. All the women are within the age range of 35 to 60 years old.

Twelve of the women were beggars previously. Three of them were doing small trading (selling household items from a headload). Another three of them were doing handicrafts. Most of them migrated to this area during that last 10 years. The reason for migration was usually the forced sale of their small piece of land. Because this area has been reclaimed recently, no one owns the land.

Family size varies from three to eight, with the average family size 4.5. Out of 81 members in 18 families only four were literate. In all 18 families, excluding the women members, only eight others earn anything for the family. The average annual income of the family before joining the co-operative was $60. After joining the co-operative their income increased to $190.

Social problems

Some wealthy people and the religious monks in the area were unwilling to accept that women should work in the field doing agricultural activities. They argued that this is against Muslim traditions. They were spreading rumours that the women were anti-Islamic and becoming Christian. Sharifa Khatun and her family of six were the first to suffer as a result of this whispering campaign. Her eldest daughter's marriage was settled when the social leaders spread the rumour that the mother of the bride was going to become a Christian. Because of this the groom's family felt reluctant to settle the marriage because of embarrassment. Sharifa became very anxious about the situation, and talked it over with other members of the group. They jointly approached the social leaders and tried to convince them that they do maintain burka while working in the field, that they are not going to become Christian and there are no non-Islamic activities in the project. They explained that they are simply working for their survival; they do not have any source of income and the society could not give them any help. At this the social leaders were mollified and the marriage ceremony completed peacefully.

The male and female relatives of the destitute women were at first very unenthusiastic. They tried to convince the women to withdraw from the group. The women convinced them by asking them to watch what the group was doing. Eventually nobody had any objections and now many other women wish to join the group.

Women's innovations

An illustration of the project women's innovative problem solving can be seen in the example of weeding. The deep-rooted weeds—which men can uproot easily—gave the women considerable trouble. The LRP agronomist advised them to put the leafy portion of these weeds under the soil by their legs by repeated walking through the lines of rice plant which they could do easily. They are doing this now and are getting good results for the following reasons.

○ This helps build up soil organic matter which means better soil structure, more water retention capacity, less resalinization and increased fertility.
○ More efficient weeding because by weeding by hand it is not possible to pull the weed out entirely. Regrowth then occurs quickly. But if most of the leafy portion goes under the soil, the weed is soon killed.
○ In addition to the weeding this method adds fertilizer in the affected zone. It removes gas which has collected in the root zone, so good accretion of soil follows.
○ This way of weeding helps pest control significantly. The eggmass is dropped and larvae damaged.

Their method of paddy cleaning is another example of the women's innovations. The cleaning had been done by the women using a winnower, taking some uncleaned paddy on to it and then shaking it by hand. The practice was very time consuming. The women by themselves tried to follow the way men do this job. They found that the usual way men do it, with the help of a gusting wind, was not feasible for them. Instead they found a way of spreading uncleaned paddy and winnowing it with a sack. In this process they spread significant amount of paddy on a clean floor and apply wind by waving a sack repeatedly over the paddy. With the force of the air straw, unfilled grains and chaff are all blown away, leaving only the cleaned paddy in a heap.

Making a haystack is yet another example of the project women's inventiveness. The usual way to make a haystack is to put a wooden pole vertically on the soil and spread the straw around it. When the heap gets high, two men from down below throw the straw bundle up to another two who catch it on the heap and spread it round. Those who do the throwing have to be strong enough. The women decided they must try a different way. They developed a way of doing it using a rope. Two ropes are tied with the wooden pole at one end and the other two ends are held by the two women standing on the heap. They drop the centre of the ropes and two women below put straw on to the rope. The women above pull the rope. The straw reaches the top of the heap by rolling along the rope.

Rice threshing is a further illustration of the project women's inventiveness. Before joining the co-operative the women threshed paddy by trampling on it. This is slow process and one woman can only thresh about 20kg paddy in six hours. To speed this up they adopted the process of using a paddle thresher. With the paddle thresher four women can thresh one tonne of paddy in six hours.

The women have also devised an easier way of land levelling. Partial land levelling is done while laddering. Traditionally, the final land levelling is done with a spade which again needs a lot of strength and the women can't do it. They developed a new method of land levelling. In this method they take a bundle of fresh plant material accumulated during ploughing and laddering, place it on high points and press it into mud with their feet. Together with the bundle, mud from high spot moves to low spot where it stays making the land more level.

Finally, the women developed their own method of seed preservation. Because the group did not have any storage facility there was a problem keeping the seeds needed for next year. They discussed the issue in a meeting and found that they needed to store about 400kg seed for a period of 6–7 months. They did not have enough space to contain them. They decided that seeds should be kept by all the members in equal shares. Thus it stands that each member has to preserve about 25kg of seeds which they can keep easily in an earthen container wrapped by a sack and polythene paper. They have been practising this and found it very workable.

Goals for the future

At present the women are getting only the single crop (a monsoon rice) which on average can provide them with enough food for six months. They cannot grow a second crop due to the high salinity and moisture stress (there is no irrigation provision) on their soil. By following the management practices developed by the LRP Agronomy unit, however, they have started to grow a second crop in a small area.

They still cannot do the ploughing, laddering and insecticide application.

The first two are very laborious while the last one is a very complicated operation. For these activities they employ labourers from outside.

Up until now they have not had any bullock of their own. If they can have a settlement built close to the farm they can buy a cow on a collective basis which they will use for ploughing purposes and to breed calves for future use.

In addition they are optimistic about doing some off-farm income-generating activities. They organized a seminar to identify the best ways of income generation in September of 1990 at Char Baggardona. Some of these options for generating income include: petty trading and sewing; bamboo products and handicrafts; raising livestock and poultry; and making mats and fishing nets to sell to others.

Manual silk reeling in India

PRABHA SHEKAR

Silk is a highly priced commodity, produced by the poor in rural areas and consumed by the well-to-do. Because of its exclusiveness in wear and appearance, silk has reigned as the queen of fabrics for over five thousand years. However, its total production (by all silk-producing countries put together) constitutes only a fifth of all fabrics, including man-made fibres, and has never been able to fulfil the high demand in the international market.

Sericulture, the process of silk production, is a highly employment oriented, low-capital intensive activity, suited to the condition of a labour-abundant agro-based economy. Although a highly complex process, it involves very little hard labour. All the operations involved are carried out in rural areas, providing employment for local communities. Because of its labour potential and the great demand for the product which fetches a high price, making it highly remunerative, sericulture has obtained a special status as one of the best activities for alleviating poverty among the rural poor in developing countries through the provision of employment and income. As mulberry—the sole food for silkworms—is a hardy plant, growing in all parts of the world, any area with surplus labour has great potential for developing sericulture. An added advantage in terms of a country's overall economy is that silk is an exportable commodity, earning foreign exchange.

Among tropical countries, India has the highest silk production, with its appropriate technology potentially suitable for any other developing country in the tropical and sub-tropical belt. Globally, India now occupies second position with its present production of about 9500 tonnes; an improvement over the 8455-tonne production of 1987. (See Table 1.)

PRABHA SHEKAR is a technologist working for SAMUHA, an NGO in Bangalore which works with silk reelers.

Table 1. World raw silk production (tonnes)

Country	1983	1984	1985	1986	1987
China	28 140	28 140	32 000	35 000	35 800
Japan	12 456	10 800	9 592	8 341	7 864
India	5 681	6 895	7 029	7 897	8 455
USSR	3 899	3 999	3 999	3 999	4 000
South Korea	2 292	2 088	2 196	2 196	1 608
Brazil	1 362	1 458	1 554	1 664	1 780
Others	2 770	2 720	2 748	2 748	2 874
Total	56 600	56 100	59 118	61 845	62 381

Sericulture in India

The sericulture industry in India is an ancient activity, dating back to a few centuries before the Christian era. Currently it is practised mainly in five states—Karnataka, Andhra Pradesh, Tamil Nadu, West Bengal and Jammu and Kashmir. Considerable efforts are under way to introduce sericulture into other states as well. The five contribute nearly 98 per cent of the country's total silk production. Out of 576 000 villages in India, sericulture is practised in about 50 000. The industry directly employs a total of nearly six million people, most of whom belong to the poorer sections of society. All operations in silk production, from silkworm rearing to weaving, are carried out in the unorganized sector at cottage level.

In the rural areas landowners cultivate mulberry, which is the food for silkworms. However, most cocoon production is carried out by farming communities in which farmer families cultivating mulberry also rear silkworms in their houses. Generally, for commercial purposes, hybrid variety silkworms are used. Silkworm eggs are available from silkworm seed production centres, popularly known as 'grainages', many of which are owned by private licence holders. Cocoons produced by farmers are sold in the regulated market, where they are purchased by the reeling community. Wherever mulberry cultivation and silkworm rearing are practised in India, there are well-established facilities for silk reeling, twisting and weaving. Formerly only Muslims and the scheduled castes among Hindus undertook reeling activities; however, nowadays it is common to find even upper-caste Hindus engaged in the industry.

Silk reeling is basically a process by which filaments from the cocoons are drawn together into a single thread. Various devices are adopted for this purpose, from the simplest contrivance, namely the *charaka*, to highly sophisticated automatic machines. High mechanization, using semi-automatic and automatic machines, has always been thought of as a substitute for cottage basins, never for *charakas*. Reeling capacity in India consists of 21 983 *charakas*, 6955 cottage basins and 8879 filatures. Most silk is woven on handlooms, of which there are a total of 182 000, accounting for 65 per cent of the country's total production. Only 30 per cent comes from the 31 000 powerlooms.

The yarn produced on different reeling machines differs in quality and therefore use; it is made into lighter or heavier, high-twisted or low-twisted

Table 2.   Employment generated for one hectare of established mulberry garden (third year onwards)

Labour activities	Irrigated mulberry			Rainfed mulberry		
	Total no. of working days required	Employment for women		Total no. of working days required	Employment for women	
		No. of days	% share		No. of days	% share
1. Mulberry garden						
Intercultivation	100	30	30	30	9	30
Weeding	100	100	100	50	50	10
Irrigation	75	15	20	–	–	–
Application of farmyard manure	20	14	70	12	8	7
Application of chemical fertilizers	30	27	90	10	9	9
Leaf harvest	600	540	90	300	270	9
Pruning	30	15	90	20	10	5
2. Silkworm rearing						
Chawki rearing	240	144	60	120	72	6
Adult rearing	480	288	60	240	144	6
Spinning and harvesting	120	72	60	60	36	6
Cleaning, disinfection and preparation for rearing	60	36	60	30	18	6
3. Post-cocoon processing						
Silk reeling	420	336	80	158	126	8
Twisting	564	338	60	212	127	6
Weaving	1 320	528	40	495	198	4
Printing, dyeing, etc.	42	17	40	16	7	4
4. Manufacture of rearing appliances	430	260	60	162	97	6
Grand total	4 631	2 760	60	1 915	1 181	62

209

fabrics. There is a specific market for each type of silk yarn, since the varieties of fabrics produced are innumerable. Depending on the type of fabric, the yarn may be subjected to pre-weaving processing, such as twisting, to provide strength and give its characteristic look. While there are certain regulations for the marketing of cocoons and raw silk, the sales of second silk and fabrics are left to the open market.

Women in sericulture

As illustrated in Table 2, nearly 300 work days per annum are generated from each hectare of mulberry, of which more than 60 per cent is contributed by women.

Most turners are either women or children, working as wage earners or assisting in a family unit. Silk reeling is also considered to be a woman's domain, requiring patience, perseverance, dexterity and considerable skill. Almost all reelers on the cottage basin are women, with only the next process of re-reeling being done by men. Nearly 75 per cent of *charaka* reelers are women. In India education is free up to matriculation, although, due to economic constraints, girls are generally made to work and only boys sent to school. However, education is not given much emphasis for any children in reeler's families, and mostly school drop-outs take up the activity. Men are unlikely to become involved in reeling if alternative employment opportunities are available.

Like any other activity in the unorganized sector, reeling faces certain conditions which are applicable to both men and women. General working conditions in reeling units differ in different areas. In most cases factory regulations do not apply; thus reelers are deprived of many benefits to which they would be entitled in other industries. A wage earner is always paid on the basis of piecework, and wages are collected every day or on a weekly basis. Wages are equal for both men and women, and unit owners also provide advances for consumption purposes which are based on trust rather than gender. The equal pay system has come into effect without the intervention of either union or association. The main reason for this is that reelers have considerable bargaining power, since the activity requires a high degree of skill which is always in short supply.

Factors affecting silk reeling in Karnataka

Development of the reeling industry

Karnataka is situated in the southern part of India. Sericulture was introduced to certain areas in the state a few centuries ago by the princely rulers of the erstwhile Mysore State. Its present organized status, however, is a legacy of the British, who took over the state and the industry in the early nineteenth century after the fall of Tippu Sultan. Because the climatic conditions were conducive for sericulture, mulberry cultivation and silk-worm rearing spread throughout the southern districts of the region, forming what is popularly known as the traditional sericulture belt, comprising Bangalore, Mysore and Tumkur Districts. More than 50 per cent of villages in the state have now adopted sericulture, producing as much as 4790 tonnes of silk annually, and Karnataka contributes nearly 60 per cent of India's total silk production.

Silk reeling, however, has traditionally been carried out. in only a few centres in the sericulture belt. Reeling centres consist of a few towns situated around a strategic point in which sericulture is concentrated, the prime factor determining an area's suitability being the availability of 'soft' water, as 'hard' water does not yield good-quality silk. In the case of Karnataka historical factors were also involved, as people in certain areas were trained and encouraged by the local princes and British rulers. Kolar Chikkagallapur, Vijayapura and Sidlaghatta in Kolar District, Rama-nagar, Kanakapura in Bangalore District, and Kollegal Yelandur and Chamarajanagar in Mysore District emerged as major reeling centres in the state. It then became a hereditary activity, skills being transferred among family members without much scope to spread to other areas.

Government involvement in the reeling industry continued in 1945 with an attempt at mechanization through the introduction of the cottage basin. Most reeling in Karnataka is now carried out on country *charakas*, cottage basins and filature basins. In recent times, using Karnataka as a model, the government is assisting the spread of reeling to other non-traditional areas/ states under a World Bank-assisted sericulture programme, by means of various training programmes and the introduction of new technologies in the field.

Cocoon and silk marketing
The growth of the sericulture industry in Karnataka was also facilitated to a large extent by infrastructural facilities developed by the government, such as a separate Directorate which was established even before Independence, a silkworm seed supply system and marketing facilities for both cocoons and silk.

Cocoons are now sold in an open auction, with correct weighing and cash sales being enforced. The Department of Sericulture also gets a large revenue, collected as commission from the reelers and rearers at 2 per cent of each transacted amount. The government's intervention as a purchaser has created more-competitive prices, and the regulated market concept is so attractive that hardly any rearer wishes to sell his cocoons outside it. The fact that the reeling capacity which consumes cocoons is higher than their production has created a regular demand, but means that there is always some shortage in supply for reelers. However, cocoons are available every day throughout the year, enabling the reelers to plan their purchases, and most use the market daily.

In 1979 the government established a silk exchange, modelled on a similar pattern to the cocoon market. There are now many branches of the exchange in major silk producing centres like Ramanagaram, Sidlaghatta, Kollegal and Chickballapur. Market procedures are similar to those followed in cocoon marketing, the product is sold in open auction with twisters, weavers and traders participating as purchasers. The government collects a 1-per-cent fee from the purchaser, but not from the reeler as he has already paid the fee once in the cocoon market.

In spite of the regulations, the marketing system for silk yarn has yet to stabilize in Karnataka, and many reelers still depend on private traders, known as *Kot Walas*. To a large extent these traders control quality of silk produced in the state by offering better prices for high-quality yarn. The silk price is therefore highly unstable, also fluctuating with the season (which affects cocoon production), the influx of imported silk and international silk prices. The main factor, however, in all transactions and price fixing is the quality of the product. This cannot be judged simply by feel and appearance, as weavers' requirements are highly specific to the type of fabric they produce. Despite many silk-testing centres established in the silk exchanges, quality assessment usually depends on the silk's performance in twisting and weaving units. Hence most transactions take place on the basis of the trust and credibility a reeler enjoys with traders. This necessitates long-term acquaintance with the traders/weavers and places constraints on new reelers, both in traditional and non-traditional sericulture areas.

Cocoon/yarn quality and uses
Within a given category, silk quality varies with the type of cocoons used for reeling, water quality, and the skill of the reeler. The raw material produced in Karnataka has yet to reach the quality which can be fed to semi-automatic and automatic reeling machines. Even at a stage when large.quantities of superior-grade cocoons are available, a considerable quantity of inferior cocoons is inevitable, and these have to be reeled on *charakas*. Presently only about 30 per cent of cocoons produced in the state are of a quality suitable for reeling in cottage or filature basins, and 50 per cent of the remainder are in the lower grade. This has necessitated the existence of *charakas* in Karnataka, and the same situation exists in new areas in which they are introduced. This means that the vast majority of cocoons produced are fit only for *charaka* reeling.

Silk yarn is produced as per the denier requirement of the weaver and, even after 45 years, there is a distinct demand in Karnataka for both filature and *charaka* silk. *Charaka* reeling is characterized by operating at high temperature and speed. However, because of the absence of sufficient

212

tension in the croissure system adopted, silk reeled in this way tends to be less compact, bulkier and have more irregularities, making it suitable mostly for weft yarn in the weaving process. In comparison, cottage basin silk is more compact, stronger and less bulky, and is usually used as warp yarn. Sometimes very fine *charaka* yarn is also used for the warp, but only on handlooms. On powerlooms, both warp and weft are usually made up of filature silk, although occasionally very fine *charaka* yarn is used as weft.

This indicates that wherever strength and uniformity is required, *charaka* silk is not so well suited, but it renders better filling when used as weft. The weft yarn used in handloom fabrics is always plied, which, to a certain extent, averages out the deformity characteristic of *charaka* reeling. The irregularities are further reduced in weaving thicker fabric, when the two- or three-ply yarn is sometimes used in three or four folds. However, the main criterion for weavers to purchase *charaka* silk as weft is the price factor, rather than the quality, and this affects the marketing of small quantities of yarn. The same is not true with filature yarn or the *charaka* silk used for warp purposes, of which bulk quantities are transacted. Most of the larger reelers with more *charakas* aim to produce superior-quality yarn.

Initially Karnataka silk was highly sought after by the Western world as dress material, and later production and marketing were well organized during the World Wars when large quantities were needed for defence purposes. Now most of the silk produced in the state is converted into fabrics in the major weaving centres of Tamil Nadu and Banaras in Uttar Pradesh and Andhra Pradesh States. However, a considerable quantity of silk is also used within the state by the local handloom and powerloom sectors.

The methodology of the case study

Selection of areas and women
This study was undertaken to try and determine the social, cultural and economic issues associated with silk reeling in Karnataka. For the purpose of the study two traditional reeling locations in Karnataka were selected, representative both of the wide range of reeling areas and different categories of reelers which exist in India. In addition, the systems prevailing in marketing, types of raw material, etc., fairly, if not fully, cover the reeling community in Karnataka itself. The two locations, namely Kollegal in Mysore District and Sidlaghatta in Kolar District, are both traditional silk-producing areas with a reeling history of nearly 200 years. However, the glaring differences in the practices adopted and prevailing situation make them rich samples for study.

Ten people were interviewed in each area. Respondents were selected depending on their involvement in reeling activity: reelers from various categories such as wage-earners working in other's units, owners of

213

independent units, and owners employing other reelers and supervisors of units run by the male members of the family being chosen.

Data collection

Data collection was from both primary and secondary sources. The emphasis, however, was on primary data, elicited by conducting interviews with women respondents belonging to different reeling sections. Innovations on their machines were recorded after general observations had been made.

Information was collected from the respondents by means of conversational interviews, lengthy discussions being held with them to elicit information on various aspects of their work. Although a profile comprising a set of questions relating to their family background, educational level, etc., was found useful as a guide during interviews, most of the answers were elicited by conversing with the respondents on an informal basis. This was facilitated by working as a team of two; while one person made conversation, it was recorded by the other. However, it was realized that villagers would be more candid if they knew that their views were not being recorded; thus it was important to note down only the points and work from memory later. Notes were then cross-checked with respondents during later visits. Since data processing was also done by both interviewers, the incidence of memory lapses was minimal.

It was particularly appropriate that the methodology used for this study should involve both group and individual interviews. In a village situation, it is extremely difficult to isolate women from their surroundings to have discussions. Another factor is that in Indian villages the visit of strangers is met with curiosity; hence the fan-following and group discussions which followed. This was found to be particularly so with the Muslim reelers of Sidlaghatta, where to interview a woman alone—for the first time at least—was impossible. It was also not beneficial, as she was treated as a part of a group and the reponses and reactions of those surrounding her—generally her family members and neighbours (and also onlookers whom the interviewers did not even know!)—as well as her own, were taken into account. Such a group was at times as large as 30–40 people, a minimum of five or six being the most common occurrence. Subsequent interviews had a more direct approach, talking to the woman directly and eliciting only her opinion on various issues.

Findings

Sidlaghatta

Sidlaghatta is situated about 60 kilometres north of Bangalore. The area is near to the border of Andhra Pradesh, which has a considerable influence on the local community in terms of culture and trade. Owing to the reeling activity, around which other trades have developed, it is quite a prosperous town, well linked with major towns and cities such as Bangalore, Kolar and Chintamani, and Salem in Tamil Nadu.

Most of the local population are Muslims and there are very few reelers from other castes or religions. Reeling is the main occupation of the urban community, agriculture and sericulture providing most employment in rural areas. Labour for reeling is mostly from within the town, and few people come in from nearby villages to seek work. This unusual situation is due to the intensive agriculture practised in the *taluk*, which provides employment to almost all the rural population and has indirectly created a dearth of labour within the town for reeling activities. This shortage has resulted in an emphasis on coupling many machines together through a common shaft with a single drive, powered by an electric motor and/or diesel engine.

In Sidlaghatta town there are 733 *charakas*, 278 filature basins and 246 cottage basins. Reeling units in Sidlaghatta are generally cramped, poorly ventilated, and always a part of the family home. This situation can be attributed to the fact that most reelers in the town are from the Muslim community, in which the *purdah* system still prevails; their houses are therefore built with very little open space and small windows. The social practices of Muslim families mean that women are unable to go outside the house, even for the purpose of supervising their own reeling unit. This makes it almost impossible for a woman in Sidlaghatta to become an independent reeler, and there are no women licence holders of either cottage basins or filature basins. At the most they help their families by supervising production and managing units within the four walls of their homes, and although local reelers have organized themselves into a silk reelers' co-operative society, there are no women members.

Sidlaghatta's cocoon market is one of the major markets in Karnataka. Here, between 15 and 20 tonnes of cocoons are transacted daily. However, the impact of the town's silk exchange supporting reelers is at present low. Fewer than 50 per cent of the reelers use the exchange mechanism for selling silk. Most of the bigger reelers in Sidlaghatta also possess trading licences, and have direct links with traders and weavers elsewhere in Karnataka as well as from outside. Many such transactions are not brought to the notice of the government, and are regularized only by their billing in the silk exchange.

Smaller reelers in Sidlaghatta and Ramanagaram face difficulties of having very little capital where high turnover is required. They overcome this by selling small quantities of silk to bigger reelers, who fix the price depending on that prevailing in the Bangalore Silk Exchange. The system is both beneficial and exploitative to the smaller reelers. It is beneficial because small quantities of silk fetch a lower price when sold in the

215

exchange, since traders prefer to purchase lots of at least 20–25kg. Thus although the price offered by the bigger reelers is much lower than the market price, it is higher than they would get at the exchange and also provides them with immediate cash to purchase raw material for the next day. However, since the objective of the smaller reelers is to produce a larger quantity of silk, they pay very little attention to maintaining a high quality, as the bigger reelers pay the same price to all their clients.

Sidlaghatta silk is very popular in all weaving centres, being regarded as the best all over India and thus attracting the highest price in the raw silk market. This is due both to the quality rendered to it by the skill of the reelers, and the properties of the water in which reeling takes place. The water in the area is known for its ability to produce good-quality silk.

Kollegal

Kollegal is about 180 kilometres south of Bangalore and has two centuries of sericulture activity behind it. The town is situated near the Tamil Nadu border and was formerly in the Madras Presidency under British rule. Its reeling centre extends to two *taluks*, Kollegal and Yelandur. The land around the town is mostly under rainfed cultivation; hence agriculture is not practised as intensively as in Sidlaghatta and is highly seasonal. With the local urban labour force mostly engaged in silk weaving, the reeling industry engages labour from the surrounding rural areas, and many of the units are situated in the villages themselves. Here unemployment is high and, except during the peak agriculture season, there is more labour available for reeling, at a relatively low cost.

The emphasis in Kollegal is thus on individual *charakas*, only four or five reelers having adopted coupled *charakas* operated by electric motor. There are a total of 1572 reeling units in the area, consisting of 4568 *charakas* and 2778 cottage and filature basins. (A filature unit which was established in the area in 1910 is still working.) Cottage and filature basins are typical of those found anywhere in the state. Reeling units in Kollegal are mainly owned by Hindu families, especially the upper-caste groups of Lingayat and Vokkaligas, and the work place is generally isolated with good ventilation. Almost the entire labour force are lower-caste Hindus, and there are hardly any Muslim reelers, although a few are Christians. Among educated youths in the area there seems to be a trend to move away from reeling. This is, however, natural, given national government policies in which certain sanctions and reservations in education and jobs are given to scheduled-caste children.

Among reelers in Kollegal, 28 women possess licences for reeling units and a few are also members of the local co-operative society. However, even the women owning an independent enterprise usually still depend on men for the marketing of silk and cocoon purchases. There has been a breakthrough in this respect with two women attending the cocoon market,

216

Spinning the fine filaments from the silkworm cocoons using a traditional charaka

although this is due to compulsion, as their husbands are drunkards, rather than their own choice. Kollegal's market is the second largest in the state, with an average daily transaction of about 25 tonnes of cocoons.

In contrast to Sidlaghatta, 80 per cent of Kollegal reelers sell their yarn through the silk exchange. The Karnataka Silk Marketing Board (KSMB), situated in Kollegal, is a trading body which has also been established by the government to support reelers in marketing and act as a buffer by purchasing and releasing stocks to keep price fluctuations at a minimum. The Board is of particular assistance to smaller reelers as it purchases even the smallest quantities of silk produced. This has helped many reelers in the area who have limited working capital to continue their activity, despite the fluctuations in the status of the industry.

More than 50 per cent of cocoons produced in Kollegal are of an inferior grade. This is due both to the variety of the cocoons themselves and the rainfed mulberry cultivation. Although of a medium and coarser variety, the typical bright yellow silk from Kollegal is highly sought after for weft purposes by the weavers of Dharmavaram and Kambakonam in Andhra Pradesh, even those whose preference is for Sidlaghatta silk regard it as second best. Weavers in the neighbouring state of Tamil Nadu and the

217

districts of Coimbatore and Satyamangalam are also major customers for Kollegal silk.

Innovations in *charaka* reeling

Innovations to reeling equipment

Many innovations in the basic design of equipment used were found in the reeling areas in the study. Almost all changes to the design were aimed at improving the drive system of the machine, while other changes included the brakes, frame and components, as described below.

One drive is the cycle chain system. It is a simpler drive system which is slightly more efficient than the handle on a traditional *charaka* and has been developed using a cycle chain. In this method the crank wheel is welded to a metal plate or fixed on to an L-angle, and screwed to the wooden posts. The free wheel is then attached to the main shaft of the reel, and connected to the crank wheel with a cycle chain. This is a very common type of drive found all over the state, wherever a single *charaka* is operated as a unit. The ball bearings present in the system make operating these machines much easier.

The second drive is a drum-and-friction wheel system. Reelers in Kollegal have found that, when turned, the cycle crank tends to move in jerks, which is not good for uniform reeling. Hence they prefer the drum-and-friction wheel system. Here a long metal shaft is inserted into the wooden posts running along the main frame of the *charaka*. A heavier drum wheel is fixed on to the shaft at one end, towards the inner side. At the corresponding end, the reel shaft has a small friction wheel which is made to sit on the drum wheel. Since the size of the friction wheel is about one-third of the circumference of drum wheel, every turn of the handle steps up the turning speed of the reel by a factor of three.

Coupling of charakas

The improvements by reelers have culminated in units in which several *charakas* are coupled together with a common shaft. These invariably have metal frames with a long common shaft connecting all the *charakas*. Each has its own drum wheel at one end, and individual reels are mounted with friction wheels. Generally four machines are coupled in this way, although occasionally units of only two *charakas* are found. At larger operating units as many as 10–12 machines are connected together by a common shaft.

A few reelers have been successful in attaching a motor to the shaft to enable coupled *charakas* to operate using power, although power cuts are a common feature in rural areas. To overcome this constraint, the unit usually has an alternative energy source in the form of a kerosene or diesel engine, and provision is also made to turn the *charakas* by hand during occasional emergencies when neither power nor an engine can be used.

Brakes

Individual units are stopped by the reeler ceasing to turn the handle. However, an essential feature of coupled units are brakes for stopping individual reels whenever required by reelers, without affecting the other reels. The brakes are simple devices incorporated into the main structure of the machine. All the brake systems found in the study were copied from one device or another.

The simple brake system, used in almost all areas, is a long rod running perpendicular to the main shaft. One end is near the drive system, attached loosely to the machine by a small shaft protruding from the main frame. The brake rod extends towards the reelers to a length convenient for them to handle. The end nearer to the drive has a small metal piece in the shape of a flag welded to the rod. When the reeler intends to stop the machine, she turns the rod (which has a small handle attached to it) to the right, at which point the metal piece lifts the friction wheel, thus breaking its contact with the drum wheel and bringing the reel to a slow halt.

There have been several innovations to this basic system. The rod as described above has in many cases a small cup-shaped metal piece attached to it instead of a flat piece. In this case, the rod is lifted and lowered within an 'L'-shaped support. When the handle is lowered, due to the action of a lever, the cup rises and holds the main shaft tightly, creating resistance in turning. In some machines a separate pulley is provided alongside the friction wheel, which is held tight when the brake is applied, thus stopping the machine.

Frames

The traditional *charaka* frame, which is nothing but four sturdy wooden posts fixed in the ground at a particular distance, is still being used by most *charaka* reelers in Karnataka, as it is relatively cheap, although not very durable. In the past most reelers have preferred to replace the frame often, rather than invest more as an initial cost. However, during recent times there have been several improvements to the traditional *charaka* frame.

Many reelers use 'L'-angle pieces of different sizes, which are welded into the frame to house various components of the *charaka*. For example, the traverse system is fixed on to an extended L-shaped metal piece from the main frame. Wherever *charakas* are coupled together, the reelers invariably use metal frames rather than wooden posts, as any variation in individual frames creates difficulties in the alignment of the *charakas* on a single shaft. Metal frames are usually die-cast, which is much cheaper when they are being manufactured in large quantities, and are a copy of those used for cottage basins.

Reels

Different types of reels are now used, specific to certain areas. In Sidlaghatta, most of the reelers operating single *charaka* units continue to use the traditional wooden reel. However, when many machines are connected with a common shaft, different types of reels are used. In order to fit the reel on to the main metal shaft of the improved device, the arms of the reel are made of metal on which wooden battens are fixed. On these reels, the wooden battens are thinner and appear weaker than on the traditional reel, but are actually reinforced by a metal supportive strip running beneath them.

Reels are usually quadrangular in shape, although in some places, for example Ramanagaram and Kollegal, the frames are hexagonal. Here, instead of four wooden battens, the reels have six, which are again supported by the metal reel frame and metal strips running along their length. Only reelers in Kollegal, and a few in Chickballapur, use all metal reels, and these are always hexagonal. Here the wooden battens are replaced by metal tubes, strong enough to withstand the pressure of reeled silk.

Traverse system

Innovations to the basic traverse system are usually made by having different types of eccentric wheel. In some areas, such as Ramanagaram and Channapatna, it is in the form of a flat pulley with a small groove running along the middle of its perimeter, which holds the belt in position. In Sidlaghatta and Kollegal it consists of a cylindrical cage sitting loosely on a steel rod fitted to a wooden post on the main frame, around which the belt is wound. In Kollegal, some of the reelers use a crude wooden cylindrical cage instead of a metal one, probably to reduce cost. (Again, reelers prefer to replace the equipment regularly rather than investing more initially.)

Ovens and basins

Traditionally the oven consisted of three stones used as a support for the basin, which also formed a fireplace. The main fuel was firewood which, although previously abundant, is fast dwindling. Without exception all the reelers in the state are now using improved ovens with fire gratings, ash pits and chimneys. This facilitates the use of alternative fuels such as paddy, peanut and coffee husk and wood chips which are available locally at much cheaper prices. Thus improved ovens significantly reduce operating costs and also improve working conditions, increasing the overall efficiency of the reeler. Characteristically, even in units where many machines are coupled together, the oven and chimneys are independent for each machine.

Many reelers in Sidlaghatta prefer to use a copper basin, even though it can be 10 to 15 times more expensive than the usual aluminium one. However, the reelers save fuel, and once the water is heated it stays warm longer in a copper vessel.

Innovations in reeling practices

Quality control
In terms of the quality of silk reeled, the *charaka* device itself has very little to offer in terms of quality control, although various other factors can be relevant.

The chemical nature of the water is crucial in determining the quality of yarn produced, its lustre and strength. As mentioned earlier, silk reeled in hard water appears dull and lustreless. Reelers have also found that certain seeds available locally give the desired quality in water and, in some areas, they use colouring agents temporarily to render the silk the bright yellow colour which increases its marketability.

Since *charaka* silk is reeled at high speed, co-ordination between the turner and reeler is essential. The speed is also regulated depending on the quality of cocoons reeled, with the machine being operated at a higher speed for those of better quality and slowed down for inferior cocoons. Pre-reeling processes such as stifling and drying are also done differently for different quality cocoons.

Drying the silk
Since the silk is directly reeled on to standard reels in the form of hanks, it is essential to see that it is dried immediately after it is wound on to the reel. This is ensured by various methods, as follows:

o The reel itself is situated at a slightly higher level, as found in Sidla-ghatta and Ramanagaram and other reeling centres. This allows a longer passage of thread, affecting drying to some extent before it is wound on to the reel.
o The reel is usually covered with a thick cloth which absorbs water from the wet silk. It also reduces hardening of silk due to the gum spots.
o In the cooler hours of the day and during the monsoon season, charcoal embers are placed beneath the reel, hastening the drying process.

Temperature control
Reeling on the *charaka* must always be done at a high temperature. Although it is difficult for reelers to manipulate cocoons while cooking and reeling in hot water at a temperature of almost 90–95°C, they are so skilled that all the manipulations inside the reeling basin are carried out with the help of a bamboo stick. Even while casting cocoons the reeler

usually handles only the reeling ends, rather than the whole cocoon which is floating in the hot water. At times when the reeler has to get the reeling ends of the cocoon from the jute (silk waste removed while cooking), she sprinkles water on to the jute to make it cool enough to handle easily.

The temperature of the reeling basin is judged by feel and maintained by adjusting the fuel supply into the oven. When the water temperature goes beyond 90°C, the reeler cools it by adding cold water which is always kept in reserve by her side.

Working conditions

Since cocoons are reeled directly from the basin at speed, water tends to splash in the opposite direction towards the reeler. To avoid this, she usually uses a barrier in the form of a wooden plank, a tin sheet or even a gunny cloth tied across the *tharapatti*.

The *charaka* oven is constructed in such a way that it leaves only enough space for a person to sit. The reeler must be very near the basin. However, since the sitting place is virtually on top of the fireplace, she spreads a gunny cloth on the area on which to squat. Although the sitting posture adopted does not allow her to rest the lower half of her body comfortably, she is used to this and does not find it difficult. Any change in the sitting posture would be unwelcome.

In Sidlaghatta, the reels are situated in a slightly elevated position, and so the turners stand while they work. This position is more comfortable for them, because while turning they do not always hold the handle. Instead they usually push it. When it makes a turn and comes back, they push it again. In Kollegal the handles are located at a lower level, allowing a turner to sit and turn. However, although the cycle crank-wheel handle is often encased by a wooden covering, which forms a grip and turns loosely around the main handle, the turners' hands in such units are rough with callouses in the palm. Sometimes in Kollegal a turner operates the handle with her foot in the same way a Sidlaghatta turner does with her hands.

After the process of reeling is completed, the reel is too heavy to be completely removed from the supporting posts. Instead the reel arms are loosened, and the hanks are slowly pushed to one end of the reel. Then, lifting the end of the reel from the wooden post, the hanks are gradually removed. In metal-framed reels one arm is made to collapse by loosening the butterfly nut which holds the reel arms in position.

Factors in technology change

Origin and transfer of the innovations

Many of the practices and much of the equipment just described seem to be traditional. However, some could also be classed as innovative, and it is

222

often difficult to assess which of the methods and machinery used by reelers are traditional and which are more recent. The modified designs have become so popular and widespread in the traditional silk-reeling area that it is now almost impossible to find an original country *charaka* anywhere in the state. However, different designs are found in the same area and the same design is also found in different regions, indicating that the innovations are probably of multiple origin.

It is difficult specifically to identify the place and time of origin of the various innovative designs of *charaka*. Discussions with reelers indicate that all improvement to *charakas* have probably taken place during the last 20 to 25 years. It is likely that during the 1940s, with the introduction of the cottage basin which is a better designed and improved reeling device compared to country *charaka*, new ideas for improving *charakas* themselves must have arisen. Evidence for this is the fact that most of the improvements and spares now used in *charakas* are identical to systems found in cottage basins.

An officer of the Department of Sericulture stated that a motor was attached to a *charaka* for the first time in Coimbatore in Tamil Nadu. Given the basic requirements of a *charaka*, an old man owning a fabricating unit there produced a design in which a motor was attached to the drive. (There are many general engineering units in Coimbatore which are renowned for developing innovative designs of various types of appliances and machines. They also make reeling devices, even though silk reeling is not well developed in the area.)

Many innovations have been adopted by reelers themselves as a response to their changing needs. Some are imposed by the master reeler or unit owner, although it is usually a two-way process, with reelers responding to the changes and demonstrating a planning process from below.

An example of how new designs may be transferred between regions is when a woman marries into another reeling family from a different area, taking with her the technology she uses. This method is found to be more prevalent among the members of the Muslim community, probably because of the woman's closer association with the husband's family. Reelers have also passed on information about innovations and copied designs while visiting relatives and friends locally or in other areas, and it is common to find designs copied from a neighbour's units which might originally have come from another area.

Improved designs of manual silk-reeling devices have been developed by the Central Silk Board, a government organization, and, in order to popularize the new technology, several schemes were set up to supply machines free of cost, subsidize loans and investments, and provide credit at low interest. However, in spite of these facilities the designs have not gained popularity, even in non-traditional areas where reeling is a new experience. This is mainly because of the introduction of the tavellette type of *croissure* in the new device, which produces a higher quality yarn, but one which no longer bears any similarity to traditional *charaka* silk. The new product is between filature and *charaka* grade, in other words, it is not suitable for either warp or weft, and as weavers' requirements on this are very specific, there is no ready market for the yarn. Owing to the resulting lack of enthusiasm among reelers for the 'improved' designs, the government programme for implementing them has stalled for the present.

Reasons for innovations and their effects

A few of the innovations described have been aimed directly at benefiting workers in the industry. Almost all changes in the design of the machine, such as the introduction of ball-bearings and improved drive systems, seem to have been directed towards easing the turning process. As the changes appear to have been developed to answer the needs of the turners, there has been a significant reduction in the drudgery and strain involved in the activity. In addition, the speed stepping-up systems incorporated in the drives have facilitated faster turning, increasing the efficiency of workers significantly. Thus productivity has also increased considerably, which has benefited the owners of the units.

Turning at a more uniform speed results not only in improved production, but also in higher-quality silk yarn. Improvements in quality are also seen as a result of the coupling of machines, indicated by the better price offered for silk produced on them. However, despite the many changes to the machine, there is practically no change in the basic principle of *charaka* reeling, and the fundamental characteristics of the silk produced remain constant. These are retained as a response to the requirements of the weaving sector.

Factors such as technical performance and productivity, which are priorities for unit owners, are the most frequent stimuli for design changes. An example of this situation is provided by the innovations to reeling equipment, which have led to an improvement in production of about 30 per cent. Although design changes such as brakes, traverse systems and types of reel have little or no direct impact on productivity, the net result of all innovations to traditional *charakas* has been higher production, through the increased efficiency of machines, and savings on fuel.

Such changes have contributed little to reelers' working conditions. Benefits to workers, if they have occurred at all, have been only secondary. Since the system is production based, the improved performance has brought about an increase in wages, although whether this corresponds to inflationary trends in the economy is debatable. However, women have seen it as an addition to their income which is also coupled with their promotion from turners to reelers. It is difficult to assess how much the innovations will contribute to health risks, although reelers claim that *charaka* reeling affects their health in the long term; thus any improvements in conditions will be beneficial. The only innovation with a directly positive effect on the working environment of the majority of reelers is the improved oven.

Some of the innovations have arisen as a response to external factors, for example the changing structure of labour market, which they in turn affect. Given the limitations in manual silk reeling, labour constraints in certain areas, such as Sidlaghatta, have led to mechanization. The labour shortage has arisen in this area for two main reasons. Given the impetus of an increase in wage, most of the turners have become reelers. In addition, the strong demand for Sidlaghatta silk has necessitated the participation of larger numbers of reelers. Since the labour force from rural areas is rarely available to undertake reeling, and reelers are indispensable in *charaka* units, the master reelers have found ways by which the turners are replaced. The innovations adopted in Sidlaghatta have also helped in gearing up the occupational mobility of a turner, who now operates as a reeler. In other reeling areas a turner would gradually be mobilized to take up the job of a reeler, but here the transfer from one to the other takes place within just six months.

In spite of such efforts, there remains a dearth of skilled workers in many reeling areas and experienced women reelers can become very powerful, with a strong bargaining position. In some cases they have forced unit owners to improve their working conditions, for example by providing a more spacious area to work in, and provide other benefits, such as an increase in wages and bigger advances.

Motorizing has reversed the basic feature of the *charaka*, which is traditionally manually operated, and has reduced labour and operational costs by as much as 50 per cent compared to the non-motorized machine. However, although there is potential for them to be absorbed as reelers, the displacement of turners in such units has in some areas considerably reduced the employment potential of the activity, and also disrupted traditional links in the transfer of skills.

Transfer of skills
Reeling has traditionally been a hereditary occupation, with skills being passed on between family members, either from the mother's or father's side. In addition, skills are sometimes learnt from friends or neighbours owning units. The mobility of workers in *charaka* reeling starts with very young girls becoming helpers, then turners and eventually women reelers. It is general practice for a turner to observe reeling activity before she becomes a reeler.

A person with no reeling experience usually enters the industry by working as labourer in another unit. It takes nearly two years to become a reeler this way, again through occupational mobility from helper to turner to reeler. However, in some units skill transfer cannot be through this

225

traditional chain, because the owners are hesitant to train new people in reeling for fear of loosing heavily in the form of waste. They thus depend on older reelers or those trained in other units. This is an additional factor contributing to the dearth of skilled workers in areas such as Sidlaghatta and Ramanagaram.

There was evidence that skills are transferred differently and are caste-based in the two areas under study. In Kollegal, the skill is passed on from mother to daughter, with the husband and father not necessarily knowing how to reel (in most cases he is an agriculturist). Usually only the male children are sent to school, and if they drop out they take up their father's occupation rather than their mother's. Daughters pick up the skill from their mothers, as they accompany them to the reeling unit from a very young age. Once the daughter is 10 or 12 years old, she finds employment as a turner and then goes on to become a reeler herself.

However, if reeling is pursued by Muslims, for example in Sidlaghatta, it is almost always passed on between all members of the family. Although some employees are from other castes, a Muslim owner tends to employ reelers from his own religion. These factors have contributed to the high concentration of reeling activity in certain semi-urban towns in the traditional sericulture area.

Access to information

The study found that women are as knowledgeable about the technologies as their male counterparts, if not more so. A woman's access to the communication system is, however, limited, particularly information about technological changes, owing to the fact that she does not frequent the cocoon market or the silk exchange. These are the main centres of communication for reelers, as many assemble there from different places to purchase cocoons or simply visit to get information on silk prices. Women feel unable to attend for various reasons, for example:

○ Their husband/father/brother, if sharing the workload, takes over this job.
○ Men are better educated and better able to assess cocoons and look after money. Women feel they can be cheated more easily.
○ In the villages, cultural constraints stop them from frequenting the cocoon market and silk exchange.
○ A woman does not want to risk her family suffering a large financial failure. Women's failures are not so easily pardoned as men's.

Each reeler respondent said that she would visit the market only if the others went.

Women's access to information and communication channels is also based to a large extent on the caste and religious group to which they belong. It is much more difficult for Muslim women to interact with others than it is for Hindu women. In spite of restrictions, most women in both religious groups obtain information on issues related to reeling through discussions with male members of the family. For example, those in the study knew about the price at which cocoons were purchased and silk sold, places of transaction and quality parameters, and were also aware of the quality of the silk produced in their units.

Women's achievements

In both organizational and technical terms, the reeling process is critically dependent on the skill and expertise of women reelers, and their contribution to the local and national economy is considerable. Reeling skills are accumulated and passed on by successive generations of women, within and between families. Despite their exclusion from active participation in many areas of the industry, most women reelers, as described, are highly aware of the forward and backward links. Although the degree of their awareness varies, depending on their economic situation, caste and religion, many are as knowledgeable about the technologies as their male counterparts.

Women wage-earners in the study perceived that they could contribute to their family and local economy and work effectively as independent reelers, while those who were already operating independently thought in terms of expanding their units. They realized the constraints they were faced with: particularly the dearth of any working capital.

The study found evidence of many innovative changes to equipment and practices in manual silk-reeling devices in the two areas under consideration. However, it is difficult to pin-point the time at which particular innovations were made and the people who first devised them. Silk reeling like most other sericulture activity, has always involved whole families, and it is thus impossible to assess in isolation women's contribution to the innovations.

It is interesting to note that all the successful innovations in reeling have been developed in the informal sector, by individual, independent reelers. Those introduced by the formal sector—namely by government—failed in the field. The main reason for this seems to have been because formal institutions did not take into account the context in which reelers operated, as indicated by their concentration on improving the quality of yarn produced. This was irrelevant to reelers, who were more interested in making the operating process easier—the focus of most of their own innovations.

Limits to women's role in reeling

A major constraint to a wider role for women *charaka* reelers is their lack of visibility. Although they constitute more than 75 per cent of the

227

workforce in the *charaka* reeling sector, in the past women have been neglected in most developmental schemes. In addition, while they are responsible for all the operational aspects of reeling; purchases of raw material and the sale of silk—which form the important forward and backward links in the industry—are handled by men. Reelers' visibility is also obscured by the fact that none of their innovations has been given any official recognition, nor any attempt made by their co-operatives to lobby for publicity through a government department.

Religious and cultural restrictions on women are wide-ranging, and make up the most significant limits to their activities. As previously mentioned, the restrictions cover areas of their life such as education and where they can go, which affect their access to information and communication channels and their level of awareness. The worst effect of these constraints on women reelers is that they prevent them from attending the cocoon market. However, although various reasons for this were put forward by the women in the study, if such barriers can be removed they may be in a position to attend. This is evident in new areas, where the activity does not have any traditional significance and women reelers do not hesitate to visit the market.

In many cases women seem to accept the restrictions without question or resentment. They view themselves always as members of their families and mothers of their children, and women's priorities are to assist them in fulfilling their basic needs. Women find it easier to manage both household work and their occupation if they are part of an extended family system, in which work is shared between members. Such families provide vital support mechanisms, and important channels for communication and the transfer of skills. However, although at the individual household level a woman may share equal responsibilities for reeling activity, a family can also be very restrictive in that her role within it, and its expectations of her, are closely defined. The situation can be worse for a woman in a nuclear family, in which she has to manage all the work on her own. This is achieved by putting in more working hours, leaving her no time for leisure and entertainment and further restricting communication with other women reelers. Given a choice, many women prefer not to work, but look after their families, indicated by the fact that when a certain income level is reached they stop working.

Even women with entrepeneurial qualities face certain limitations, and many younger and more educated Muslim women wish to escape the *purdah* system. Those who are exposed to the mass media and associate with other caste groups having more freedom find it especially difficult to bear the religious barriers put upon them. Some of the scheduled caste (SC) have gone as far as converting to Christianity to achieve higher social status and get benefits from the church. First-generation converts are found to be more flexible in getting married to other SC or allowing their children

228

to marry either Christians or among SCs. However, since the benefits and sanctions provided by the government to SC have increased over a period of years, reconversion to SCs has been more frequent. Another factor in this has perhaps been the discrimination against converted SCs by members of their caste.

Control of technology

Factors such as women's access to information and ease of communication also affect their ability to respond to changes in their working environment. As there are no women master reelers, one does not discover their reaction to changing trends, and independent reelers tend to imitate the larger operators. The wage-earner, the woman in this instance, is fully aware of the fact that a change in technology—for example, introduction of motor-reeling machine—is helpful only to the owners of the establishment, but there is little she can do to influence the decision. Since women's aware-ness in the capacity of wage-earner/independent reeler is as good as, if not better than that of their male counterparts, their inability to contribute to bringing about changes in technology could be viewed from a class, as well as a gender, perspective.

There are no formal organizations such as co-operatives, banks or training institutions dealing directly with reeling activity, or women's associations working for the interests of women reelers. Even if such organizations did exist, they would be unlikely to possess the capacity for lobbying policy makers. In terms of decision-making in local commu-nity matters, the power relationships between women and men are also very unequal. This is despite the changing political structure which gives reasonable prominence to women at the local level. In the local governing body, namely the *Panchayat*, the Karnataka government has reserved a minimum of 25 per cent of seats for women. However, as this system is relatively recent, only a slow change for the better can be expected.

Large amounts of working capital and initial investment are required to support a reeling unit. Many sanctions and priorities are given to women in the present credit system, and, realizing the lack of funding opportunities for women, the government is targeting credits for them through World Bank-aided programmes. In general, however, the relevant information has not reached them. Although scheduled-caste women are more aware of such schemes and what is available, this does not necessarily bring about any positive benefit as they are often hindered from participating by the manipulation of middlemen, and funding agencies dealing with co-opera-tives have not tried to target women reelers because they are not members of any of the reelers' co-operative societies.

Women who are enthusiastic about improving their standard of living are those who are aware of the economic factors involved in reeling and ready to take risks to obtain credit to expand their business. Risks in reeling are thought to be minimal, provided women have a thorough understanding of the technology, as the raw material is available locally and there is a ready market for the product. A disadvantage for a man or woman working in the silk industry, is, however, the fluctuation in prices and the instability of the silk market. A particular factor hindering women from taking up reeling on their own is that any loss of money in business is not treated kindly, while a man's failure is accepted in a casual manner. A women's ability to take risks is directly related to the caste and class to which she belongs. Destitute women have the highest degree of risk as, owing to their total lack of participation in the market, they are almost totally dependent on male relatives or neighbours to transact business outside on their behalf.

Recommendations

It should not be forgotten that reeling is almost always a family enterprise, and any attempt to isolate women from their family framework will not achieve the desired result. Even the government has realized this and, in its attempts to spread reeling skills, usually moves a whole family of reelers from a traditional location to provide a model in a new area. What is important is that the responsibility, work and economy shared among family members should be more flexible, without women experiencing constraints due to the many barriers which exist.

Unless women are encouraged to participate in the purchasing of cocoons and sale of silk, they will never get their due share of recognition. The government should facilitate women's participation in marketing through encouragement, sanctions and reservations.

Women might be more prepared to participate in marketing if they were allowed to work as a group. In extreme situations, an all-women's co-operative might also be able to overcome the hurdles which have prevented women reelers becoming independent. There should be wider official recognition of the innovative technologies of reelers; in particular they should be drawn to the attention of development planners. Doing this would have several subsidiary benefits, for example:

○ Sericulture development programmes modelled on these, more appropriate, technologies, would be more acceptable.
○ As India provides a model for tropical sericulture, recognition of these innovations would have an impact on the sericulture industries of other countries. The technologies and methods developed in India could be appropriate to most developing countries in the tropics and sub-tropics, which are currently introducing sericulture.

Carpet making in Nepal

PRABHAR THACKER

This study is the result of a project studying Women and Technological Innovation. The fact that women particularly possess knowledge that is quite different from or complementary to that of men requires an understanding of indigenous knowledge systems and of the local decision-making framework which is crucial to the planning of technical intervention. Development agencies are beginning to understand that the rural poor possess a more extensive knowledge of local environments and production systems, than is generally accepted by Western scientists. Specialists in technical assistance are usually men who are influenced by their own cultural perceptions, and thus tend to view women as 'non-technical'.

The long-term objectives of the project are, first to encourage and support local and regional capacity to analyse issues related to technology and women, and second, to safeguard or improve the position of women as users of technology and as basic producers.

The short-term objectives of the project were:

○ To document indigenous innovation cases and their importance to off-farm production in the south.
○ To draw lessons from the cases as to how technical assistance can make greater use of local women innovators in the design and development of new technologies.
○ To develop and facilitate links between research and action-oriented organizations into inter-regional collaboration.
○ To develop and maintain a regional base for knowledge and understanding of technical innovation among women.

The initial step towards this was in the form of a workshop in Colombo, Sri Lanka, where five researchers from India, Sri Lanka, Bangladesh, Nepal and Britain discussed the major issues to be addressed and methodological

PRABHAR THACKER is a researcher who works in Manushi, a women's NGO in Nepal which she helped to set up.

231

approaches that would reflect a participatory research mode. The underlying theme in the discussions that emerged was: *Innovation by women cannot be considered in isolation from the issue of empowerment and conscientization, which ultimately affect women's ability to organize themselves and change their lives.*

Nepal's carpet industry

Keeping in mind the need to focus on the software (human) aspect of technology and how it is linked to the rural sector, the carpet industry is ideal to study. The industry thrives on a strong rural-based network where female labour contributes significantly to the value-added component of the end product in the form of exotic 'Tibetan' carpets for export. A highly labour-intensive activity where technological input has been deliberately accorded less emphasis by the government, as a protective measure to ensure employment-generation opportunities (particularly in the rural areas), the carpet sector, which was initially a rural-based household activity, has recently blossomed into a leading export sector of the country.

Information and documentation about the carpet industry is both insufficient and inadequate. Most reports take the form of feasibility studies and reports preoccupied with technical improvements and market strategies. While most reports do fleetingly mention a high incidence of female labour in the manufacturing sector, there is no information on the socio-economic conditions of these workers, or on the implications of technology on their work, despite the fact that Tibetan carpets top the list as maximum earner of foreign exchange, after tourism. The objectives of the case study on women in the carpet industry in Nepal are therefore:

○ To identify specific areas of work where the concentration of women is found to be high.
○ To examine a specific activity wherein technology has been introduced.
○ To record women's own perceptions of interventionist forces and their responses (as primary users of technology).
○ To highlight policy implications affecting technology and make recommendations for women's access to technology.
○ To develop and maintain a regional base for knowledge and understanding of technical innovation among women.

The carpet industry in Nepal as an example of off-farm employment in the countryside needs to be explained in the light of four broad factors: its origins; socio-economic factors including migration and environmental issues; implications for women and technology; and policy implications.

232

'Tibetan' carpets arrive

Following the occupation of Tibet by China in 1959, and the mass exodus of Tibetan refugees into Nepal and northern India, Tibetan rugs and carpets, almost unknown to the outside world, became popular either as luxury items in the form of exotic hanging pieces, as utility items for winter or as rare collection pieces. A few pieces which may have reached museum collections in the West through Western travellers, remained unknown. Barter trade between Nepalese and Tibetan merchants prior to 1959 may have brought these carpets into some Nepali households, though most of these unique pieces went unnoticed, for they were rarely displayed.

The study concerns itself with hand-knotted carpets with a wool pile. These carpets are commonly known as 'Tibetan' carpets in which the hand-knotted feature gives them a uniqueness and high reputation in the export market. The knotting or twisting characterizes each single unit. Pile threads are knitted or twisted in a complete turn around by at least one warp thread, and are kept in place by the insertion of tightly woven weft threads.

There has been a noticeable and drastic change since the 1960s in terms of knot density per square metre. The average density of carpets manufactured by the Carpet Trading Company of Jawalakhel (one of the largest manufacturers) in Nepal until the early 1970s, consisted of 70 000 knots per square metre, with a weighted average of 3.80kg per square metre, which denotes a finer pile. The criteria for quality by which carpets are judged are based on quality of the materials used, colour fastness and density of knots. In comparison, carpets being produced now have an average of only 48 000 knots per square metre. There has also been increase in average weight amounting to about 5kg/m^2. This change was dictated by the demand for heavier and beefier carpets from abroad, particularly OCM/UK in order to withstand the rigorous process of chemical washing, which most carpets undergo in the respective countries of export.

While carpets for export are manufactured according to these specifications, those manufactured for local sale in Kathmandu (basically for the local tourist market) still retain some of the older and more traditional aspects, both in terms of product quality and design. Locally sold carpets are thinner in pile and more intricate in design. Some of them depict the traditional dragon and other emblems of significance in Tibetan religion and culture. The density of knots of these carpets range between 60 and 80 knots per square inch. Most commercial designs, on the other hand are simple, sparse in design concentration and lighter in shade and colour.

Knotting density has always been one of the unique characteristics of Tibetan carpets. In recent times, however, simplicity of design has had an adverse effect on workmanship. The level of weaving skills required is much lower than for the traditional pieces in which the iconography is

233

dominated by mythical beasts (usually tigers and dragons), lotus and peony flowers—clear links to the ancient Chinese cultures. The treatment of the motifs and the style of coloration are also quite different.

Carpet weaving today forms part of this larger craft: knitting and producing woollen products as primary necessities to keep warm under harsh and cold weather conditions in the mountains. Population pressure, absence of employment opportunities and environmental degradation, besides other variables that have not been included in this report (such as inaccessibility, remoteness and fragility) have isolated mountain people in a state of continuous poverty.

The history of the carpet industry which has come to occupy a strategic role in Nepal's industry as the second-largest earner of foreign exchange, is thus very closely linked to the history of the Tibetan refugees in Nepal, which began in the early 1960s through the mountain's passes of Dolpa, Mustang, Rasuwa, Humla and other carpets renowned in this area. The continuous efforts of the Swiss personnel in SATA and other expatriates with business connections abroad, helped in building up a ready export market. In 1968 a total of $3380m^2$ of carpets had been exported by the Carpet Trading Company alone at a total value of Rs950 000. Despite intermittent disturbances in the carpet industry, caused mainly by fluctuation in raw material supply, price variations and problems of fuel-wood supply, exports have been gradually increasing, to create further demand for product standardization and quality control.

As carpet making is based mainly on traditionally acquired skills, Tibetan refugees brought with them their natural talents in wool carding, spinning, weaving and other related activities. Though weaving of rugs known as 'radi pakhi' has always existed as a side activity among the indigenous people of the higher mountain regions of Nepal, particularly among those of Tibeto-Burmese stock, the unique feature of Tibetan carpets was an added asset that boosted the scope for product improvement in both quality and design, skill acquisition and product diversification. This created in impetus for the woollen sector and for other related activities, for which a ready pool of human resources already existed at individual household level.

The carpet industry and activities associated with it, despite their combined contribution to Nepal's economy and to employment generation has gone largely unnoticed. It absorbs a large segment of the economically and socially disadvantaged such as the landless.

Production and trade links

The working arrangements in both production and marketing are complex and dependent on interlinking which decide the success or failure of small manufacturers who are mostly dependent upon orders from large factories.

234

Units which have no export potential are at a disadvantage. Direct links with large exporters ensure both steady business and a regular raw material supply. Women entrepreneurs operate in the small-scale categories, given constraints in mobility and lack of access to capital. Largely dependent on a strong informal network of operations, women encounter difficulties in negotiating and bargaining. Women entrepreneurs therefore rely on male members of the household for most transactions.

It may be noted here that there are distinct categories of businesses which form part of the carpet industry and trade and yet function as independent, semi-independent or dependent units.

Main wool importers are Himalayan Wool Company; Wool Trading Company; Nepal Wool Imports; Tibetan Wool Sales Pvt Ltd; and Jugal Wool Trading in the private sector. There is only one wool-importing agency in the government sector, Gharelu Silpa Kala Bikri Bhandar. Most large wool importers are also major exporters of carpets.

While the bulk of manufactured carpets is imported by wholesale importers, for example OOM, carpets are also manufactured for sale in the local market usually to tourists. There has been no assessment made of the demand potential for these locally sold carpets which are mostly purchased as souvenirs. The long-term implications of this mode of supply which is geared heavily to Western tastes and design (quite alien to the aesthetic and spiritual characteristics of Tibetan arts and crafts) cannot be overlooked. As an export-oriented industry based on external demand in terms of quality and design specifications, the gradual loss of artisan-based skills, traditionally acquired and generationally reproduced is quite evident. During the course of our study, there were numerous occasions when this view was expressed by women workers with long experience in this sector, as well as by employees and government officials. It was also put very aptly by Kesang Dolma, a woman entrepreneur who began work in the carpet sector as a refugee weaver and has over the last 15 years, established her own enterprise. According to Kesang 'It has become a rarity to find people skilled in weaving the traditional intricate designs of the original Tibetan carpets. The demand is for modern designs.'

Export and market potential

Basically there are three types of exporters in the carpet business:

○ Formal carpet industries: registered within the department of cottage and village industries. These are involved in manufacturing as well as indirect export of their products.
○ Order-based exporters: these are not involved with manufacture but place orders through manufacturers.

235

○ Buyers/exporters: these are exporters who do not place orders with manufacturers, but purchase locally for export.

In the wake of rising exports and its potential for foreign exchange earnings, the Nepalese Government has indicated keen interest in supporting and expanding the carpet export trade through various marketing strategies that will look into design development, improved production methods and quality control. This will include not only the finished product (carpets) but the raw material aspects such as, quality of raw wool, wool yarn and quality of dyeing. Demand projections indicate further expansion and intensification of this sector for export promotion. With this concern in mind, the government recently undertook a feasibility study of integrated wool yarn processing services in Nepal. This study was undertaken by a private consultancy firm as part of the programme of activities of the Export Service Centre (ESC) and an implementing agency of the government. This in-depth technical report justifies the establishment of an integrated wool yarn processing unit which 'chemico-mechanically scours wool and hand picks it for mechanical dyeing'. Right now, high priority is being placed on technological input for export promotion.

Growth trends and performance

The carpet industry was the first to hit the billion-rupee mark in Nepal's exports to the international market during the fiscal year 1988/9 (see Table 1). Since then growth trends in carpet exports have been increasing rapidly. The major markets for export have largely remained unchanged. These are Germany, Switzerland and the United Kingdom. Though export potential of handmade carpets in the USA is high, and is said to have quadrupled in the last decade (with business transactions amounting to one billion dollars

Table 1. Export of Nepalese carpets in square metres

Fiscal year	Volume of carpets (Rounded to nearest 1000m^2)	% Growth of previous year
1981/2	99 000	–
1982/3	151 000	52.5
1983/4	263 000	74.2
1984/5	227 000	(−13.7)
1985/6	330 000	45.4
1986/7	465 000	40.9
1987/8	802 000	72.5
1988/9	914 000	14.0

Average annual growth: 40 per cent
Trade promoting Centre Overseas Trade Statistics, 1989.
Source: DECORE, 1989.

236

a year), the Nepalese share in the US market is small. Tibetan carpets accounted for a mere 0.7 per cent of the total imports of oriental rugs into the US during the first six months of 1988.

When starting a carpet business, the cost of one loom is about Rs20 000. A person wishing to start a business must have a minimum capital investment of about Rs50 000. If a ready source of wool is ensured, the business will be more attractive.

According to small manufacturers who were interviewed in the study, their main problems are:

○ lack of basic investment capital;
○ inability to get bank loans;
○ large discrepancy in returns from sale of product;
○ irregular supply of raw wool and vulnerability to fluctuations in the export trade market; and
○ lack of access to export market information and trends.

Most of this was substantiated by Kesang Dolma, small-scale entrepreneur, who spoke of her experience trying to get a bank loan, 'I was told to pay them Rs50 000 if I wanted a loan of three lakhs. I was not willing to do this. So I did not get a loan. There are many men and women like me who are uneducated, and have no power or access to people in the bank to help us.' Even under straightforward conditions the requirements of numerous visits, the intricacies of filling out the forms and the opportunity costs incurred due to time spent on commuting, are disincentives strong enough to dissuade the small entrepreneur from using bank lending schemes.

Methodology

The study is based on primary and secondary data generated from the study itself and based on literature reviews and personal communication. Field surveys were conducted in four industries within the Kathmandu valley. Of these, two industries belong to the formal sector and the other two to the informal. In order to obtain a representative sample of both the sectors, one factory in the formal and one workshop in the informal were selected in Kathmandu. The same representative sampling was applied to Patar District. Apart from these, numerous informal discussions were held with both owners and employees during numerous visits made to factories and to rural villages.

The study was limited to Kathmandu valley, Patar and Kathmandu districts mainly because there is the biggest concentration of carpet manufacturing business and trade activities in this area. Also, the absorption capacity of female labour in the formal sector is highest in these areas, as is the use of female household labour in the rural peripheries. The other reasons for using these three districts relate to time and money.

The study covers a sample group of 52 women within the factory-based (formal and informal) system of work. A sample group of 13 women from each of the four factories consisted of three spinners and eight weavers selected by random sampling. Weaving and spinning account for the highest concentration of women workers. In addition, technological changes have affected these areas of the work process more than any other.

The study used structured and unstructured questionnaires, group and individual interviews with owners/managers of factories and workers, informal group discussions with rural home-based spinners, and a one-day discussion with selected women respondents were the main methods used for obtaining information and cross-checking. A total of eight key informants included the following: two expert technicians; two government officials; one carpet expert and a livestock expert specializing in sheep.

The entire study was conducted by the same researchers which allowed for participant observation. The study was based on both qualitative and quantitative data, the former bearing particular significance in relation to the need to analyse women's own perceptions and responses in relation to their work, their worth and their experiences as women workers.

The selection of the weaving and spinning villages in the study is based on information obtained from carpet exporters, merchants and government officials in Kathmandu. The primary consideration in the selection of these regions was that they should be representative of relationships to conditions in the production process. In view of the decentralized nature of activities within the carpet industry in Nepal, this case study is a representative sample which is illustrative rather than statistical. The need to understand the process of technology and women's responses meant establishing connections in the villages (Lobhy in Patar District and Balkot in Kathmandu District).

The first section is based mainly on the questionnaire and presents the general socio-economic conditions of women working in the carpet sector at the factory or workshop level and at the home industry level. Spinning and weaving are the work areas that the study focuses upon. Implications of technology are significant in these areas as well. Socio-economic variables are discussed mainly within these and other activities within the organized and the unorganized forms of work.

Socio-economic profile of women workers

Age group: Women of varying ages are found in this sector. The majority of women were between the ages of 15 and 66 years. There is also, however, quite a large proportion of children between 10 and 15 years old who are active in weaving and spinning. Smaller children have been excluded from the sample due to difficulties arising out of incomplete or inaccurate information. These children aged between five and seven years of age assist their mothers in reeling spun yarn—such assistance from small children is prevalent in both the factory and household situation. Usually women over 55 are found in spinning and ball winding. Weaving requires extra energy, effort and concentration, resulting in the dominance of younger women.

Ethnic groups: Ethnic groups most commonly found consist of women from the Brahmin, Cheteer, Nawar, Tamarg, Rai/Limbu and Dhimel/Majhi communities. One of the four factories in the study puts out spinning for homework in one village. Most Tamarg, Rai and Limbu women are migrants from the hills. While Dhimals and Majhis are new migrants from the plains in southern Nepal.

Migration: Out of a total of 52 respondents, nine are non-migrants. Forty-three are migrants whose place of origin is different from the present residence or district.

A strong kinship network exists in the rural areas which has a strong influence on the rural/urban links. This is reflected in the carpet industry where migration determines the structure, composition and turnover of the workforce. Friends, neighbours, relatives and community are main sources of information for contacts in the city and for work in the carpet industry. This pattern of kinship is prevalent both in spinning and weaving in both organized and unorganized work. Spinning occurs mostly at household level where non-migrants are largely found. Factory/workshop spinners are mostly migrants.

Marital status: 60 per cent of the respondents are married women; 4 per cent are separated (divorced or female-headed households) and 36 per cent are unmarried. Most women in factories are sole income earners and supporters of the household, despite the fact that they are married. Male members are found to be either jobless or do not care for the household (this information came out in the course of our one-day discussion with women workers).

Education: Of the total 52 respondents, 77 per cent are illiterate; 8 per cent are just literate and 15 per cent have studied up to primary level. Illiteracy is most pronounced among homeworkers who are unaware of the wages they earn (per kilo of wool) for spinning, despite the fact that they have been spinning for several years. Most homeworkers regard their spinning- and yarn-related activities (for example ball winding) as a part of their domestic work, and not as formal work. Lack of education and awareness among women workers is a strong contributive factor to the exploitative nature of work in this sector.

239

Work history: Almost 75 per cent of women workers had been involved in other work before their present stint at carpet making. Most of the former work falls in the categories of waged agricultural-related work, knitting, domestic work, ready-made garment making, textile weaving, construction work (roads and houses). Some had worked simultaneously on two jobs.

Thirty-eight per cent of the women respondents have still retained a second job, in addition to their work at carpet making. At household level, spinning is a side activity during spare time from farm and domestic work. During the agricultural slack season, spinning becomes an important form of off-farm employment.

Mode of entry: The main sources of information regarding availability of work are friends and relatives. Recommendations from the same sources to contact persons such as middlemen and agents is also another mode of entry into the job. Advertisements also attract 20 per cent of workers.

Working hours: Variations in working hours range from two hours to 16 hours per day. About 31 per cent of women work 7–10 hours a day; about 25 per cent work 11–13 hours, 21 per cent work 14–15 hours and 11 per cent work 2–5 hours a day. Women working only during free time (with no fixed working hours) amount to 12 per cent. Most of these women are home spinners who do not work regularly, but during what free time there is from household chores, caring for livestock and farm work. During the peak agricultural season and during festivals, women's volume of spinning reduces.

The carpet industry falls under the cottage-industry sector irrespective of the size of employment or scale of investment. The Factory Act, thus, does not apply to this sector. Therefore, there is no fixed working time and hours. About 6 per cent of women work from 4 in the morning. Most women (about 62 per cent) start work from 6 to 7 a.m. and about 60 per cent work from 7 to 11 p.m. at night. About 15 per cent women do not have any fixed working time. Factory workers break from work for a half hour to two hours for lunch, and again half an hour to two hours for tiffins. From general observation it appears that migrants work longer hours and take fewer breaks. This is mainly because most migrants live within a group system where housework is organized on a rotation basis. For example, cooking, cleaning and shopping is taken in turn among the workers.

For most of the home spinners, it is free-time work. And for some households, this work is the only or main source of income in which case they also work regularly and intensively. Among home spinners in most cases more than one family member (mother and children/especially daughters) is involved in spinning. Most home-based workers are dependent on more than one factory or wool dealer, and obtain wool from many places.

240

Since factory-based spinning and weaving is piece-rate work, there is flexibility in working hours and time. Women work according to their convenience and are not constrained in mobility either. Clever juggling of household chores and spinning allows them to engage in other part-time work like domestic service or seasonal work.

Despite flexibility in working hours in time, the continuity and co-ordination of work as a joint activity entails considerable skill. The quality of carpet reflects the quality of its weavers. Depending upon the size of the carpet, weavers have to work simultaneously with partners at the same loom. This requires regularity, concentration and continuity of work. As a joint activity it has less flexibility. Women who have more household responsibilities and small children are unable to do weaving though it brings in more income than spinning. Preference among those women for small-size carpets means less earnings because the export market is oriented to large-sized carpets.

In both spinning and weaving women are under the supervision of middlemen. Their rates of pay, working times and hours are set by the middlemen. One middleman will have between three and nine employees for whom he provides food (two main meals and afternoon snacks). The snack is served at the workplace as a means of saving labour time. These middlemen force them to work long hours. They are often bullied and threatened with dismissal from the job if they want a break.

Wages and income: Variations in income levels are apparent both within the formal sector itself and between the formal and informal factory workplace. In the formal sector the wage rate at one factory is Rs315 per square metre, for Grade A carpets and Rs300 per square metre for Grade B. Grade A refers to greater knot density, evenness of yarn, evenness of borders and design, and the absence of visible cotton threads. Other factors include quality of dye, blending of raw wool, etc. In the unorganized sector, variations are less pronounced, amounting to a flat rate of about Rs25 per m^2, irrespective of intricacies in design which determine the amount of time spent weaving. According to the employers, the weaving of intricate designs generally rotates among the weavers.

Wage rates for spinning vary from factory to factory ranging between Rs11 to Rs15 per kg. One person can spin about 3–4kg of wool per day. Home spinning rates are lower (Rs10–12 per kg). Women complain of difficulties encountered in getting their fair share.

Organization of production

Ease of operation, affordability of investment, availability of labour and the lack of government supervision and monitoring are some of the factors that have motivated numerous middlemen, agents and large factory owners to enter the area of carpet manufacturing and trading. Major manufacturers and exporters are invariably male, as are middlemen and agents. Distinct advantages accrue to them as a result of the above-mentioned factors and the internationalization of carpet exports.

Typology of work

For families at subsistence level, a Tibetan carpet will not be manufactured for home use; it is unaffordable. The local market in urban areas caters mainly for tourists. Most rural households in and around Kathmandu have taken up spinning as a major non-farm activity to supplement household income. Spinning and weaving are the main activities that fall within the dispersed category of work. The cost of a traditional wooden or hand-operated spinning-wheel is about Rs120 000; an iron one which is sturdier will fetch Rs250 000. Since women are usually alone tending to housework and field-work, spinning is an activity which can be done single-handedly. Some land-poor households with large families are dependent on carpet weaving and other off-farm employment activities for their livelihoods. Traditional wooden looms are used in rural households. Households engaged in weaving are fewer than those engaged in spinning for the weaving process requires at least two people to work simultaneously at one loom.

Mechanization

The recent introduction of mechanization into the carding of wool has already wiped out the highly labour-intensive processes of cleaning raw wool, teasing and blending—which were the early stages of production. A single machine with minor accessories or attachments can take over jobs that fall primarily into the domain of female labour, and was performed at household level. The argument about mechanization and female labour put forward by factory owners, managers and supervisors is: machine carding has relieved women from the strenuous work, accompanied by pain due to hand carding; it has allowed women to work more efficiently for higher productivity in spinning; and has not adversely affected their income which on average remains unaffected due to the increase in spinning.

Responses from the women themselves were varied. While most of the women at both factory and household level did agree with the above, there would also be consensus among them about the necessity of putting in long hours spinning (of machine-carded wool)—an activity not devoid of health hazards. The carded wool is much finer and contains tiny particles which are very easily dispersed into the air during spinning; these cause respiratory problems.

The world market for Nepalese carpets capitalizes on its 'hand-made' quality. These carpets have thus monopolized the market in a way that is unique, for these thick carpets have no rivals. Even India which produces 'Tibetan carpets' uses machine-spun yarn. And though the products may look identical, carpet experts can always tell the difference.

The lucrative nature of this sector has caused the mushrooming in the number of middlemen and agents. Some operate on a large scale and have distinct 'domains' of operation in the villages while others are small informal workshops that operate in a single room.

Mechanization of carding has eliminated the drudgery of hand carding and the harmful effects of fibre ingestion. In terms of the timing of production there was one significant difference. The reason for this is because both hand carding and hand spinning have been simultaneous activities performed individually. The elimination of hand carding has freed some labour that has then been redirected into spinning. The negative impact of mechanized carding on women's labour and income that comes from it, however, is quite apparent.

Underuse of female labour

The carpet export market is especially vulnerable to slumps. These have a negative impact on the carpet industry in general in Nepal and so affect female labour. The slump in carpet demand has meant sending less raw wool for processing and spinning for carpet making. Our visits to factory sites revealed a consciousness among women workers about slumps in the international market. Women were being given a mere 1–2kg of yarn to spin. On an average, one person can spin about 3–4kg of wool in a nine hour day. Spinning takes place entirely on a piece-rate basis, in both formal and non-formal sectors. The piece-rate measure of work even under normal conditions of wool supply holds down the productivity of female labour and deprives women of potential returns from full employment opportunities. It also provides a safe cushioning effect for employers who are saved having to provide regular salaries to employees during a slump.

Access to technology

Though hand carding involves laborious time and energy and work tools consist mainly of coarse brushes with risks to health, one may assume that mechanized carding has relieved female labour for more productive work spinning and provided them with upward mobility in the production process. This needs, however, to be considered not in terms of single cluster of related activities but within the overall production process. Mechanization of carding is concentrated in urban Kathmandu. This has distanced technology and other benefits derived from it away from women in the rural areas. Technological input in the carding process has robbed women of their work and placed it in the hands of men. Training in the use of technology and skill development caters to men as users of technology— which also brings with it status at work. Mechanization of carding has provided job security to men who have subsequently been brought into a regular or permanent category of factory workers with all the benefits that accrue to permanent staff members—medical benefits, pensions and leave.

Decentralized production

Because the carpet industry is entirely export oriented, requirements of initial capital investment are low and the potential high for profits. The industry's major production processes are spinning and weaving which imply the maximum amount of female labour on a flexible piece-rate basis which is concentrated in labour-intensive areas of production. This provides a lucrative area of investment. As an export-based industry it also receives ample protection from the government whose industrial policy is export-oriented. Moderate capital requirements and availability of credit through government-supported lending schemes and its high potential for export have allowed this industry to flourish on an *ad hoc* basis.

The decentralized mode of production through dispersed units within the rural periphery of urban Kathmandu is a highly fragmented labour process which is highly dependent on female labour participation and organization. Thus, the organization of production within the woollen goods and carpet sector is arranged to maximize government benefits and profits through minimization of capital investment by using a cheap, unorganized female labour force. This has helped to reinforce the alienation of female labour both within the internal labour market of the factory, and within individual households. The implications of this on women's control over their own work within the overall production process, the end product, and the subsequent processes of trade and marketing became quite evident.

The system and its implications on the improvement of women's status as a conscious stable female workforce leaves little to be said. Most employers covered in the study expressed their opinion about the dispersed mode of production as:

○ Quite 'natural' since major operations such as spinning and weaving are heavily dependent on female labour.
○ The dispersed system is a consequence of expanded activities and increased production based on convenience in terms of location, rental costs, availability of labour and taxes.
○ Organizing under one roof is too expensive due to high maintenance and overhead costs.

244

Hierarchical job categories

The skills involved in the carpet industry are relatively simple and can be easily learned through observation and practice within a few days. The availability of labour for such work is easily found among women. The conspicuous scarcity of men at certain levels denotes their dislike for work which is repetitive, monotonous and where pay is dependent on the amount produced.

Responses from women regarding the absence of men within these categories of work were varied: 'Men are lazy and cannot sit for long hours at the same work'; 'Men have other options for work'; 'This is a woman's job'.

At one of the factories visited enquiries were made about experiments with the introduction of new tools or modifications in the tool design within the factory. We were informed that pedal-driven spinning-wheels had been introduced as prototypes. However, women did not find it easy to operate. Essentially, responses from women indicated that: 'sitting on the floor and working is easier'; 'this is the way we work at home'; 'co-ordinating the leg and hand is difficult'.

There was no attempt to train women in the use of this new mode of spinning either. According to employers and supervisors, the pedal-operated wheel would not have increased productivity. This resistance to the new model from the women themselves and the indifferent attitude of the employers, could have excused factory owners from training responsibilities.

Susceptibility to sexual divisions and bias

It goes without saying that while the 'private sector' activity is delegated to women, the trade, marketing, buying and negotiating activities are dominated by males. The masculinization of all jobs outside the production process ensures domination over women's work and output. In other words men benefit for women's labour through trade expansion. Almost all employers, agents, contractors interviewed had pat reasons ready: 'women are not mobile to work as agents'; 'they find spinning and weaving easy to handle'; 'Women cannot work at machines'; 'Most women prefer to stay at home and spin than go to the factory to work'.

These sorts of statements made by men reflect two basic issues. First, sexual divisions in general, and 'sexual bias' in particular, both combine to form one part of the arrangement within which technology in the broad sense, is governed. The sexual division of labour in the form of: who does what, who is entitled to what, who decides what, helps sustain the arrangement in terms of this broader issue of technology and production. These statements also throw light on male perceptions of stability in the patterns

245

of social arrangement through systematic sex biases about, who is doing what, and who is producing what.

Female specialization in spinning and weaving whether in the factory or inside the home, is looked upon as an extension of the private sphere of activities though they may be performed within the 'established' arrangements of the factory. They reflect sex biases that are central to the understanding of the inferior economic condition of women especially poor rural women. It is, therefore, tradition just as much as modernization that needs to be analysed.

Susceptibility to the business cycle

Women are consistently allocated those jobs which fall into the lowest categories where demands in terms of skill, training and decision-making are minimum. The total dependency of this industry on external forces at both ends (namely, the raw wool supply from abroad, and in the export of the finished products based on the demands on the international market), dictates a delicate and vulnerable situation. Given this susceptibility the industry will be highly affected, and, since female labour has the largest share of total labour in this sector, females will be most affected. Women are thus exposed to this double susceptibility.

The condition of non-migrants is far better than that of the others. They benefit from the support of their immediate family. Most of the migrant workers said they were aware that they could earn about Rs1500 a month at the given rate of Rs15 per kilo of wool; spinning 4kg a day. But they put themselves at risk by allowing themselves to be completely dependent on the agent for work as well as for accommodation. Second, they also expressed a sense of loyalty to the 'job agent' who accompanied them from the village to Kathmandu.

Women spinners at the household-level work less intensively at spinning due to constraints of time. Most householders looked after their own land and livestock, so are not thus totally dependent on cash income, as in the case of migrant labour. Advantages for home workers are the proximity of the workplace together with its compatibility with household work. Another is that children contribute time and labour input into spinning which adds to their returns. The major disadvantages are that the income for spinning is very low; household work does not allow free time; opportunities for socializing at work are rare.

Sexual harassment

The vulnerability of women workers to the advances of their male co-workers and superiors should not be passed over. In one factory, the owner made it quite clear that sexual taboos did not exist among most of the ethnic groups, particularly those belonging to the Tamarg and Dhimal communities which represent a large cross-section of women in the carpet sector in Kathmandu. They are used to mingling with men and are not constrained by social taboos of other ethnic communities. Accordingly, he explained that falling in and out of relationships is quite common among these women. There had, so far, been no untoward incidents where women had complained about such harassment. He felt it was quite natural given the 'openness' of their society's practices.

A few incidents reported by the factory owner, however, do imply the prevalence of harassment. For example, a woman weaver whose work was being continuously rejected by the supervisor as being inferior brought this to the notice of the factory owner. The owner who related this to us said that upon enquiry it turned out that the supervisor had been making advances to this woman for a long time but had failed in his attempts. Subsequently, he had found a convenient way to get back at her. During our study women were most reluctant to discuss this aspect.

In another factory we were informed about harassment from outside the factory premises. Most women work at the loom till late hours of the night. In some instances they have been harassed by men lurking outside the premises. Factory owners have subsequently made arrangements for these women to have additional security when they leave the factory premises at night.

Kesang Dolma, a Tibetan woman entrepreneur who has been involved in the carpet industry for 30 years and began her career as a refugee child worker at the Jawdalehed Refugee campt at the loom, has a deep understanding of the problems faced by these vulnerable women workers.

Kesang, who has been operating her own factory for over 20 years, looks upon women workers not only as employees, but as women needing guidance. She realizes that being poor, uneducated and young, and mostly migrant, they need to be helped in their personal lives as well. Kesang says she has not been very successful despite her years of close association with women workers, for some women so easily get entangled in relationships— often with married men in the neighbourhood. These men generally live off the earnings of women, and it is not uncommon to find one man with multiple relationships which ensure him a steady income and a comfortable life. These women are often abandoned after they have had children; their situation then becomes very serious. In some cases, women are able to find people willing to adopt a child.

Training and the concept of 'salary'

In the carpet industry the terms 'skilled', 'unskilled' and 'semi-skilled' are used very precisely. The resource of skill is dependent on the quality of output. In the area of weaving, this factor is of prime importance. Training takes place on an informal basis with the trainee sandwiched between two workers at the loom, and so the skill is acquired quite easily.

During the study, it became markedly clear that the concept of salary is unique in the carpet sector. All the girls and women questioned were on a regular 'salary' basis. However, closer questioning revealed that there exists an intricate network of employment agents and contractors who recruit young women for weaving and spinning where the demand for female labour is very high. This is particularly the case with factory recruitment. Most new recruits are accompanied by a neighbour or relative or somebody from the same community in Kathmandu where they are put under the charge of a contractor or middleman known as the recruiter. Provided with food and lodging they receive a 'salary' which is in fact only a portion of the total amount due to them. In some cases, a distinct bondage was clearly discernible wherein young girls and boys have no choice but are tied down to render services to one factory under constant threat of being tracked down and punished for breach of contract by the middleman.

Coir workers in Sri Lanka

KAMALA PEIRIS

Coir fibre is a product derived from the coconut husk. Three main types of fibre are manufactured in Sri Lanka: white fibre, necessary for making superior grades of yarn, and 'Bristol' and 'mattress', both by-products of brown fibre. White fibre is the most costly, and results from a natural chemical process involving pre-conditions of timing and retting procedures which ensure that its colour is retained. Its production thus requires more complicated procedures and highly developed organization than that of brown fibre, which is more straightforward. White fibre is not marketed in its raw state but processed into yarn, ropes and—most recently—finished products. These are sold locally and for export.

Brown fibre is made in areas north of Colombo, in which nuts are used for the production of copra and desiccated coconut, and in the coconut triangle. The focus of white fibre manufacture is an area running along the coastal belt of Western Province, south of Colombo, into Southern Province. In statistics showing shades of white fibre produced in different districts, Galle District outdoes the rest by far, producing the fibre which brings the best income to coir workers.

Women and coir

Most coir production is organized on an informal basis; the majority of workers are women in small units or in households, using hand-operated tools and machinery. Although industrialists have from time to time examined the possible advantages of mechanized production (including spinning), these ideas have been always rejected on the basis that the relatively low costs of female (and child) labour could never be equalled by mechanization. Hence, in spite of exploitation of the product, the white

KAMALA PEIRIS set up and co-ordinates the Siyath Foundation in Sri Lanka, which works with low-income women's groups.

fibre industry has remained a home industry and source of employment—
mainly for women—throughout the centuries.

The number of women involved in the industry has never been properly
assessed, and most assumptions are very low, owing to a disregard of the
time spent on 'invisible' tasks and the informal features of coir production.
For example, in 1979 the Food and Agriculture Organization (FAO)
estimated that there were between 14 000 and 24 000 workers in the white
fibre industry along the south-west coast of Sri Lanka, with a production of
6–7000 metric tonnes of yarn per year. However, comparison of these
figures with estimates of yarn production in the region indicates that the
former have been compiled without a clear idea of the actual working day
of a coir worker. Very few of the workers—unless they are young women
without household responsibilities—are able to work eight hours a day, and
the number of working days per year is also over-estimated. On the basis of
250 days of work per year, a more realistic estimate would be 24 000 to
26 000 workers, and when an estimated number who are involved in the
further processing of fibre into finished products is added, the total could be
in the range of 26 000 to 30 000 women.

In addition to the general problems women face in Sri Lankan society,
they experience particular hardships as a consequence of being workers at
the lowest levels in the coir industry. For example, lack of a regular supply
of raw material, the machinations of traders, the informal quality of their
work as they dry, clean fibre and make yarn in the confines of their own
premises, and restricted mobility which precludes them from going out of

Table 1. Gender division of labour in the coir industry

Process in coir production	Gender of majority of workers
Husking	male
Transport by cart	male
Making husk pits	male
Cleaning husk pits	male
Filling husk pits	female/male
Emptying husk pits	female
Hammering soaked husks	female
Drying fibre	female
Cleaning fibre	female
Spinning rope by hand	female
Spinning a superior quality by hand	male
Spinning rope by machines:	
sitting	female/male
standing	female
Transport on foot	female

Source: Study on the potential of women workers in small-scale coir organizations in Sri
Lanka, 1983.

the village to search for bargains in husks, fibre or to sell yarn all prevent them from acquiring the best advantages from their work.

The white coir industry shows a clearly demarcated gender division of labour, women doing the most unclean, back-breaking work, as illustrated in Table 1.

A further comparison between men and women may be made to show how wage levels compare between the two. For example, in 1979 a man earned Rs50 plus a coconut for 10 minutes' work climbing a coconut tree, while a woman earned Rs50 for an hour of beating husks or emptying pits. Although rates have increased since then, the disparity remains just as wide. Further, it is considered acceptable that a woman should work over a longer period of time to earn the same amount as a man. Thus the lower value of her work is related to a lower value placed on her time. For example, in 1990 a woman beating husks as a source of employment is paid Rs10 per 180 husk pieces.

Another factor that invisibly affects women's incomes is the male-dominated management structures of trading companies. For instance, a collective of yarn makers supplying an exporting company has found its product consistently graded low by male workers in charge of grading. Nevertheless, the women did not succeed in convincing the superior (again a male) that the grading was defective. The relationships between traders of husks and yarn also squeeze women's meagre profits. In the final analysis, poverty levels of women in the yarn trade indicate that many of them have very little hope of overcoming their plight if they work in isolation.

Further details on the relationships between different traders in the coir industry, and their strategies to deceive women workers, are provided later.

Objectives and scope of the study

The introduction to this book suggests an extended definition of the word 'technology': that in its widest sense it is not only machinery—large or small—or even practical methods, techniques and processes, but also concepts and thinking processes—the whole behavioural paradigm; in short an ideology. In this context appropriate technology is a network of practical voluntary actions which are consonant and compatible with the capacities and simple thought processes or behavioural patterns of all economically disadvantaged, and hence vulnerable, groups.

The rest of this paper describes an experience of the development and practice of this ideology by women workers in the coir industry. It is argued that this experience deserves to be included within the scenario of appropriate technical innovation. The field of activity under consideration in this study is the use of white fibre for coir yarn production. The processes and tools being used comprise both hardware—simple tools, and software—practical processes and theoretical behaviour paradigms. Of these, the tools and practical processes are described in this section, while the development of women's organization and behavioural strategies are discussed later.

Husk and fibre supply

The majority of husks made available to the white fibre industry are supplied by private traders operating from a village base. The larger traders own up to 100 or more pits, and all traders make as much as 30–40 per cent net profit. Sometimes they operate as both husk and yarn traders, supplying women with credit and setting off yarn against it. In this way they increase their profits, as women with not much education can be cheated by the complex numerical calculations involved.

Although overall availability of husks is not a problem, a shortage is felt in Galle District where the project under study is located, and this can affect white fibre production. In Galle, yarn making is a popular income-generating activity for women, and its retting capacity has been exploited far above the other districts. During the lean period of nut harvesting in Sri Lanka (August to February each year), the problem of husk shortage is further aggravated and buying of yarn by traders also drops drastically. Traders who have holding capacity prefer to buy large stocks when husk prices are low, as the yarn can then by bought cheaply. Hence the income of women yarn makers is also badly affected at this time.

Compared to past levels, profits for husk traders are now dwindling with rising inflation, and coir is no longer regarded as a way to easy riches. Hence wealthy entrepreneurs are pulling out of the trade, and smaller ones are competing violently to maintain reasonable profits. A reduction in husk trading in the villages further reduces the meagre independence of women, who are then forced to buy machine-made fibre at higher prices.

Mechanization of husk processing

For generations white coir fibre in the southern coastal belt has been produced using traditional retting processes. However, in recent times a new development is to pre-crush the husks. It is argued that the retting time (and thus working capital) can be drastically reduced by mechanical crushing before retting to enable easy penetration of water, thereby hastening the bacterial activity which loosens the fibres. Husk crushers have been introduced into many areas in the southern coastal belt by the Export Development Board (EDB) from the early 1980s, following export promotion and privatization policies by the state.

The total cost of a crusher with necessary ancillary investment for installation is Rs2 000 000, almost half of which is given as a grant by the EDB. However, such an investment is beyond the capacity of low-income coir workers, unless they are organized into large, strong collectives; consequently the beneficiary is the rich trader (*mudalali*) who has capital to spare.

Although the use of husk crushers does not displace traditional labour, it does increase the unit cost of fibre production. This extra cost is passed down to the workers, who also lose the small supplies of husks which they used to ret and process themselves, because the rich crusher owner buys all the husks in the area at higher prices to feed his crusher. (The latter needs at least 8000 husks a day to run at full capacity.) The workers are therefore forced to buy fibre produced by the crusher at the higher price.

A further development in the late 1980s has been the introduction of mechanized coir extraction technology. At present there are seven projects established in Southern Province for the mechanical extraction of white fibre. While two are managed by the Department of Small Industries, others are owned and managed by the private sector—again with financial and other forms of assistance from the EDB. The workers' negative reaction to this development is because of their frustration at some of them losing work as husk beaters and others being forced to pay higher prices for fibre. The higher price paid by exporters for yarn from hand-beaten fibre than that paid for machine-made fibre also indicates that the final processed product is not as high in quality as that beaten in the traditional way. This was aptly described by an old woman worker who, throwing up her gnarled and knotted hands, demanded 'Why do we need other machines than these hands?'

A survey of coir products in 1976 showed that about 52 per cent of yarn producers resorted to hand spinning, 35 per cent used hand-operated spinning machines, and the rest a mixture of the two. There are advantages and disadvantages of both methods. Hand spinning is an independent activity, undertaken by each worker separately depending on her own timetable, and can be carried out either in the shade of a tree or inside if hot or rainy. It can also be done at night. Although it is more time and energy consuming than machine spinning, it compensates by paying better.

Machine spinning must be carried out by three workers together; thus their working output depends upon the availability of common time and their individual abilities. This can lead to much tension unless workers are from the same family. While this may seem a disadvantage in the working situation of single workers, for promoting attempts at cohesion—as was done in the project under study—the need for such a group of three facilitated the process of bringing women together into larger groups for productive work. In addition a sense of sharing and caring could be experienced, and analysis more easily undertaken, in a group situation.

Yarn quality determines its selling price. Good manually spun yarn from hand-beaten fibre has a high twist, is thin and is the highest priced of all yarn, presently at Rs22–4 per kilogram. Machine-made yarn from hand-beaten fibre, hand-spun yarn from machine-made fibre and machine-made yarn from machine-made fibre fetch lower prices, respectively. However, while only about 2kg of hand-spun yarn can be made per day per worker, production can be doubled using a machine.

Qualities of yarn are less standardized in Sri Lanka than in India, where they have been identified as falling along a defined grading system. The Department of Small Industries in Sri Lanka distinguishes only five grades of yarn, depending on the thickness and the number of twists per inch. A further complicating factor is the absence of standardized colour for Sri Lankan yarn. The divergences in quality of raw husks, the duration and efficiency of retting, and deviations when selecting fibre for colour before beating all produce a yarn of variable end quality.

End users

Using white coir as the basic raw material a wide range of products is manufactured in Sri Lanka, from traditionally produced hand-spun two-ply coir yarn requiring no investment in machinery to sophisticated powerloom coir mats and mattings which involve heavy capital expenditure. Each of these products is produced from a different quality yarn.

The local market is not interested in a good white colour, requiring several varieties of yarn for the production of mats, mattings, brushes, for direct consumption by local industries and for household needs. This has hampered efforts by export firms to obtain the qualities they require from local middlemen. Although the companies demand better varieties of yarn, the quantities involved are small when compared to the Indian export industry (the percentage of total yarn export from Sri Lanka is only 5 per cent, compared to 95 per cent from India).

In Sri Lanka local trade in yarn is monopolized by five or six traders based in Colombo. They build up stocks brought to their warehouses by suppliers and sell, at the highest possible price, to buyers who come from all over the country. Except for the disruption in activities resulting from the recent conflicts in the country, their trade has received no set-backs or fluctuation in profits, as local consumption of coir products is still rising.

In contrast there is at least one yarn trader—and often many more—in every village down the south coast. While the traders north of Galle produce for the local market, the good white colour of yarn beyond Galle makes it the main area of operation for export companies. Again from further south towards the south-east coast all yarn is sold locally, usually to the east. Local traders often resell to larger traders, thus forming a chain of suppliers up to the largest traders, who hold monopolies, or to the exporters. The business relations between local traders and export companies are usually of a long-standing nature and beneficial to both parties. The larger companies provide stable outlets, and are the most popular clients from the traders' point of view. It is not unusual for traders to expand their businesses over time and become powerful members of their communities. They then employ workers in units in their home compounds so that large quantities of predictable quality yarn may be produced.

Compared to local trade, exporters of coir products have in recent years faced serious difficulties owing to a slackening of demand caused by mat manufacturers reducing their yarn requirements, the impact of the world-wide economic recession, the inflation rate in Sri Lanka and higher shipping rates. Since coir is no longer profitable, companies which export coconut products today do not consider it one of their main areas of activity (despite their investment in mechanized equipment for the manufacture of coir products).

Some smaller firms, however, which used to supply the larger ones have now branched out as exporters themselves, although they tend not to manufacture finished products and have only a limited number of yarn-supply points along the coast. Making use of the Free Trade Zone facilities, some local firms have also formed joint ventures with foreign firms and been funded by foreign donor agencies. Export sales of finished coir products have increased over the last few years, but all companies still rely on yarn exports supplied mainly from the south. The problems of exporting yarn have made the Sri Lankan Government itself acutely aware that, if the country is to retain its coir export income, a shift to the production of finished products is necessary.

Strategies of coir and yarn traders

Delaying payment and forcing suppliers to deliver on credit is a major characteristic of the coir trade, with the exception of the largest exporters and their main suppliers. Other suppliers usually deliver on credit, receiving post-dated cheques, and this type of delivery is continued down the line to the level of the village yarn collector. Often women workers are also induced to deliver on credit but, if there is more than one trader in the village, this usually fails. Such competition between local traders is advantageous to women workers as long as they operate alone, but if they form organizations which can compete with the traders the latter find ways to wreck such ventures.

A major difficulty of women coir workers is that they are at the mercy of two types of village traders, namely those dealing in husks and those dealing in yarn. The coir trade is a highly competitive, energy-consuming exercise; if a trader is to make a reasonable profit, he must find devious ways to augment his income from it. Selling husks or fibre is the first activity in the process of yarn making which binds the trader to the yarn maker. Although occasionally, when women can afford it, they have small pits of their own of varying sizes, these are vastly outnumbered by the pits owned by traders. Hence the latter have a virtual monopoly of husk-retting operations, possessing the resources to purchase green husks and own their retting pits. They therefore control the supply and pricing of retted husks, irrespective of how much hardship is caused to the workers. Examples of particular strategies adopted by husk traders are as follows:

○ He rets husks for shorter periods, resulting in harder retted husks. This reduces the time during which he has to tie up his capital, but involves buyers in husk beating work that is more time and energy consuming.

○ He sells by lots of 100 husk pieces (three are called a 'hand'). Formerly the husk of a whole nut was split into four pieces (100 pieces give 3.3kg of yarn), now five or even six are usual (100 pieces give 2.5kg and 2.1kg respectively). In locations where there is much coir activity and a shortage of husks, they are split into up to 10 or 12 pieces. The higher the number of pieces, the higher the trader's profit.

○ As all retted pieces are not of equal softness or colour, he mixes the unbeatable hard ones and those of a darker colour with the better husks. He does not allow grading at the point of sale, and women have to suffer with a lower grade of fibre resulting in lower priced yarn.

○ If workers complain about the husks, the trader threatens to sell to outside villages. (Often he prefers to do this if the husks can be moved in bulk.) Thus women have to buy even second-grade husks at his price.

○ Even when he sells within the village, the trader opens the pit (usually containing about 5000 pieces) only after he has found enough workers to buy the entire contents. If he can afford it, it is preferable to wait as the quality will improve with time and he can sell at a higher price. Therefore women cannot obtain husks as and when they want them. (Workers owning their own pits will remove husks in small lots—as many as can be beaten at one time.)

○ Giving husks on credit is preferable for the trader as he can baffle women through complicated calculations when they have to pay back in kind (yarn). In some cases he earns interest as high as 144 per cent. He is also assured of a regular yarn supply as the women are bound to him through credit.

○ In the rare instances where workers pool resources to buy a pit, the trader tries to block this by any means at his command. There is evidence of this from court cases in south Sri Lanka in which the *mudalali* (trader) used force and technical legal advice to prevent women from making their own pits.

○ The fibre trader often sells short weight as the workers do not own weighing scales. In addition he adds pith, dust and uncleaned fibre which is also mixed in terms of colour. Thus some of what the women buy has to go to waste and the fibre must be graded for colour before making different varieties of yarn.

The yarn trader has his own strategies:

- He uses different kinds of units for buying yarn so it is impossible for workers to assess which is more profitable; for example he buys by the kilogram, by skeins of a given length and number of strands, or by Rs10-worth of fibre.
- When he wants to increase the price, instead of doing so directly he asks for five strands instead of four as the standard for each skein.
- In large companies yarn supplied is kept back for a fortnight (ostensibly for moisture loss), and invariably the weight finally decided upon is less than what was brought in.
- How grading is carried out for each lot in such companies is not known to the workers, who have to accept the various grades decided upon by company employees.
- In contrast, the small village trader buys at an even average rate (somewhere between the highest and lowest grades), and pays immediately as if he is doing the workers a good turn; hence women prefer to sell to him, because they do not have to wait for the money. However, they know that when he sells he will make a profit on the whole transaction by dividing it into different grades. Further, from the big company he also gets a bonus for supplying in bulk, which is pure profit for him.
- This trader does not pay extra if the weight of the bundle of yarn brought has one or two hundred grams extra. Instead he pays the woman for the exact number of kilograms, lets her go, then calls her back and gives her Rs10 for the bus fare, as if to show his benevolence.
- The trader provides credit for any urgent needs the women have, so binding them to himself as his regular suppliers. The women find it necessary to ask for credit for their incomes are so low.

A graphic example of the dual monopoly of husk and yarn traders functioning together to cause severe problems for coir workers is when export-oriented firms sometimes raise their buying prices in order to meet orders on time. However, although they themselves are receiving a higher buying price from the company, the village yarn traders hold down the prices they pay the women for as long as they can, knowing that the women are not aware of company policy. However, the husk traders with more contacts outside usually find out and raise their husk prices. Generally it takes months before the women can induce the yarn traders to raise buying prices even slightly, and only after they have taken measures such as limiting their production or reducing yarn quality.

Further details of women's strategies against the traders will be seen later.

257

Village-level coir organizations

Any organized activity in coir production at village level in Sri Lanka has been primarily the result of initiatives from outside, and from two main sources: government departments and/or non-government organizations (NGOs). The most significant sources of government activity are the Co-operative, Rural Development and Small Industries Departments and the Export Development Board. Some examples of the involvement of the latter two departments in coir have already been mentioned.

Independent organizations working with coir producers are either at national level, such as Lanka Mahila Samiti (a large women's organization) and Sarvodaya, or small individual groups along the south and south-west coast. The former are large organizations which span the whole island and are involved in many different activities. In coir production they tend to act as 'umbrella organizations', with small societies or groups formed specifically in yarn-producing areas to improve the economic prospects of their members. Influential and concerned individuals in villages have also formed small independent organizations based on foreign funding, supplying aid either as cash or technology, like spinning sets. Sometimes the government will jointly run a project with an NGO, or have a part in it.

The following are further examples of organizations currently working in coir at village level.

Co-operatives

Throughout the country there are co-operative societies whose members are productive workers in different fields. The organizers and officials of rural co-ops are generally the village élite, and their success depends on how much time, effort and leadership that such individuals are prepared to devote to the ventures. Early problems such as the misuse or misappropriation of society funds led the department to introduce more stringent legal restrictions for co-operatives, and greatly to expand its own cadre of supervisory officials. To aid in restricting possibilities for corruption, co-op officers are transferred frequently. Formerly the small industries department appointed instructors to work with coir co-operative groups and bought up the yarn produced. However, since 1982 this situation has changed, particularly in Galle District, here both instruction and purchasing facilities have been discontinued.

Most of the problems of rural co-ops stem from their methods of organization. Leaders can become autocratic and paternalistic and over-zealous in their duties, leading them to frown on innovative activities and to treat genuine mistakes and actual frauds alike. They frequently overawe the office bearers of associated smaller women's groups. Many of the rules and regulations now enforced, for example that a large proportion (up to 45

258

per cent in some cases) of co-operative profits must be geared to purposes other than distribution among workers, are counter-productive in that they make participation difficult for poor villagers. The intricacies of these rules also reinforce the latter's dependence on the better-informed élite or co-op officials, and prevent them from participating effectively in the organization. The temporary nature of the official's association with a particular society means they do not become personally concerned about the members' plight or gain their confidence. Some societies also have problems with the lack of a clear market for their produce, and there are no arrangements for central handling, transport or co-ordination of co-operative activities.

Rural development societies

In coir-producing areas, some rural development societies (RDSs) form an organizational structure within which women can work collectively. However, such societies encounter similar difficulties to those experienced by co-operatives, as office bearers are also members of the village élite whose interests often conflict with those of the poor. In addition, RDSs are all-purpose organizations, obliged to focus attention on many aspects of rural development. Consequently, coir workers' interests are only served in so far as they do not infringe on those of the body of members as a whole. As membership of RDSs is open to both sexes and the majority of office-bearers are men, there are often conflicts of interest and poor women coir workers are paid scant attention. The government officer in charge of the societies can rarely solve such difficulties, as he or she does not have specific technical expertise and has to supervise a large number of groups.

Department of small industries

Another avenue of employment for coir workers are complexes organized by the department of small industries (DSI). This type of facility has been available in Sri Lanka for over 30 years, providing economic benefits to workers who earn a daily wage. Departmental instructors at each work-place, under the guidance of the Assistant Director in the particular administrative district, make decisions over issues such as production and sales. In one section of the complex husks are processed into fibre, which is then passed on to another section where different grades of yarn are produced according to the requirements and orders received by the department. During the last few years a number of measures—such as crushers and decorticating machines—have been introduced, with a view to improving the industry as a whole.

This change in policy to a more development-oriented, macro-level organization competing with private trade is advantageous at national

259

level. However, the condition of women workers in individual complexes can deteriorate unless particular care is taken to safeguard their interests. Other specific difficulties with expansion include ensuring a constant fibre supply, which depends on obtaining husks in bulk. A general problem with the type of assistance provided by the DSI is that although in the short-term workers are freed from the problems of obtaining raw material and marketing the product, in the long run it does not develop indigenous awareness of their problems or capacities for finding solutions. Thus if such a complex is closed down, women are back to their original position at the mercy of individual traders.

The women's bureau

This government institution providing opportunities for women to engage in the coir industry started a few years ago, funded both by the state and foreign aid sources. As a new organization the bureau has had a tremendous task to build up its strength and reach out to as many women as possible in the country, and it has the further responsibility for equitable distribution of its support. For each of the bureau's projects, selected women are given general training, including information on government services available, health, sanitation and family life. Then each chooses a specific area of activity, one option being coir, and is given further training in this area and a grant (not exceeding Rs1000).

Although on the whole the bureau is functioning well, there are some problems. The individual basis of activities means there is a lack of opportunities for women to work as a collective group, and the outright grant is not conducive to promoting a self-sustaining spirit. In addition, several of the bureau's officials responsible for the local organization of work are actually men.

Talalla

A few years ago this location was selected by Agroskills, a management consultancy firm (commissioned by the Export Development Board) for a project to provide long-term assistance to women coir workers. The basis for the choice was Talalla's proximity to a lagoon already used for retting, indicating significant local interest in the product. Initial outside assistance was the installation of a husk crusher in a shed in the garden of a village teacher, and later a fibre-cleaning machine was also provided. The teacher formed a society of coir workers who were given credit to buy husks and a market for the yarn they produced. In addition, a local bank agreed to grant loans to society members. Crusher operation and maintenance and administration of the group were the responsibility of Agroskills.

A major problem with the project was ensuring a regular, and large enough, supply of husks. A trader from the interior was contracted to deliver on a regular basis, but several local women who themselves owned husk pits chose not to join the society, and the crusher usually operated significantly below full capacity. The society's yarn was bought by another trader, but problems also arose here as its quality was frequently below his requirements. In addition women fell behind with their repayments, both of bank loans and credit for husk purchases. To reduce dependence on Agroskills and enable them to withdraw from the project, plans were made to make the society a limited liability company, with shareholders to be the yarn producers and others interested in their welfare. Although shares were priced low and limits set on the number any single person could own, poor workers still found it difficult to become involved in the company, and many of the founder members were the village élite.

Kalupe

The mat-making centre in Kalupe arose out of a study undertaken by a Dutch researcher who lived in the village for a year, discussing with the coir workers their situation and helping them to crystallize their ideas into a proposal for an action project. Funds were provided by the Dutch government. An early problem was the quality of yarn produced, and a retired instructor from the DSI was employed to provide training in this area. The higher quality yarn was purchased from the workers by a woman employed for this purpose and, when enough had been collected, production of the finished product—mats—began. The DSI also supplied a building for the centre to use, and a cleaning machine; boards and tools were purchased from project funds. Marketing outlets were found in a number of European countries and in a local tourist area. After the first three years the centre was self-supporting and even making a small profit.

As a condition of joining the project, women have to produce a certain quantity of good yarn and obtain spinning sets. Some are trained as mat-makers, during which time they are paid an allowance. Women come to the centre daily to work (the boards on which the mats are made are too expensive and unwieldy for them to use at home), but it does not operate as a factory and they are free to go home whenever necessary to attend to household chores. Payment is on a piece-rate basis, but there is a responsibility to share work when an order has to be executed. Women are given advance loans by the centre to buy husks, and the People's Bank recently agreed to provide additional loans for other purposes.

The project is managed by a Board of Management comprising workers' representatives, yarn producers, teachers, a treasurer and secretary and DSI officials, with one of the latter acting as president. Complementary to the technical activities, efforts have been made to develop the women's individual and collective capacities—for example by rotating management responsibilities, and providing information-gathering trips to other coir projects and selling points in the main towns—and they meet regularly to decide which suggestions their representatives will put forward at board meetings.

In spite of the project's apparent success, several problems remain. The centre's strict requirements for high-quality yarn limit the number of women who can be employed, and they remain at the mercy of local husk traders. Reliance on one product and a single export channel is also seen as risky (there have been slack periods owing to a lack of orders), and there are plans for diversification in the near future. Although the project has successfully avoided being taken over by the village élite, the women's own involvement in its management has been slow to become established. This is partly due to the fact that the DSI officials were accustomed to working in a traditional hierarchical structure, and also, although women were already used to working in small units of two or three, many have had problems becoming actively involved in a larger group. Thus they tend to remain dependent on a few individuals who dominate the project. Conflicts sometimes arise between the women at the centre and independent yarn-making groups in the area, as their interests clash with each other.

The coir project

The coir project was initiated in 1983 by Siyath Foundation, a Sri Lankan NGO which works at grassroots level with poor rural women. The ideas which formed the basis for the project were partly inspired by the Rural Development Change Agents Programme. The latter began following a national workshop in 1978, which aimed to make an in-depth analysis of the country's rural development policies and programmes in order to determine a new direction. Drawing on traditional concepts of self-help, a basic approach was defined to view development in fundamental humanistic terms as a process of overall development of people and their potential, involving participation and self-reliance as corner-stones. These were to be generated by the intervention of catalytic agents who would identify suitable entry points to rural communities and assist people to articulate their felt needs and realize them using their own initiative, skills and local resources. The training of these 'change agents' (facilitators) at village level was problem-oriented and practical and a very egalitarian approach was consciously adopted.

Based on this philosophy, the Siyath Foundation decided that group formation, open discussion and collective activity could be used as the mode of operation for coir workers. The women are supported to achieve total fulfilment as human beings, in relation to acquiring more independent collective values as well as striving to reach their economic aspirations. The aim is to achieve these twin goals through the release of their creative

262

energies and thinking processes. Self-reliance and development of the collective personality of the organization of these women are the basic elements of this new strategy. The basic premises are that:

- Poor women do not view their lives in a fragmented manner, separating the economic from non-economic aspects.
- If they actively participate as subjects rather than as passive objects in the development process, they are able to move from a condition of survival to one of directing their own actions towards economic independence.
- A sensitive and flexible approach without rigid top–down procedures can reinforce this process and permit experiments to be multiplied and grow in scale.
- Informality, simplicity and lack of rigid procedures are features essential for success in the activities of women workers.

Such experiments allow widening of the political space which poor communities can enjoy. Siyath's approach is specifically characterized by such elements as:

- Concentrating only on women coir workers.
- Stimulating their organization through trained facilitators (change agents), based within the villages for a certain time, who work not by means of authority or highly specialized skills, but through personal involvement and example. Such a cadre of persons thus is welded to local people by the sharing a common value system and a simple philosophy appropriate to village life.
- Beginning on a small scale and expanding step by step.
- Keeping the groups of coir workers small, allowing for interaction and participation by all.
- Rotating all special jobs so that responsibilities are borne by all members.
- Using only non-directive guidance in training, thereby giving women confidence to handle problems on their own.
- Avoiding large-scale capital investments which will prevent workers feeling that it is their own venture.
- Allowing for great flexibility so that women may progress at their own speed of decision-making.

Siyath had selected its facilitators in 1984 and, following training, they introduced themselves into villages in the project area. This had to be done on their own merits, and was not an easy task in the local context as there was often considerable suspicion to be overcome. Once they had gained the village women's confidence, the facilitators' main roles, with support from Siyath, were awareness building, group formation and non-directive guiding of groups in problem-solving.

263

Data collection

A variety of techniques were used in collecting data for this study. First, personal participatory observation was undertaken to identify the processes—both practical and psychological—that were being used in the various operations of skilled manual work, as well as for action and reflection. The women workers themselves clarified ambiguities, and differences of opinion were discussed in detail until a common consensus was reached before documentation. Next, both activity specific descriptions and sequential questioning through in-depth interviews helped to fill in the gaps in order to arrive at the full picture of the women workers' vocational milieu, which gave purpose and direction to the efforts to improve their lives. The data thus derived were also checked against information gleaned from surveys and direct observation.

In this regard group interviews, held in the context of the monthly regular meetings at which change agents articulated their personal viewpoints and perceptions, added the final touches and completed the many-faceted picture, seen from different perspectives. An understanding of how the women chose their priorities—not only in terms of options available to them, but also in self-evaluation and evaluation of their peers—was obtained through promoting the growth of their own ability for ranking among alternatives, based on fine discrimination; an exercise they enjoyed and realized was invaluable to further refining their analytical thinking processes.

Comparison of technology levels was achieved by undergoing a personal and collective process of reflecting on their own activities, self-perceptions and acceptance as members of the community at large. Mechanisms used for this included the women looking critically at themselves and their peers before, during and after their innovative experiences. The main researcher, while involving herself as a partner and sometimes a guide in this reflection process, also used other conventional methods such as discussion with external actors who influenced and were influenced by the silent revolution which was taking place in the quiet village community of which these women workers were an integral component, and desk study to bring in the wider dimensions which had a bearing on the industry that gave them their livelihood.

About the villages

The two locations selected for study, Dodanduwa and Hikkaduwa, are in the district of Galle along the southern coast of Sri Lanka, 115 kilometres from Colombo, and within eight kilometres of one another. Dodanduwa has project operations at four sites, Hikkaduwa at five, one of the latter being the Kalupe mat-making centre. The two locations are characterized by a high degree of landlessness: 45 per cent in Dodanduwa and 15 per cent in Hikkaduwa. Analysis by size of landholding shows 69 per cent in the landholding category in Hikkaduwa and 38 per cent in Dodanduwa have highly uneconomic units, ranging from four to 10 perches. This is barely sufficient for a dwelling unit, and does not leave any land for the cultivation of garden produce which could reduce money spent on food in these subsistence-level families.

In both locations unemployment is rampant—more so as women seldom venture outside the village to find employment, except for traditionally 'female' jobs such as teaching and nursing. Hikkaduwa is close to a tourist resort, which afforded some opportunities for work until the recent disruptions. The men fish in the two villages, but seasonally; it is impossible during the monsoon. Males among the families in Hikkaduwa are mainly engaged in casual work as coconut pickers and toddy tappers, with a few working in lime kilns. This type of employment does not yield them a steady income, particularly in a situation of over-supply of labour.

Hikkaduwa women, however, take on coir work on a regular basis throughout the year. They manufacture a variety of yarn types which are sold to several small traders who operate in the village, or to the centre at Kalupe. The centre acts as a model to the women, and helps to raise the level of their aspirations. However, although it provides a market to some for their yarn, opportunities for becoming involved are limited, as previously outlined. Educational facilities are available close at hand, but a number of young women in Hikkaduwa leave school early and lapse back into illiteracy. In this location the problems of landlessness and caste differences are also particularly acute.

The situation in Dodanduwa is slightly different. The community here is more homogeneous and has not been exposed to, and disillusioned by, too many aid projects. The educational level in this location is also higher than that in Hikkaduwa: only a few adult women are unable to read and write. However, in contrast to Kalupe, coir workers in Dodanduwa do not engage in yarn making throughout the year, and the varieties they manufacture are limited to two or three. This restriction has created in them a certain inflexibility and a resistance to attempt the manufacture of better-quality yard which could fetch higher prices. The trading situation also differs, as women workers in Dodanduwa are in the grip of two powerful traders who appear to control all stages of the village industry, from husks to markets.

Although the Dodanduwa women continued to be isolated from each other, after some discussion and awareness creation they were not averse to trying out a new approach to their work. One of the collective activities they already undertook was a form of informal forced saving, or *seettu*, in which they each put by some money regularly and took turns to receive a lump sum which could be used for more substantial activity.

265

Strategies of women workers

This section attempts to identify and differentiate the progress in strategy formulation articulated in practice by three different categories of coir workers:

○ Unorganized vulnerable women workers functioning as isolated individuals.
○ Organized groups working in a location-specific institutionalized mode.
○ The organized informal group, bound together by a commonly accepted programme of action to which all the women are committed.

The common practices adopted by traders, as outlined earlier, indicate the nature of the problems faced by all women in the coir industry. Specific examples of the categories of workers described above are, first, women in the two village locations before the start of any project activity; second, those associated with the Kalupe Coir Centre; and, third, women at one of the sites of the coir project initiated by Siyath Foundation.

Unorganized workers

In response to the traders' sharp practices, even very vulnerable single workers have developed counter-strategies of their own. When one considers these strategies one wonders about the obvious ignorance inherent in faraway planners' preconception that the poor are not capable of finding creative solutions to their problems. The 'tactics' of the poorest coir workers are as follows:

○ They steal husks where possible from the traders' pits.
○ They pick up others' husks which float away from the pits when there is flooding.
○ With fibre obtained on credit they manage to keep back some to sell as yarn (for cash) to another trader.
○ They reduce the quality of yarn until the trader increases the price.
○ They sell yarn with a little waste, saving time by not cleaning the fibre well.
○ They mix dark yarn with white, packing the off-colour skeins in the middle of the bundle.
○ They wet the yarn or mix it with sand when selling is being done by weight.
○ They shorten the length of each skein slightly. When this is done for a number of strands, the total length can be considerably reduced.
○ They make the twist slightly looser so that time, labour and fibre may be saved.
○ When they have to sell yarn that does not strictly meet the criteria of the trader, they take it to him at night so he cannot easily see the blemishes.

266

○ They sell yarn of different varieties at different prices, in order to use as much of the fibre as they can.

Organized institutionalized workers
Women at Kalupe also attempt to increase their profits by using tactics against the yarn and chain makers, their own organization and traders in the following ways:

○ They make the yarn chains required for mat-making loose, so that sewing is easier but the mat loses its stiffness.
○ They put brown yarn in the middle of the mat where it cannot easily be noticed.
○ They use cheap dye which may fade quickly.
○ They estimate their labour time for each mat higher than it actually is, so the price of the mat rises, making is unsaleable.
○ They attempt to get paid each fortnight for the mats which are still unfinished on their boards.
○ The lazier but more vocal members pressure others at meetings to share profits, not according to the number of mats manufactured, but equally among all workers.
○ They use their knowledge on rupee devaluation and profits that can be made from selling abroad to argue with the export traders to whom they supply mats.
○ They have acquired competence in pricing, including estimates for administration and related costs, and can use convincing reasons to justify their pricing mechanism.
○ Originally they attempted to make claims for credit to buy yarn, trying to manœuvre their own organization into a position of 'enlightened matronage'.

Organized informal group
Based on the strength of the methods already used by women as creative solutions to their problems, the following strategies were developed by means of extensive two-way dialogue between change agents from Siyath and women in a village in Dodanduwa:

○ The women built organizational mechanisms and support systems in which they had confidence, over which they had control, and which they could use to gain their own ends.
○ They began with activities which they could undertake with their own resources, and which they felt could be implemented with success. This success helped to give them self-confidence so that they could go on more sophisticated projects.

267

○ Then began the process of conceiving ideas for further development, and planning, implementing and managing them as practical actions.
○ Later still they began to make claims, bargain and demand resources available from the social system (for example, extension services, credit and infrastructure facilities and training).
○ Side-effects that came from these successful and diverse activities were to increase the number of group members and lead to ideas being shared with other groups.

The above broad strategies were broken up into a step-by-step sequence, not decided upon at the start but evolving gradually out of the regular discussions undertaken by the group as time went on. The sequence began with specially trained facilitators, committed to support the workers with empathy, entered the village without any authoritative external influence and lived among the poor until they were accepted as individuals in whom the poor could place their confidence. Many days were spent by these facilitators in informal discussion with each poor woman about her own condition in life. After a general understanding of the contradictions in their socio-economic environment was achieved by this means, the poor women realized their common predicament and, through the sensitive mediation of facilitators, decided to meet informally in small groups to discuss their difficulties together.

These groups of a few members from neighbourhood families them-selves identified their common need (for example, indebtedness); they were never defined for them by the facilitators. Then only the groups decided to take some collective action, however small it might be to start with. The groups also decided to keep their numbers low, so that all could voice their opinions, to meet every week, and to avoid formal structures. It was agreed that informality was essential to promote openness and self-confidence, to enable everyone to contribute towards common decision-making, and to aid creative thinking. From the beginning, groups decided to develop their own rules. The facilitators supported these views and helped members to articulate them by asking encouraging questions. The women also decided that responsibilities associated with the functioning of group and related activities would be borne in rotation by each of them. This was because they wished to avoid the likelihood of individuals seeking to exercise power over their peers.

Their first collective action was to devise a practical method for accu-mulating savings by contributing weekly to a fund, the amount being decided by themselves. Each week's collection was distributed among those members who needed loans for investment. Other practical collec-tive actions (for example, buying husks or fibre and selling yarn together) were undertaken gradually, as the group's resources grew over time. Problems in group functioning were tackled as they arose, by forming (through discussion and consensus) fresh rules which were enforced by social pressure among members. Problems and solutions which worked or failed were analysed meticulously and in depth by all members together at the regular weekly meetings, and conflicts were resolved by consensus, thus helping to forge and strengthen the sense of group cohesion.

The facilitators too came together regularly to analyse their roles, in order to help themselves to remain 'democratic mediators' and not 'autocratic do-gooders'. As time went on and the number of groups multiplied, facilitators found it difficult to attend all weekly meetings. At this stage the groups, on the basis of criteria they themselves identified, selected some among their members to be 'intermediary change agents' who could gradually take on some of the responsibilities of attending and mediating at meetings, keeping general records relevant to all groups, and so on.

Once group funds were sufficiently large, the women devised rules for lending money to members with very low interest rates. (Repayment remains very high even after 18 months of action.) At this stage the individual groups formed a larger collective in which elected representatives from each met regularly, and a collective fund was also established. In each location this fund lends to a group which then provides individual loans to members, based on the rules which it has devised. The larger collective fund was thereafter deposited in a bank, partly as a savings fund and partly as an account from which money could be withdrawn to lend to the groups. With the greater sophistication in handling funds acquired over time, it is now the collective which either supplies husks or fibre or gives loans for their purchase.

The women learnt to travel to other towns—even to the capital city—to find more lucrative markets for the large supply of yarn the collective was now buying from members. At this time groups also started buying at a slightly lower rate from non-members. Similarly, women ventured out to other areas to buy fibre at lower prices to supply to members, always seeking the best bargains available.

The need to record group decisions and minutes of meetings, in rotation by as many members as possible has encouraged women to increase their literacy levels. Some who could not write at all at the beginning, with others' help become literate in this way. On an *ad hoc* basis, assignments were sometimes given by the group to one of the members to make inquiries about certain business matters. Groups then demanded better access to information and looked for possibilities for meeting organizations of other groups, working with similar participatory approaches, in order to learn and share experiences. During the period of conflict in southern Sri Lanka (1989) when many village activities came to a standstill, the women planned (through the change agents) and succeeded in sustaining their activities, although the agents could not function in such close co-operation as they had done previously.

269

After they had learnt the discipline of regular repayment of loans, groups requested and were offered substantial funds—partly loan and partly grant—to augment their savings in the bank, so that they now operate a regular revolving fund. They have also purchased a building for holding meetings of the collective, storing fibre and yarn, etc. The women are fully aware that Siyath's aim is to move out as soon as the collective is able to carry out all its functions independently, and are now strengthening the capacities of their own change agents to take over the responsibility of running it. (They are planning for a future in which, with their own funds, they will be able to compensate change agents who are yarn makers for loss of work during the time they spend on administration of the collective.) Hence the groups are laying the groundwork for the self-sustenance of the collective, and planning actively and hopefully for this new phase in their operation.

There were other economic benefits not so easily quantifiable. First the members who, before the group started, had been making only one or two varieties of yarn using unclean fibre are now more particular to grade the fibre and make about six different qualities of yarn. By this means they are able to sell it at a higher price. Second, before the collectives began the village had only about 30 spinning sets. Now most of the workers (63 women) own their own spinning sets. Third, the amount of yarn produced by members varies greatly. While one makes about 280kg monthly and earns a profit of between Rs1200 and Rs1500, another who has a sick baby and is unable to devote so much time to coir work can make only about 5kg per month, earning just Rs50 profit. The great flexibility, sympathy and understanding the group has developed is indicated by the possibility of such a woman being accommodated as a member. Fourth, women have learnt to compare the profits from different kinds of yarn using cost factors such as the quantity of raw materials, the quality of the product and time spent in production. Finally, by selling to the export trader they have learnt about the advantage of the bonus given if yarn is sold in bulk. This was new knowledge to them.

Women's self-perceptions

The facilitator and Dodanduwa group members who discussed this aspect together came up with the following as advantages they gained through being in the collective. Although these are intangible feelings not measurable in concrete terms, the joy they showed in identifying the benefits in a collective discussion was proof enough of their sincerity. The feeling of togetherness and sense of belonging have helped them as poor women to overcome their isolation and antagonism towards each other. They see that this has grown out of the realization that they themselves—rather than others who exploited their labour—could enjoy all the benefits of their own efforts. The open discussions at meetings and the collective thinking they

270

can generate has given each of them the self-confidence to say 'I, can do this or that activity for our collective'.

Since this collective activity began, six other societies have been formed in the village. These societies have conventional patterns of work and hierarchies with office holders. Members of the coir collective who also attend these meetings are now used to giving open criticism of all activities they see as not beneficial to the larger group. They say that 'our collective does not need those hierarchies as we know what is best for us'. They also state that through the experience they have gained of argument and counter-argument they are able now to hold their own when in conflict with the office holders. Hence the women's participation even in other societies has grown and the contribution they make in them is very evident. They have realized the value of getting organized together for the common good of all. They say 'It is we, the poor, who can see our problems and all their ramifications', and 'it is attempts like ours that help and enable the villagers to recognize the human potential of the village and to use it collectively and well'.

Management experience has been gained through the practical experience of rotating responsibility for funds, keeping records, using money wisely and repaying loans. Women now use this experience in the management of their own personal funds. Writing ability has been developed through their need to keep records in turn. Women have also learned to deal with government officials and offices. Those who used to go to the traditional village élite for help in filling out forms and undertaking formal transactions can now either carry out such activities on their own or seek help from a fellow member.

The women analyse how one of them has improved herself through this industry. They discuss how they may learn lessons from her wise decisions. They also look at others' actions critically. Speaking of the actions of a treasurer in another society they say 'it is we who gave him that office, so we have a right to question his actions'. Self-criticism and humility are other traits they have developed. In describing this they say 'how can we criticize others if we don't look our own shortcomings in the face?'

About collective activity they said:

o The idea of 'I and me' gets pushed to the background.
o We gained strength to bargain with the trader.
o The money we collected together gave us a sense of pride.
o We can sell this large stock of yarn now because we did it together. If we had not done so, we would still be in debt to the trader.
o Now we have a place of our own and this happened because we got together.

There is now more evidence of co-operative activity in situations where fellow group members need help. Now women voluntarily offer to assist at

271

occasions like weddings and funerals in other members' houses, whereas before, if they did so, it was done reluctantly and only through a feeling of obligation. They now even mediate in their neighbours' problems. One member said 'although it is not my problem, I helped to solve it because they are all our people. Tomorrow I may have a similar problem. Then I know I am not alone, that my colleagues will support me.'

In household work, too, order and organized methods of work have been introduced. Economic use of money, winning a sense of respect from family members—even husbands—and contributions to decision-making are other advantages they have gained. One husband's earlier comment was 'if I bring money into the house with my occupation, why does my wife need to beat husks? Why can't she do the housework and be satisfied?'. Now he says 'when I cannot earn any money, it is my wife who feeds us'. The wife says 'I will try to work harder and save my husband from undertaking such a dangerous job, going far out to sea to catch fish. I will feed him and my children.'

The facilitator stated that at the beginning when she first went round the village talking with yarn makers, they used to say 'we do this to earn a few rupees from day to day. What real profit do we have?' Now the same women say 'if we do this industriously it is as good as a government job. Now it is rare that we don't have some money in hand and we are able to put away some savings.'

A few young girls from coir group families have volunteered to help in improving the health status of the village. They have been trained to help in health clinics, and hope to start a programme to bring health awareness to the members of the collective. Since the women are now able to handle outside aid, they will seek government resources for upgrading the village latrines. Most revealingly, there are also some boys who are now working in the coir industry, which was never a man's occupation before the collective started.

The women are now realizing the importance of the need for a larger but loose management structure to support them as their organization grows.

Comparison between village organizations

It is obvious from the above description of women in the coir project, and earlier discussions of other organizations and government departments involved with rural coir workers, that many different attempts have been made to assist them, with varying results. Although the more formal approaches of the government and some NGOs may seem to have been more successful initially, particularly in terms of logistic and economic benefits to women workers, other factors cast doubt on their longer term 'appropriateness' and sustainability.

The introduction of mechanization of coir production is an example of the type of intervention which often worsens women's plight. Problems associated with mechanization itself are capital cost, the resources needed for full utilization, and the knowledge required for its correct use and maintenance. In addition, it usually leads to men taking over the production process, direct displacement of women's labour, and their becoming even further removed from project management. For example, the crusher at Talalla could be put to use profitably only by the formation of a limited company, which precludes any participation in decision-making by workers who cannot afford to buy shares, namely, the majority. This is not to say that mechanization is always damaging to women, as it could potentially relieve them of some of the most unpleasant and difficult tasks in coir processing, but it needs to be introduced with care and a special commitment to safeguard their interests.

The formal and large NGO projects described earlier show little potential for flexibility to react to new problems and changing circumstances. In addition, few were planned with a view to self-sustenance, which makes them dependent on regular external support and vitiates the purpose of encouraging women to manage their own affairs. More particularly, when the project withdraws—for whatever reason—coir workers are left just as badly, if not worse, off than before.

In contrast to larger-scale attempts, the coir project began by involving local women in articulating their problems and needs, and helping them to see how they could meet these themselves. This 'conscientization' process, which came about through the change agents' efforts, seems to have been successful in the sense that women were fully aware of the nature of the situation of exploitation in which they found themselves, and determined to tackle it. Such determination and a newly created sense of belonging to a group were shown, among other activities, in the preparedness of members to contribute to common savings and credit funds. Even though the amounts involved may seem small to an outside observer, the contributions were meaningful for women living on the absolute minimum, and the funds provided an economic security which was highly valued by members. Siyath's approach ensured that, from very small beginnings, its groups have built up a whole spiral of self-supporting effort and the ability to tackle further problems as they arise. In addition the organization includes the capacity to embrace error. Commitment is to action rather than capital investment, and rotation of responsibilities means there is less likelihood of individuals seeking to exercise power over their fellow workers. However in terms of the numbers of groups and members, the size of the project is still small. This is probably mainly due to the relatively long time taken over group formation, inherent in Siyath's approach of stimulating the self-development of individual members, and groups themselves, through facilitators in a common learning process. In this phase, difficulties relating to family circumstances in particular can

273

greatly hamper women's participation in activities, and need to be over-come. Self-confidence and skills must also be built up.

Compared to more formal projects, progress has also been slower on the economic side, and marketing and product development have so far not received much attention. Siyath feels that the slow and careful formation of its groups is to be preferred over the quick establishment of those with solely material incentives, although facilitators have been confronted with the problem that other projects come into its areas offering direct material benefits, and in one location this did cause their groups to fold. However, the remaining coir project groups now exhibit considerable potential to expand their activities, and this expansion will be carried out and managed by the members themselves, as Siyath plans shortly to withdraw and go on to repeat the process elsewhere.

Food processing in Sri Lanka

PADMINI ABEYWARDENE

Optimism about the potential of food processing in Sri Lanka is based on the seasonal over-abundance of indigenous fruits and vegetables which are only marginally used. A fair portion of the produce perishes where it was grown, unable to fulfil the food and nutrition needs of poorer groups in the country. At least 55–60 per cent annual wastage has been reported, due to losses caused by various factors along the post-harvest chain, and while producer prices fall very low during periods of glut, urban consumers pay exorbitant prices in city markets.

Food-processing gains are vital in a country as poor as Sri Lanka, where they are battling with a growing problem of under-nutrition. This has particularly serious consequences for the health of the most vulnerable groups in the population. Compared with the 1980–82 figures, the 1987 Nutrition Surveys showed a marked increase in chronic under-nutrition among children in the age group 6–35 months, and data indicate the progression of this condition into the pre-school and school years. Recent emphasis on the second growth spurt in adolescence and the consequent focus on the nutrition needs of the 'girl child', prompted by her potential as a guarantee against malnutrition in the next generation, underlines the urgency of developing appropriate measures to reverse this situation. Analysis of the nutritional problems involved indicates a primary calorie shortfall in food intake rather than one of protein inadequacy as, in an overall situation of calorie deficiency, the protein intake is first used to fulfil the energy requirements of the individual.

Problems of food inadequacies contributing to under-nutrition have been further aggravated by the increased strain placed on the poor, and on women in particular, by the decline in 'real income' following the structural adjustments implemented in the country, and more recently less aid around in general.

PADMINI ABEYWARDENE is a social scientist who works on a freelance basis with the Centre for Women's Research in Sri Lanka.

275

The jak *tree is indigenous to Sri Lanka; its fruit is popular among rural people*

The waste of available produce in a situation of food insecurity underscores the urgency for greater concern in refining the low-cost processing technologies traditionally used by rural women, in order to contribute to optimum use of energy-rich garden produce, and at the same time to stimulate agricultural production in the relevant lines, for the possible end effect of improving the quality of life for the country's poor.

Women and food processing

In Sri Lanka as in the rest of the world, the area of food processing is traditionally associated with women's sphere of interest, and thus is subjected to overt gender discrimination in relation to aspects of technological innovation in the production processes. Apart from the few male-managed large firms using modern production technologies which have recently entered the food-processing scene, and the fewer instances of urban women with education and capital emerging as entrepreneurs in the relevant field, the efforts of the vast majority of rural and urban women engaged in food-processing activities in the informal sector are largely invisible—despite their crucial contribution to both the household and national economy. Their invisibility appears to be an extension of the concept of dichotomy in gender roles and the traditional over-emphasis of the maternal role of women, to the exclusion of the multi-disciplinary tasks that poor women in particular perform every day. A consequence of this is the failure, both by society and women themselves, to recognize their contribution to economic productivity, and instead to view such tasks as an extension of women's 'housewifely' obligations.

The objectives and scope of the case study

The main objective of this study was to attempt to analyse in depth the innovative technologies of rural women, with the major focus on the poor. Specifically, the study sought to:

o assess rural women's participation in both 'hardware' and 'software' technology processes in relation to the selected line of study, namely the sun-drying of *jak* and breadfruit;
o identify the innovative skills of rural women, and assess their awareness of technological processes and their application of decision-making capabilities in the choice of technology in sun-drying of the selected products;
o identify constraints to innovation by, and participation of, women in development efforts; and
o make recommendations for including women as full and equal partners in the process of development.

In view of the different culinary traditions visible among the three principal ethnic groups in Sri Lanka—Sinhalese, Tamils and Muslims—the study attempted to obtain ethnic group-specific information in relation to the lines of enquiry, and to observe cross-cultural links which influence the adoption of technology by women. Within the sample of Sinhala women, an attempt was also made to observe variation in practices between the two main sub-groups—the low-country and up-country populations.

277

This study on women's innovative technologies is made in relation to the processing of two garden crops which are commonly found in most parts of Sri Lanka, namely *Artocarpus heterophyllis*, known as *jak*; *Kos* (Sinhala); or *Pelaka*, (Tamil) and *Artocarpus communis*, known as breadfruit (English) (*Del*, Sinhala; *Eeri Pelaaka*, Tamil). The extent of cultivation of the two products in the dry zone, and their nutritional values, are given in Tables 1 and 2.

The *jak* tree is indigenous to Sri Lanka and grows in most parts of the country. Its fruit is used for food, the bark for timber, leaves for animal food and the dead wood for fuel. Average tree height is approximately 25 feet, with trees bearing fruit in about the third year. Most trees bear fruit once a year, generally during the *Yala* season (May to September), although a few bear during the *Maha* season (October to April), and

Table 1. The extent of cultivation of *jak* and breadfruit in the dry zone (ha.)

Year	Jak fruit	Breadfruit
1980	10 099	2 523
1981	17 190	4 980
1982	17 180	5 000
1983	17 700	4 980
1984	16 750	4 890

Source: Department of Statistics, Agricultural Information Division.

Table 2. Food composition of *jak* and breadfruit (per 100g produce, raw weight)

Nutrients	Measure	Jak *bulbs*	Jak *seeds*	Breadfruit
Energy	kC	51	151	113
Protein	g	2.6	4.3	1.5
Fat	g	0.3	0.4	1.5
Carbohydrate	g	9.4	32.6	26.0
Calcium	mg	30.0	35.0	25.0
Phosphorous	mg	40.0	126.0	Nil
Iron	mg	1.7	1.2	1.0
Vitamin A	μg	Nil	Nil	Nil
Carotene	μg	Nil	25.0	Nil
Thiamin	μg	50.0	180.0	100.0
Riboflavin	μg	40.0	50.0	60.0
Niacin	mg	0.2	0.5	1.2
Vitamin C	mg	14.0	17.5	20.0
Moisture	g	84.0	70.0	60.9

Source: Food composition tables, Medical Institute, Sri Lanka.
Note: The calorie content of 100g of produce dry weight would be considerably higher due to the reduction in moisture content.

some at both times of year. There is also a shorter hybrid variety, which starts bearing fruit at 18 months and has a year-round crop.

Harvesting the fruit is usually carried out by men who climb the trees, although fruit available at a lower height is plucked by women using long poles. *Jak* has traditionally been a popular food among the rural people, consumed directly as a cooked food, ripe as a fruit and in a variety of preparations in its processed form. Consumption of this fruit was widely popularized during the war-time food scarcity by a Sri Lankan philanthropist, affectionately called '*kos mamaa*' (*jak* uncle), who distributed improved varieties of plants throughout the country.

Although not indigenous, breadfruit is grown in most parts of Sri Lanka, the extent cultivated being lesser than that for *jak* (estimated at approximately a quarter of the area). Tree height is approximately 15–20 feet. Breadfruit has a highly seasonal availability, more so than *jak*.

As in the case of *jak*, plucking is mainly undertaken by men climbing trees and occasionally by women with the aid of long poles. Popular among rural families of all income levels, and the urban middle class and the poor, the fruit is directly consumed in a cooked form or cooked after processing by sun-drying.

Organizations involved in processing

In addition to direct consumption, processing of *jak* and breadfruit into secondary products by sun-drying has traditionally been performed by women at household level. Extension agencies such as the Farm Women's Extension Programme of the Department of Agriculture, and non-governmental agencies, such as Lanka Mahila Samithi, have shown an interest in the dissemination of improved methods of processing. Most recently a few industrial firms have started processing these products through canning. In addition, research and development institutions, such as the Industrial Development Board and the Ceylon Institute for Scientific and Industrial Research, have developed a variety of processing technologies for these products, one of which is sun-drying—the technique used universally by rural women in Sri Lanka.

Criteria identified for the selection of districts and locations for study were: one, the availability of *jak* and breadfruit in home gardens, in common lands or in government reservation land near people's dwellings; and two, the residence of families representing the principal ethnic groups selected for study.

The limits on communication imposed by the relative inaccessibility of the traditional Tamil areas due to the civil unrest, and the difficulty of locating an adequate sample of indigenous Tamil families in an environment that satisfied the first criterion above, necessitated the selection of families currently residing in a suburb of the capital city, but who had

279

originally practised processing of the selected produce in their previous homes.

Selection of, and access to, sample women

A sample of 80 women, the most senior in the family, was selected on the basis of one per family from five locations: four in the two districts of Kalutara and Kandy and one in Colombo District. Within this sample there were 20 each from the Tamil and Muslim ethnic groups and 40 from the Sinhala group—20 from the low-country and 20 from the up-country locations.

The Muslims were selected from a predominantly Muslim pocket of residence in Kalutara District. However, half the number of Tamils in the sample were selected from among plantation workers in Kandy District and half from among those who had had processing experience in their traditional rural areas, but were actually residing in a suburb of Colombo.

Access to rural women was made through non-government organizations (NGOs) working at grassroots level. Sarvodaya, a leading secondary NGO in Sri Lanka, provided the necessary contacts for identifying eligible women for the sample in Kalutara District. The initial group meetings with the rural women, with back-up support from the NGO, provided an opportunity to discuss the subject of the study in relation to its central themes. These groups then participated in the selection of eligible women and the most suitable sun locations for the study. Final selections were made at the second-round meetings on the basis of lists compiled by the women themselves, in consultation with the pre-school teachers who were also social mobilizers for Sarvodaya.

In Kandy District the approach was through a grassroots-level NGO, Anthodaya, which as the name suggests was in the service of the 'poorest of the poor'. Discussions with the NGO's steering committee and women's programme workers once again paved the way for a village-level meeting and selection of families for interview, together with the assistance of girls from the village who accompanied the researcher and her assistant to the homes of interviewees.

Access to the plantation women in the sample proved difficult, despite the introductions and contact made through the good offices of a tea nursery holder living in the vicinity, himself an ethnic Tamil. Apart from a Sinhalese line room resident who was from a neighbouring village and who worked on the estate as a tea picker, the Tamil estate women were diffident about providing any information, compelling the researchers to attempt the interview at two other sets of line rooms. It was only at the third line room that a satisfactory response was obtained in terms of demonstrating a 'readiness' to discuss—and here it was the men who participated in the discussions, even competing among themselves to provide information.[1]

The Tamil group from Colombo District was reached through the Women's Education Centre of Colombo.

Link people identified for interview were:

○ Traders dealing with the product in the main vegetable market in the city and those operating in suburban farms.
○ Collecting agents and suppliers to the canning factory dealing with the product.
○ Women in households supplying fruit to the collecting agent.
○ Research and development institutions working on food-processing technology in the selected product lines.

Instruments of enquiry

Informal dialogue, with emphasis on participant interaction and observation, was the principal mode of enquiry used for the study, and to facilitate this an open-ended, semi-structured questionnaire was developed. It indicated the main areas in which information was sought, and was conceived not as a primary tool of investigation, but for its value as a useful 'support' and reference point around which the dialogue could centre.

Wherever possible, the intention was to conduct discussions in the homes of participant women to enable observation of food-processing-related activities, the socio-economic environment, and household relationships in the families selected for study. In conducting discussions in their homes, the researcher and her assistant were often accompanied by a few of the participating women themselves. This appeared to contribute to the relaxed informality which the dialogue assumed, the credibility of the information obtained, and an awareness of their role and contribution to the household economy by the women.

Socio-economic background of the women processors

In the sample of women interviewed, with the exception of the single case of an 18-year-old girl who was the most senior woman in the household (since her mother had gone to the Middle East for employment), 48 per cent were in the age group 50–69 years, 28 per cent between 30 and 45 years and 24 per cent in the over-70 age group.

In relation to educational achievement, 21 per cent of the participants had no schooling, 37 per cent had educational levels between grades 1 and

---

[1] The researcher recognizes that the perceptions of the male Tamils interviewed may differ from those which would have been held by the women on the tea estate.

281

3, 15 per cent between grades 4 and 6, 10 per cent between grades 7 and 8, and 15 per cent had studied in grade 10 and above.

Family income levels of participants showed 45 per cent in the food stamp category, and hence below the official poverty line. About 21 per cent, although not on food stamps, appeared to be well below the poverty line, judging from the employment pattern of the subjects, as well as that of their husbands or grown-up children who were employed as casual labour in the nearby plantations or in their own or neighbouring villages, hence making their source of income both irregular and inadequate. The estate Tamil families too fell below the official poverty line, in spite of their assured minimum wages; however, their quality of life appeared to be equal to, or even beneath that of the rural poor.

There was also a small percentage (6 per cent) of middle-class families in the village sample. This had a teacher, a bus driver and a petty trader in the household. An even smaller percentage (3 per cent) of high-income group families were suggested for inclusion by village support groups, in view of their active involvement in food-processing activity. The urban Tamil families in the sample (12 per cent) were distinctly élitist, enjoying high levels of income and education. Belonging to an ethnic group accepted as being traditionally industrious and thrifty, the women in this group had much experience to offer and at the same time were able to express with greater clarity the intricacies of their knowledge.

Link people and their role

Small traders
The three small traders (in processed *jak* and breadfruit) with whom discussion was held at two suburban fairs were rural women between the ages of 58 and 64. They were mothers or grandmothers in their households and lived with either a married son or daughter. Thus they were not the main earners in their households but were engaged in this activity, according to them, to contribute to household expenditure.

These small traders at suburban fairs sold processed *jak* and breadfruit with an assortment of garden produce, such as lime fruit, leafy vegetables, papaya, betel and even curd. Their scale of operation was essentially small, yet catered to the needs of unsophisticated customers and earned a small profit for them. They collected the surplus from households in their villages and sold it, along with whatever produce they had of their own, playing almost a 'middleman role' yet without 'middleman profits'. One of the women mentioned that the scope for this activity was becoming increasingly limited: 'times are hard . . . less fruit is available for processing as there is a big demand for fruit for direct consumption, and whatever processed fruit there is is barely sufficient for subsistence needs, leaving little for sale'.

Retailers in the capital city

Of the two retail traders interviewed, one was a 53-year-old woman and the other a man of 36. Both had stalls in the busy vegetable market. As in the case of the small traders, processed *jak* and breadfruit were only two of the products they dealt with. They also sold processed cassava, pulses and fresh fruit.

Retailers' supplies of *jak* and breadfruit were obtained from distant places in lorries which brought other types of rural produce to the market. The produce was collected from rural fairs and village homes, and was delivered to the retailers once a week or sometimes once a fortnight. The quantity of *jak* and breadfruit was small—usually one or two sacks, each weighing approximately 40–45kg. There was a considerable gap between purchase prices and sale price, giving these traders a fair margin of profit. However, the scale of operations was limited and did not appear to provide much income opportunity for rural women.

Commercial processing

Supply of *jak* and breadfruit for commercial processing centred around the collecting agent, who obtained the raw and immature fruits required for the purpose from rural areas on immediate cash payment. Plucking of young fruit correspondingly reduced the quantity available for direct consumption or processing; however, the availability of ready cash was too attractive an offer to be rejected by the households living in such poverty.

Discussion with women in supplier households indicated that the older women were conscious of the adverse effects of this practice on the food availability at household level. They were thrifty by nature and stated that they disliked destroying the young, be it man or nature. To the young women interviewed it did not matter—immediate cash was useful in buying necessities, and money coming from the sale of fruits helped them to some extent. 'There were still fruits around,' they said, as 'the even slightly over-mature ones were rejected.' Besides, these young mothers themselves engaged in casual labour and did not have much time for processing work.

In both *jak* and breadfruit it is the mature fruits which are selected for processing. The preliminary stage of cutting the *jak* fruit was commonly done using an axe or a long-handled *manna* knife. The fruit was most often cut into four portions for easier handling, the centre core chopped off and the seeds and flesh, known as 'bulbs' (*madulu*, Sinhala) separated. Usually recognized as women's work, the study showed many instances where husbands and sons assisted the women in this activity; in fact men in the estate-sector Tamil population performed it more often, as women worked more hours than they did in the plantations and hence were away from home for a considerably longer period.

Jak bulbs are sun-dried either boiled (blanched) or unboiled. It is important to note that no washing is done at any stage in processing, as it is accepted that exposure to increased moisture by washing in water would have negative effects on sun-drying.

Sun-drying of boiled jak bulbs

Slicing: The two main methods used were slicing lengthways or crossways. However, within these was considerable variation in detail. Slicing lengthways was done using the knife, when the bulb was often cut into two almost mechanically. Alternatively it was torn lengthways with the fingers which, the women said, minimized shrivelling during drying. With this method more variation was possible, bulbs being torn into three, four or six pieces depending on their size.

In addition to the practices families were used to and those which they learned from others, there were instances of innovative efforts which indicate a conscious choice of technology. The women made it clear that fruit which was considered too mature had necessarily to be sliced crossways, as it would facilitate quick drying—a critical factor in handling over-mature bulbs which are more liable to spoilage if drying is delayed. They said that if such bulbs did not dry well they emitted an obnoxious smell (*pilunu*, Sinhala) and promoted fungus growth (*pus*), making the product unfit for consumption. There were other women, particularly from the Tamil urban sample, who as a general practice had adopted fine slicing, crossways.

Blanching: Immersing the cut produce in boiling water for a 'short time' was a practice adopted by most of the women interviewed. As for the preferred quantity of water in the clay pots used for this purpose, some stated that a 'correct' amount would be to have the water approximately five inches above the level of the raw material placed inside the pot. This was certainly a tricky assessment in view of the several variables, such as the size and shape of the pot, in a situation where no measurement was possible. Unlike the case of boiling rice where the widely adopted 'finger measurement' could be used as the testing is done in cold water, when blanching such a measurement was impractical as the raw material had to be added to already boiling water. It was clear that it was the women's experience, based on observation and practice, that guided their judgement in relation to such fine measures of quantity which were of direct relevance to the quality of the finished product. Women were quite confident that, for blanching, the water should be at boiling point at the time the raw material was put in; the expression often used was *bibulu enakan natanna ona*, or 'bubbling hot water'.

284

Optimum time for blanching varied between three and six minutes. In this response the women attempted to relate a proven activity to precision in time—an exercise totally alien to rural women using their traditional knowledge and innovative strategies in the very much kitchen-related exercise of food processing. A distinction was made between the time taken for fruits of 'correct' maturity and those which were 'even slightly' over-mature; the latter type, they maintained, should take less time in blanching than the former. A further distinction made was between fruit which was 'more starchy' than others—in addition to being able to distinguish between 'more' and 'less' starchy fruits when they were cut, women appeared to have identified the trees in their garden and neighbourhood as those bearing more and less starchy fruit. Their conclusion was that bulbs from more starchy *jak* fruits required less time for blanching.

Being totally dependent on the faculties of sense, it is probable that there were slightly more than marginal variations in the application of such indefinite assessments. There were instances where women mentioned that the processed *jak* developed *pus* or mildew, and this they attributed to some error in handling on their part. Accuracy in blanching, which they called 'boiling slightly' or *yantham thambanawa*, was critical to the processing, as over-boiling at this stage made the product susceptible to attack by weevils (*gullas*, Sinhala) and could not be corrected by increased emphasis on the drying procedure.

There was also evidence of experimentation and innovative effort in this area by some women. They had found that steaming was an improvement over blanching, as there was no direct contact with water (almost taboo in household-level sun-drying, as water was recognized as an agent which influenced the moisture content), and it gave more control in achieving the desired state of 'readiness' in the product.

Use of salt: Another factor in the blanching stage was the inclusion or omission of salt. This was an area of controversy, with apparently contradictory reasons put forward by the women for either method. In addition to its taste value, salt was used by some as a preservative against insects or spoiling, while others thought that its addition would make the product soggy and hence encourage mildew. The practice of using salt was seen to be more common among those in the urban Tamil sample, although there were a few among the other ethnic groups who also added it. The Tamil group also added salt to increase the thickness of the slices, otherwise said to be 'paper thin' when dried. In addition to salt the group added some saffron to the boiling water, both for reason of colour and as a protection against attack from insects.

Draining: Slight variation was seen in the methods used by the women interviewed. There were some who took the raw material out of the pot with an aluminium perforated ladle and put it into a *kirigotta*, which was a large strainer made out of local reed. Some turned out the contents with the water into the *kirigotta*, allowing the water to drain out through it. Others covered the mouth of the pot with a *nebiliya* (lid), drained off the water into a container and placed the pot covered with *nebiliya* back over a very low flame, allowing any remaining water to evaporate.

Although each method and the equipment used varied slightly from the others, they all focused on the achievement of a single requirement, namely the removal of water and subsequent reduction of the moisture content as much as was possible. Another factor in the strategies was that those who had adopted the practice of turning out all the contents at once on to the *kirigotta* thought that this helped to ensure greater uniformity in product texture.

Sun-drying: Drying was done on a variety of surfaces, depending on the resources available. Those who had rocks with flat surfaces in their neighbourhood used these for drying. According to them this yielded the best results, provided they had adequate sunlight, as they knew that heated rocks maintained their heat over a greater length of time. In this way prepared produce was spread evenly directly on the rock.

Spreading the produce on reed mats was the more common practice. In addition, dried woven coconut branches, *palmyra* leaves (in Jaffna), sacks made of jute, zinc sheets (if they were not rusty) or whatever was available was used by the women for this purpose. An additional contraption used in Jaffna District for drying was a low table (*pandal*). An advantage visible to the women in this method was the hygienic aspect of keeping the produce on a raised surface; in scientific terms it may also have offered greater scope for air flow, a vital factor in moisture control. Protection from crows attacking the produce was attempted by most women by keeping a mirror on an opened-out black umbrella, which it was believed would scare the crows away.

A slight difference noted was that some of the women held the view that, after the water was drained out, the product had to be kept aside for a while for slight cooling, prior to taking it out for drying in the hot sun. Women in all groups believed that to obtain the best results in drying, it was necessary to *atha gaanna*, or run one's hand lightly over the produce, to enable gentle turning over of the pieces so that all surfaces would benefit from the direct sunlight. This appeared to be an extension of the practice adopted in the drying of paddy for hand-pounding or milling.

According to the women the time taken for drying was anyhting between two and four days, but this no doubt is subject to a whole set of variables.

Insect repellents: The sun-drying stage showed up further differences in practices adopted by women for the control of insect pests. These differences appeared to be according to ethnic group. Tamil women at times used margosa leaf as an insect repellent during sun-drying. Muslim women used lime leaves or lemon rind, which were dried together with the produce— the pungent smell, they said, drove off the insects. Some Sinhala women too had learnt to add these herbal preservatives, perhaps from their Muslim neighbours.

The test of adequate drying: Sound and colour seemed to be significant factors in assessing adequacy of drying. Rural women expressed this state of crispness as producing a 'crackling' sound, *kara-kara gaanawa*, when one's hand was run over the produce, or sounding *takas* when broken in two. Difficulty in biting on it was also a criterion used by some.

Storing and using the products: The women mentioned that these processed products could be kept in good condition for a period of approximately four to six months. This was their objective too, in terms of time, as in the context of household processing the foods were meant to be consumed in the *avare*, or off-season, when fresh fruit is unavailable.

The smoke-chamber or *duma* was of central importance, as it was there that these products would eventually be stored in an assortment of containers.[2] Simple clay pots used for everyday cooking, jute sacks, woven baskets, tins and even paper bags, were among the containers used. Some of the women spoken to substantiated their preferences for using a particular type—to some, clay pots with the mouth of the pot tied up with thick paper were superior to a tin, while to others the jute sack or the woven basket provided an opportunity for any residual moisture to escape, and for the heat and smoke from the *duma* to penetrate and help in preservation. It was also evident that the use of paper bags and tins was a fairly recent adaptation, as women mentioned that pots and woven baskets had been the containers commonly used in their traditional homes.

It was their unanimous view that processed food should not be taken out of storage for consumption until at least four weeks had elapsed, and that it should be handled hygienically, leaving no room for pollution, or *idul*, to take place. According to traditional custom, it was usually an older woman in the family—the grandmother or mother—who had the task of removing the food from the *duma*, 'but now', they said 'times have changed'.

Sun-drying of unboiled jak *bulbs*
This was a less-popular method of processing as its success was dependent on good 'sunning'; it was therefore undertaken only during dry spells of

---

[2] The *duma* is a wooden contraption built immediately above the cooking hearth, just below the smoke escape chimney. It therefore provides both heat and smoke to the products stored on it.

bright sunlight. (Lack of adequate opportunity for quick sun-drying both discolours the product and gives a bitter taste.) To speed up drying, the *jak* bulbs were cut into fine strips crossways. No salt was added, to guard against the produce becoming soggy and consequently mildewed (due to fungal growth). The drying and storing methods adopted were the same as for boiled-dried *jak* bulbs.

Correctly handled, the product should keep from three to four months—a slightly shorter period than the boiled-dried *jak* bulbs. Women from the Kandy District, who at times carried out unboiled processing, added that a few lime leaves or lemon rind were included during drying for additional protection against insect attack, to which the unboiled-dried *jak* bulbs are more susceptible.

Jak *seeds*
These are processed both boiled and unboiled, the two methods endowing the product with substantial differences in texture and flavour. It is important that only the seeds of mature or ripe fruit are used for processing.

Boiled jak *seeds*
Boiling: With the outer covering intact, seeds were boiled in a pot of water covered with a lid, often a *nebiliya*, on a high flame. The approximate duration of boiling required was indicated by some of the women as about one and a half hours. The length of time is subject to several variations, such as the type of stove used—for example, a simple three-stone fire or an energy-conserving cook-stove. A more reliable indicator used by women to determine adequacy in boiling was 'observation'. They were of unanimous opinion that the outer covering of the seed had to be very slightly cracked—not underdone, yet not 'too much', they said, or the seed would be too soft and susceptible to attack by weevils.

Use of salt: As in the case of *jak* bulbs, the study revealed differences of opinion on this matter. While some women had their own reasons for the use or non-use of salt, others maintained that they followed the traditional practice which prevailed in their ancestral homes.

Draining: This was done either by ladling the seeds out into a *kirigotta*, or by pouring the contents with the water into it. Draining all the water was critical to the sun-drying process; the women therefore often put the seeds on a mat, allowing the water to dry, and then put them out in the sun. Four or five days drying in bright sunshine is required.

The test of adequacy in drying was again the 'crackling' sound of dryness; another indicator used was difficulty in biting on the seed.

Storage: Processed *jak* seeds were stored in jute gunnies, pots, tins or paper bags which were placed on the smoke rack (*duma*). Ethnic group-related differences were visible: Muslims tended to use more tins and paper bags for storage, Tamils woven baskets or clay pots, and most of the Sinhalese pots or gunnies. When a clay pot was used, some of the Tamil women in the urban sample lined it with two or three chunks of charcoal, then added the processed product, and continued with this same order of packing in alternate layers, finishing with a layer of margosa leaves on top. After this the mouth of the pot was securely bound with thick paper and then it was placed on the *duma*. The charcoal, they maintained helped to keep the produce moisture-proof, while the margosa leaves protected it from insect attack.

Unboiled jak *seeds (*Weli-kos eta, *Sinhala)*
The central feature in this processing method was the use of sand in which the *jak* seed lay buried, to be taken out for cooking at a time of need—usually in the '*avare*', or off-season. While mature seeds were suited for this process, the women stressed the importance of keeping the seed away from water to prevent sprouting, which would counteract the qualitative change it undergoes in processing. It was explained by some that the *hilum* (*pekaniya*, a direct translation of the word umbilical cord) permits the absorption of water; hence the special care needed to keep it away. Well-managed processing, they said, yields high-quality seed with added 'flesh'.

Selection of sand and seeds: There were several views on the selection of sand. Some used a special mixture of dried river sand and anthill clay—*humbas mati*; others used common garden sand, collected and dried in the shade.

It was only the very mature seeds that were used, especially those of the ripe *jak* fruit eaten as a desert. Women and children often collected such seeds from under the trees, and they are first dried in the shade on garden sand, to prepare them for processing.

Processing: One of the following three methods was used:

○ Surface of mud floor: a dry place was selected for this purpose, often in a corner of the kitchen (leading to the popular expression *kos-eta mulla*, or *jak* seed corner). The most common method was to arrange the *jak* seed and prepared sand in alternate tiers.

Among the finer details elaborated by the women was the need to press down each layer of sand firmly to form a tight packing without allowing much air space between the layers. This, they said, was important in guarding against attack by termites and ants. An advantage of the arrangement was that it enabled the addition of seeds to the '*jak* seed corner' as and when they were available, continuing, however, to maintain the alternate layer.

In certain homes a slight variation was observed with the construction of a four- to six-inch-high mud partition, separating the *jak* seed corner from the rest of the kitchen.

○ Cavity dug in mud floor: the principle followed in this arrangement was the same as in the *jak* seed corner, with layers of prepared sand and *jak* seeds arranged in alternate fashion in a cavity dug in the kitchen floor (mud).
○ Use of containers: containers of several types—old clay pots of a large size, tins, discarded galvanized buckets and sometimes wooden boxes—were used, and seed and sand again arranged in alternate layers inside them.

A novel arrangement described by one of the women was to make these tiered arrangements in individual 'ball-like' fashion, each ball or cluster comprising about 100 *jak* seeds. An advantage was that one could take out only the required quantity of seeds without disturbing the whole arrangement.

Pericarp
This thin layer of shiny material covering the seed was dried unwashed in the sun by being placed on a mat or other available surface. Being fine in texture, drying was quick and was usually completed in one day. Not a widely adopted practice, this was seen among the Sinhala groups, both up-country and low-country.

Storage was usually in clay pots, with the mouth tied with thick paper, which were put on the kitchen smoke rack (*duma*).

Breadfruit

As in the case of *jak*, breadfruit was processed either boiled or raw, the former being the more common practice.

Preparation of the fruit
Three distinct methods were observed in the preparation of fruit for processing:

○ peeling off the outer skin with a knife;
○ scraping the outer skin with the aid of a spoon; or
○ boiling the whole fruit without scraping, and then peeling off the skin with a knife. This was a less common practice.

In all these methods, the inner spongy core was removed and not used for processing.

Sun-dried boiled

There were three variations seen in boiled sun-drying:

o the raw material was sliced fine, blanched and sun-dried;
o the whole fruit was boiled (in cold water), sliced and sun-dried;
o the fruit was cut into large chunks, blanched (in boiling water), then sliced and sun-dried.

In the blanching procedure, there were finer differences observed—some immersed the fruit in boiling water for two or three minutes, while others removed the pot of boiling water from the fire, kept it aside for approximately two minutes until the vapour escaped, and then added the sliced breadfruit to it. A critical factor in all three procedures, however, was to guard against over-boiling.

Sun-drying unboiled or raw

The procedure adopted was to slice the fruit and sun-dry it raw. Though apparently simpler than the former method, according to the women interviewed, this was more risky as:

o the sliced raw material had to be sun-dried immediately after it was sliced, to prevent the *kahata* or staining which otherwise took place;
o the slices had to dry well in bright sunshine for at least four to five days to prevent spoilage.

Gender roles

Stereotypical gender roles, as well as instances of role deviation, were evident in the performance of tasks in the field of food processing. The former portray the heavy workload borne by rural women in a dual role of performing household duties and earning income. Women in the sample claimed responsibility for the efficient functioning of the household in addition to their child-bearing and child-rearing roles. Beginning with a basic responsibility of cooking, their tasks included fetching both water and fuelwood. Some of them also contributed to family income through employment—for example, as casual labourers, school teachers, older women as mat weavers, and in the estate sector as plantation workers. There were others who worked in their home gardens and contributed to the food needs of the family, and hence to 'expenditure saving', while a few were able to earn income through sale of the surplus.

The sample of middle-income Tamil women interviewed, though obviously relieved of a direct income-earning responsibility, maintained that in their traditional homes in the north of Sri Lanka they were responsible for all household work. Household-level processing of *jak* and breadfruit, which had its own economic value, was therefore very

291

much their concern. This was also true of some of the women in other ethnic groups—Muslim and Sinhala—although they too were not directly engaged in employment.

In food processing the only male task so identified was the plucking of fruit by climbing the trees. Processing work, in addition to its 'food relatedness' was, in the set up of the village, performed in kitchens while seated on the ground, on a very low bench approximately six inches from the ground or on a coconut scraper of a similar height. As one woman put it: 'this is work done seated on the ground and men are not used to it'. Men usually sit on the single bench or rope-woven bed placed on the open verandah in the homes of the poor.

Organization of labour

The traditional villages in which the survey was conducted provided evidence of strong social relationships within the community. Women who handled a large quantity of produce were often supported by relatives, friends or neighbours. This was particularly the practice among the Tamil families interviewed; there were some others, however, who had developed their own strategies.

Irrespective of whether women received support from others or not, they recognized the need for organizing 'processing days'—making relevant changes in their normal work schedules. This was also prompted by the need to commence processing activities early enough, to be ready for drying when the sun came up. Prior to the day, women collected extra fuelwood and had it in readiness, and took out their large cooking pots and had them washed and ready, or else borrowed such pots from their neighbours or relatives. Similarly, those who possessed large mats,— magal, or the smaller type, took them out for the purpose and 'sunned' them the day before.

If there was scope for choice, women mentioned that they preferred a school holiday for processing, as they could get their children to help with the work. It was interesting to note that the women, poor as they were, tried hard not to keep children away from school. Most of the women interviewed stressed that it was necessary to 'prepare' (plan) for processing work, as all related activities had to follow on in quick succession; delay in any particular activity could adversely affect the finished product.

Skill transfer

The main method of skill transfer was within households, with information being passed from one generation of women to the next. Another, more indirect method was the exchange of processed food when some new line of processing was being tried by a household. An example was a woman who attempted unboiled sun-drying of *jak* bulbs and shared the results with some of her neighbours with whom she had strong social relationships.

Adapting the processes

Some women had developed their own coping strategies in relation to aspects of the technology. For example, there were those who chose to cut the breadfruit first into large chunks without slicing it directly; in chunk form, they said, the raw material could even be kept overnight without spoiling—if they could not get through the slicing work in time for sun-drying.

Location-specific problems, such as constant rain in areas which had had ample fruit production, were other constraints the women had to battle. In these places, or elsewhere when there was inadequate sunlight, they would still save the sliced produce by resorting to alternative means of reducing moisture content. For example, some used to spread out the raw material on thick sheets of paper and place it in the smoke rack in the kitchen. They would put it outside whenever there was sunshine, returning it for smoke-drying when the sun went in. They continued with this in alternate fashion—a labour-intensive and costly procedure in terms of time and energy—in order to achieve a degree of drying and thereby save the product.

Food security

For rural women, these products provided security in meeting the food needs of the family. Processed *jak* and breadfruit were used during the 'off-season', and cooked at least three times during the week. This often helped to supplement the main meal or provide a substitute for the staple food—rice, yam, indigenous preparations from wheatflour, or bread—in time of want or when they chose to cook a simple meal to save time for some other important activity. In addition, the products lent themselves to the preparation of a variety of tasty dishes which often provided an accompaniment to the staple. Converted into a sweet with the addition of sugar or honey, and perhaps some coconut, they were a substitute for sugar to drink tea with; or else made into a 'fry' with the addition of chilli, they provided a nutritious afternoon snack for the family.

Preparations of sun-dried *jak* and breadfruit were particularly useful on rainy days when roads and shops were inaccessible and vegetables scarce. The lack of demand for casual labour for outside work during wet weather curtailed income-earning oportunities for the rural poor—both men and women—and it was these processed foods which helped poor families through such difficult times. They were also widely used for feeding hired labour during the rice-harvesting period, a variety of tasty preparations were put in the food packs or *embula* which women carried to the fields for the labourers.

Importantly, women said that the products helped 'to fill their stomachs', as they were considered 'heavy', and thus postponed hunger pangs, both in children and adults. In situations of dire poverty this appeared to be a strategy deliberately adopted by women, conscious of their responsibility for feeding the family, to reduce artificially the demand for food to meet the limitations in supply. It was also observed that, given the choice, rural women attempted to achieve some balance of diet. Commenting on the use of *jak* and breadfruit, one of the slightly better-off women said they would include such processed food in place of potato, local yam or *wattakka* (pumpkin). However, it may well be that such choices are unavailable to the poorer women who struggle to keep their families from starvation.

Food sharing and sale of the surplus

Social relationships within communities, and the culture of sharing observed among all ethnic groups in rural society, were clearly demonstrated in the area of food. Food sharing and food exchange have traditionally been associated with friendship and acceptance of other people. In the households surveyed, it was common practice to share processed food in both uncooked and cooked forms. For example, when one household had a surplus or if a new method of processing was being tried out. There were also examples of the products being given to families who did not do processing themselves, and in one instance a woman mentioned that she supplied home-processed *jak* to her married brothers and sisters who lived in another district.

Food sharing was also seen to perform a clearly supportive function, as those having a stock of the products often gave them freely to those in need. Such awareness of social obligations to the disadvantaged was clearly demonstrated when one of the women stated that she processed whatever surplus she had specifically in order to be able to do this. The women's role of providing alms to the temple was another motivating factor for processing.

Although geared to meet household needs, poor women also attempted to sell their surplus of such food whenever they could, in order to obtain much-needed hard cash for purchasing essentials for the family. Preparations using *jak* and breadfruit were often sold as a snack food outside rural schools. To sell larger surpluses, some women were assisted by the small traders and retailers who collected supplies from rural households. However, such links were few and far between.

Summary of women's achievements

The study shows the poor rural women's awareness of the many different food-processing strategies, together with knowledge of their relative advantages and disadvantages. The women had 'their reasons' for choosing a particular technology, and showed confidence in their ability to make such choices. They were confident too in the measurements and indicators used to determine time-related operations, such as the period necessary for blanching raw material. At the same time, they accepted the possibility of errors occurring in the methodology, and appreciated that new forms of technology which would minimize such errors could reduce their workload and provide opportunities for earning income. The innovative techniques and coping strategies they adopted, and their levels of awareness, demonstrate their readiness for change.

An attempt to match women's technologies with scientific thinking shows much logic in common. The short period of immersing the raw produce in boiling water—three to six minutes according to the women in the sample—is fairly close to the two- to five-minute range advocated for blanching by developed technology, and the 90°C requirement in temperature specified by the Industrial Development Board is that described by the rural women as 'bubbling hot'. While developed technology specifies blanching in a 22 per cent sodium-chloride solution, it is seen that the addition or omission of salt posed a problem to the women, who held conflicting views on it. On the aspect of drying, the women were unanimous on the need to achieve crispness for keeping quality; this they attempted to achieve by turning the product over by hand several times while it was being dried to ensure all surfaces were dry.

The women in the study also demonstrated considerable organizational and coping achievements. Although operating mostly at the level of the individual household, without any formal organization, the study indicated significant informal organization and networking within families and communities on a day-to-day basis. In addition, women planned ahead for problems they knew might arise, and were able to adapt their usual operating patterns in the face of unexpected difficulties. However, many problems still remain with respect to the future role of rural women in food processing.

Constraints to an expanded role

One major constraint appears to be the equating of household-level food processing with women's food-preparation tasks, in line with the overall perception of their role as housewives, resulting in the marginalization of the economic and technical aspects of women's food-processing activities. A consequence of this overall perception is to make rural women in the informal sector invisible to development planners, extension agents and to society at large. Information on new technologies is thus mainly male-directed, making knowledge of such processes virtually inaccessible to rural women, and reducing the opportunities for them to improve their technical capabilities and play an expanded role in development.

The prevailing myth that women are not technology oriented has the effect of directly bypassing women in attempts at technology dissemination. Much interest has been shown in *jak* and breadfruit processing by the relevant research and development institutions in Sri Lanka. New techniques have been developed for small-scale production of quality products with improved appearance and longer keeping quality. The low-cost dehydrator, developed by the Industrial Development Board of Sri Lanka, attempts to achieve controlled drying to ensure optimum moisture reduction through the combined effects of the three basic elements: temperature, humidity and air flow. Through its extension wing the IDB attempts dissemination of information on low-cost technology, and provides technical support to persons interested in making such units. It is reported that 15 dehydrators, capable of handling a variety of fruit and vegetables, have been set up in the country since the technology was developed three years ago. However, it may perhaps have been the result of male bias in dissemination by IDB that a man has adopted the dehydrator for processing *jak* and breadfruit, a traditional area of women's work.

The subsistence level at which household food processing takes place, despite its money-saving support to the family, fails to provide an adequate economic incentive to poor families needing hard cash to purchase the essentials of life. To the younger women in the study, casual labour at rates even less than minimum wage therefore appeared more attractive. These women also showed a definite preference for the sale of surplus fruit for commercial processing through canning, and were moving away from the tradition of processing that they had been used to. Another disincentive to them was the amount of time required for processing, in view of the many tasks they already perform both within and outside the home. The burden of younger women's work appeared greater due to the absence of the support system provided in the traditional extended family situation. In addition to the traditionally perceived 'women's tasks', new ones have now emerged in terms of earning income, taking children to pre-school, and the social obligations of participating in community development activities.

Recommendations

The recommendations made here are an overall objective of the study: namely to provide increased scope for the integration of women in development by providing the groundwork for making the critical leap from primitive to modern technology, within a context of sustainable development. The following recommendations were made by the researcher, following discussions with the women participants in the case-study.

o Research and development institutions working in the area of food processing to work in collaboration with rural women, building on women's knowledge and needs, rather than developing a technology and offering it to the users.

o A concerted effort to be made for product development at the level of household or community-based technology. This would require an in-depth study of technology currently used by rural women and the provision of an affordable and effective technical input, with refinement of existing technologies whenever appropriate, to ensure the development of a marketable product which could be handled by the women themselves.

o Rural women to be provided with a comprehensive extension package, including information on credit and entrepreneurship development, and with follow-up support.

o Forestry programmes to be re-oriented to provide for the cultivation of food crops, such as *jak* and breadfruit in particular, whenever feasible. (It is felt that community forestry programmes would provide greatest scope for this activity.)

o Government to take necessary action to ensure that information on new technologies is made available to women and men, on equal terms, and that appraisal of development projects includes an 'impact on women' assessment.

o Donor agencies to ensure that projects funded by them provide equal opportunities for the participation of women, and that more flexible indicators are used in women's projects in view of their orientation towards a group doubly disadvantaged—in terms of both class and gender.

Conclusion

Defining technology as the hardware, skills, and organization of production, and recognizing the concepts, thinking and behaviour patterns linked to these, helps to identify both the content and processes of adaptation and innovation by women. The case studies illustrate that women can and do adapt the techniques, skills, organization, management and behaviour associated with production better to suit their own circumstances, and that these adaptations are not confined to a single technical area or sphere of knowledge. As women's skills in daily life range across a number of activities, so does their capacity to innovate. They are able to link experiences, skills and difficulties across different tasks, and their solutions to technical problems are not confined to ideas of improving equipment, if adapted techniques or modified organization are more appropriate or more accessible. The organizational and skills aspects of technical change are interlinked, however: as well as gaining strength from working together and tackling the business aspects of coir buying and selling collectively, the Sri Lankan coir workers also learned new or improved production techniques from each other.

Nor is innovation solely confined to the technical areas traditionally associated with women's work. Although many of the case studies illustrate innovation in areas of traditional knowledge, the Bangladesh agriculturists, Venezuelan hydroponics workers and Chilean builders indicate that women are also capable of taking on and adapting new ideas and new technology, and moving successfully into non-traditional roles. It can be argued that the movement of women into non-traditional roles should itself be regarded as a form of innovation.

The *Do It Herself* work underlines the fact that 'technology' is strongly engendered, not only in the hardware that people use, the knowledge that they have or the processes that they carry out, but also in the ways in which they organize themselves in response to change. In order to begin to understand technical innovation by women, it is necessary to identify and examine key aspects of the relationships which exist between women and technology, men and technology and between women and men in any particular set of circumstances.

298

Women, men and technology

Both women and men's use and adaptation of technology is formed by the economic, social, cultural, political and geographical contexts in which both sexes live, but which each sex experiences in a different way. These different contexts will lead to the development of different, though over-lapping, sets of knowledge, including technical knowledge, and different patterns of thinking and behaviour in relation to that knowledge, which may be analysed as separate, interrelated models of technological under-standing. Thus any external event, such as conflict, famine or structural adjustment, will stimulate different responses from, and place different pressures on women and men. 'Technology' is part of this response: for both sexes the circumstances in which they live in any society will affect quite differently their respective priorities with relation to the use and innovation of technology.

Within the complexity of people's lives, there are several key social factors which fundamentally affect the way in which technology is accessed, used, adapted and adopted by them, and which operate in quite different ways for men and women.

○ *Cultural roles and status*: people's use and expectations of technology are firmly embedded in the roles and status which any society tradition-ally allocates to them. In many cases, for example, women are respon-sible for the preparation of foodstuffs and for the health, welfare and survival of the family, whereas men may be responsible for providing an income from paid employment. A number of technological implications derive from these roles. The ability to travel, meet with other technology users, see different techniques and equipment in use and share informa-tion and raise credit is, for example, a function of ascribed roles, and it should be recognized that in many countries, women are less able to travel away from their communities, and mix freely with outsiders. Access to education is also partly a function of cultural roles, which affects, among other things, people's abilities to read and understand technical information, or learn about the existence of different types of information. In most countries women find it more difficult to enter into science and technology education (see, for example, Andam, 1990), and in many countries of the South, fewer girls than boys enter or complete primary school, so the literacy gap between men and women continues to widen (UN, 1991). The social status which accompanies roles affects not only women's and men's self-esteem and self-confidence, but also their abilities to influence local development plans, which can lead to key technical decisions (such as the choice, location and management of grinding mills or wells) being made without taking account of men's and women's different technical perspectives and priorities. The existence of domestic violence is also a function of cultural roles:

299

South American researchers identified it as a hidden factor in women's access to technical knowledge and information. When it occurs, it prevents women from operating at full capacity, or from achieving their full potential; at worst it may cause lasting physical or psychological damage. The *threat* of domestic violence too is a constraint which may limit women's participation in community affairs (for example, by preventing them from attending meetings in the evening to learn new skills, or from travelling to attend a training course) or which may leave them afraid to question the heavy workload imposed upon them or to ask for help.

○ *Traditional knowledge and skills*: people will always have usual or preferential access to different types of technical knowledge. There are no 'rules': in some places women are potters and in others men. In some places women tend animals, and in others men do this. Women and men may both engage in farming, but may use different methods, produce different crops or farm for different reasons. The perceptions that each sex has of technology, and their expectations from it, are formed within the technical knowledge that they have and the processes with which they are familiar. It may be necessary to ask questions about which kinds of knowledge are considered more important, how different kinds of knowledge interrelate, and how different technical concepts may be transferred to other areas of technical activity.

○ *Workload*: the amount of work entailed by the different roles and responsibilities of men and women will encourage or constrain access to and use of technology, through overall time availability and the patterns of time use. A heavy burden of tasks which cannot be shared or held over (such as the daily reproductive activities usually carried out by women) will limit participation in 'new' developments or training, because there is simply less time available both for initial learning and for the activity itself. In such cases, a lessening of existing workloads, if recognized, may have to form part of technical assistance. Less obviously, existing patterns of time use affect technology use and uptake by women and men. Where activities take place more or less continually throughout a day (as is often the case for women and reproductive activities), techniques and technical processes will be adapted (or able to be adapted) to this pattern. Any 'free' time that is available is so only in small amounts and at irregular intervals. Where activities take place in discrete blocks and/or work finishes around 5 or 6 p.m., as is often the case for men, especially those in paid employment, the technology too will be suitable to working over longer periods of time. Similarly, any available time is likely to be found in larger blocks. These factors not only affect people's ability to attend training courses, but may fundamentally affect the way in which a particular process or piece of hardware is designed.

300

For the purposes of analysis, women's and men's relationships with technology can be regarded as separate but related frameworks of priorities, use and innovation. As already noted, however, case studies illustrate that these different frameworks are not equal. They are altered and adapted, and to some extent defined, by interactions and relationships of interdependence between them. These may be interdependencies strictly relating to process, such as supply of materials or labour, where one sex grows something which the other processes, or where one sex provides labour to the cultivation of a crop by the other. There may also be relationships prescribed by the wider environment in which people live and work, such as rights over land or natural resources. Important features of such interactions and interdependencies are the ways in which they embody relationships of power relating to access to and ownership and control over technology, including the final product.

Questions about payment for labour, ownership of land, housing and equipment, common property rights, and access to profit or cash from sale of a product, help to identify the nature of links between women's and men's use of technology, and begin to highlight areas where inequality or disadvantage may exist. The case studies illustrate, for example, how women's use and adaptation of technology may be constrained by difficulties in accessing materials, exploitative behaviour by middlemen, restricted access to markets and political decision-making, and heavier domestic work-loads.

Innovation

Innovation in the informal sector can be prompted by a number of factors. Scarcity of natural resources, migration from rural areas to cities, drought, wars, and changes in markets can all stimulate technological innovation, as well as the search for new opportunities. Poor people are not usually in the position of having the risks they take supported. It is to be expected therefore that any technical adaptations that they make will strongly reflect the risks that they feel they can take.

Given an understanding of the engendered nature of technology use, it is possible to begin to identify characteristics of technical innovation within a given set of circumstances. This will relate both to the detailed *content* of innovation and to the broader factors which stimulate a particular type of response. Factors that lead to the development or innovation of a technology have to be considered. Are the changes 'defensive'—responding to deteriorating circumstances, like those mentioned above—or are they more proactive—creating or taking advantage of opportunities to improve livelihoods? When circumstances are clearly deteriorating, technical 'innovations' may not be the same as technical 'improvements'. Women in Zimbabwe do not view the use of tamarind seed to eke out scarce maize

301

meal as an improvement, but as a defence against starvation. Similarly the *mechero* women on Tacna, Peru, would prefer to have access to electric light to enable them to work in the evenings.

Examining women's technical innovation within a framework of technology use, it is possible to identify features which reflect the priorities that women have and the conditions in which they operate:

○ In many parts of the world women are responsible for the health, welfare and survival of families: the adaptations which they make often reflect survival as the strongest priority, and will always reflect their different responsibilities.

○ Technical adaptations by women may not be improvements: they may be changes which enable them, for example, better to adapt to shortages of labour or food, but may not represent preferred solutions.

○ Such innovations are likely to be low risk, not because women are inherently conservative, but because an awareness of risk is essential to survival.

○ Women's days are usually full: innovations therefore tend to take place within and during existing activities in kitchens and fields rather than apart from them.

○ Shortage of time means that innovations will tend to be small and consist of adaptations and incremental changes to an existing process or technique rather than major changes to products or roles.

○ Any crisis affects disproportionately the lives of the poor. Because women feature predominantly among the poorest, technical adaptations that they make are often *defensive*, reacting to circumstances over which they have little control, rather than *proactive*, seeking or creating opportunities.

Women and innovation

The kinds of innovations that women are able to make vary according to a number of factors such as technical area, available resources, the socio-economic environment and local priorities. All innovations and adaptations are the result of a process of enquiry, of problem identification and solving and of trial and error, similar to that carried out in research and development institutions. The fact that women may be carrying out this process in their own kitchens or homes does not make it less valid, but it does mean that research methodologies (including PRA techniques) should be reviewed to examine their sensitivity to obtaining information about less visible or less recognized activities.[1]

---

[1] There is anyway some debate over whether or not PRA techniques exclude either women themselves or women's knowledge; see Mosse, 1994.

The types of innovation that women are able to achieve depend on their understanding of interaction between the environment in which they are working, the technical processes which they are using and the implications of macro-policymaking. Four different possible scenarios are illustrated by the case studies, and there may be others.

○ With household activities such as *jak* fruit processing, women's understanding of the process is usually high, and their ability to modify and innovate within these parameters is also high. Little recognition of technical skills and knowledge at this level means that women have control, and that there is little interference with experimental processes, although it also means that capacity at this level is rarely identified, supported or built on. Neither is it given the status of 'technical' knowledge or linked into other technical areas.

○ As a technical process begins to involve a more public sphere of operation, with women working from home but as part of a larger industry, women's technical understanding and/or capacity to innovate may be more restricted, if it is not recognized and supported. Women silk reelers, despite their technical skills and undoubted contributions to technical innovations within the household, will not realize their full technical potential until they understand better the other areas of silk production, and are able to participate in business on an equal footing with men. Coir women in Sri Lanka were similarly restricted until they were able to organize themselves differently and build up their knowledge of the whole coir production process. The success of the shea butter producers in West Africa was helped by their finding an engineer who respected their knowledge, understood their reasoning and was prepared to translate their priorities into criteria for technical design.

○ Once production moves into a factory setting, as in the case of the carpet weavers of Nepal, women's understanding of the process and capacity to innovate may become severely constrained. The environment in which they are working is beyond their control, their self-image is low and they are vulnerable to exploitation.

○ When women are introduced to a new area of technical activity, which is usually the result of planned intervention with non-government or government organizations, the potential for innovation is high, but dependent on the institution being prepared to recognize women's abilities, facilitate experimental skills, work with local priorities and believe in local control. The Bangladesh women farmers and Chilean builders provide good examples of how this may be done. If an institution has a fixed technical agenda, or a desire to remain in control, then innovative potential will be constrained. The insulated cooker case study from Chile illustrates how definition and resolution

303

of a problem outside of the community can lead to an inappropriate piece of hardware.

What is the future?

There are four areas in which technical assistance programmes or programmes of activity with women could help to take forward some of the insights gained.

First, there is a responsibility to recognize the technical knowledge and skills that women have, and to design projects that build on and strengthen those skills through the sharing of technical knowledge with the women whose lives depend on it. One of the lessons of *Do It Herself* is that it is an empowering experience for women to realize that their knowledge is not only technical but also valuable, and that this realization leads to the women themselves consciously exploring, strengthening and sharing the expertise that they have. Women's own processes of enquiry are as important as the content of technical knowledge, because they represent a capacity to respond to the kinds of rapid social, political, economic, environmental and/or technical change which are currently a feature of life in many countries. Focusing on processes as well as content requires new approaches by development practitioners and technical assistance specialists. It means a shift towards identifying and valuing local knowledge systems and local capacity, to providing inputs to means as well as ends, and to sharing of the 'know why' as well as the 'know how' of technology development.

Second, there is a need to communicate technical information in a form that is appropriate to women. Many women do not read, and most do not read English, which is the main language of technical communication. Technical writing can be inaccessible even to English speakers. Other ways of sharing information have to be encouraged: visits between groups in different areas, use of technical information in literacy programmes, and local-language participative radio programmes or video are some activities that have been tried, but there are many other areas to explore.

Third, consideration should be given to sharing the insights gained with the people who make decisions about development at policy or programme level in order to achieve a policy environment which is more sympathetic to and supportive of the technical contributions of women at grassroots level. Individually, organizations may have little strength or voice, but collectively, using examples from work in many countries, it should be possible to convince decision-makers in governments and multi- and bilateral donors of the fact that many of the poorest people in the world depend for their survival on the innovatory technical skills of women, and that women's scientific and technical knowledge is too valuable to ignore.

The fourth area of work is the work within organizations. Recognition of the value of women's technical skills needs to be reflected in the thinking, procedures, and projects of an agency or organization. This may involve rethinking what is meant by the words *technology* and *expert*, what processes determine the *choice* of technology, what assumptions underlie transfer of technology, at whom *technical assistance* is aimed and for whom or with whom technology is designed. Further thought may be needed about processes of technology development, and how these may include or exclude particular groups of people or particular types of knowledge.

The thinking, methodologies and rhetoric that have developed over the last ten years around the use of participative approaches in development, may, as Mosse (1994) points out, have served to marginalize not only women, but also the kinds of information that do not fall neatly into the categories expected by trainers and facilitators. The *Do It Herself* work indicates that more work is needed on methodologies which help to identify not only the content of less visible or unrecognized contributions, but also the behaviour, processes and concepts which underlie the use of technical knowledge, particularly by women.

References

Appleton

Andam, A., *Remedial Strategies to Overcome Gender Stereotyping in Science Education in Ghana*, Development SID, Rome, 1990.

Anderson, M., *Technology Transfer* in Overholt, C., Anderson, M., Cloud, K., Austin, J., *Gender Roles in Development Projects*, Kumarian Press, Connecticut, USA, 1985.

Baud, I., *Women's Labour in the Indian Textile Industry*, IRIS Publication No. 22, IVO, Tilberg, 1983.

Baud, I. and de Bruijne, G., *Gender, Small-scale Industry and Development Policy*, Intermediate Technology Publications, London, 1993.

Baud, I., *Gender Aspects of Industrialization in India and Mexico*, in Baud, I., de Bruijne, G., *Gender, Small-scale Industry and Development Policy*, Intermediate Technology Publications, London, 1993.

Bhalla, A.S., James, D.D. *New Technologies and Development*: *Some experiences in 'technology blending'*, Lynne Rienner Publishers, Boulder, Colorado, 1988.

Carr, M., *Blacksmith, Baker, Roofing Sheet Maker: Employment for rural women in developing countries*, Intermediate Technology Publications, London, 1984.

Carr, M., *Sustainable Industrial Development*, Intermediate Technology Publications, London, 1988.

Evans, A., *Statistics* in Ostergaard *op. cit.*

Gamser, M., 'Innovation, Technical Assistance and Development: The importance of technology users'. *World Development*, Vol. 16, pp. 711–721, 1988.

Gill, D.S., *Effectiveness of Rural Extension Services in Reaching Rural Women: A Synthesis of Studies from Five African Countries*, paper presented at FAO Workshop on 'Improving the Effectiveness of Agricultural Extension Services in Reaching Rural Women', Harare, Zimbabwe, 1987.

Hillebrand, W., Messner, D., Meyer-Stamer, J., *Strengthening Technological Capability in Developing Countries: Lessons from German Technical Co-operation*, Working Paper 12, German Development Institute, 1994.

306

Lemonnier, P., *Technological Choices: Transformation in Material Cultures Since the Neolithic*, Routledge, London and New York, 1993.

Lewanhak, S., (1992) *The Re-evaluation of Women's Work*, Earthscan, London, 1992.

Mazza, J., *The British Aid Programme and Development for Women*, War on Want, London, 1987.

Mosse, D., 'Authority, Gender and Knowledge: Theoretical Reflections on the Practice of Participatory Rural Appraisal', *Development and Change*, Vol. 25, Institute of Social Studies, The Hague, The Netherlands, 1994.

Ostergaard, L. (ed.), *Gender and Development: A Practical Guide*, Routledge, London and New York, 1992.

Sen, A., *Gender and Co-operative Conflicts*, WIDER Publications, Helsinki, 1987.

Stewart, F., *Technology and Underdevelopment*, Macmillan, London, 1987.

United Nations, *The World's Women: Trends and Statistics, 1970–1990*, United Nations, New York, 1991.

Whitehead, A., Bloom, H., *Agriculture*, in Ostergaard, *op. cit.*, 1992.

Machicao Barbery

CARITAS Documents.

Diccionario Enciclopédico, SOPENA, Barcelona, 1991.

Maskrey, A., Rochabrun, G. (eds), *Si Dios hizo la Noche sin Luz: El manejo popular de tecnología*, ITDG, Lima, 1990.

Montaño Sonia (Co-ordinator), *Invertir en la Equidad*, UDAPSO, La Paz, 1992.

Bustamante Gomez

1. National Commision for Energy, *Balance de Energía 1971–1990*, Santiago, Chile, 1991.
2. National Institute for Statistics. *II Encuesta de Presupuesto y Gastos Familiares. Volume III*, Santiago, Chile, 1977.
3. Urquiza, Alberto, *Reacondicionamiento Energético de Viviendas de Sectores de Bajos Ingresos*. First National Congress on Energy, Volume I, Santiago, Chile, April 1990.
4. Jordán, Rodrigo *et al.*, *Uso de Combustibles en Sectores Urbanos Marginales de Santiago*. First National Congress on Energy, Volume I, Santiago, Chile, April 1990.
5. Espinoza, Daniel, *Energía para el Desarrollo Urbano Marginal: el caso del Campamento Nuevo Amanecer*. PRIEN, University of Chile. Santiago, Chile, 1986.
6. The Municipality of La Florida, *Diagnóstico Comunal, PLADECO* Santiago, Chile, January 1993.
7. Walker, Eduardo *et al.*, *Planificación desde la comunidad: Ampliando el campo de lo posible*. CIMPA, Santiago, Chile, 1987.

8. Razeto, Luís *et al.*, *Las Organizaciones Económical Populares*, Programme for Labour Economics (PET), Second Edition, Santiago, Chile, 1986.

Arancibia Ballester and Salinas Briones

Renacer union, '*Proyecto*"*Construyamos la Esperanza*", *Población* Villa La Chimba', Santiago, Chile, 1990.

Ramírez, Apolonia, '*Renacer en Conchali*' PET, Santiago, Chile, 1988.

Arancibia, Marcela, The dilemma of women in the public and private sectors in the field of housing, planning and environment in Denmark: The vision of 10 young Chilean professionals, DHS Publications, Series A, Ediciones TVS, 1991.

Rivero, Francisca, '*La Mujer Popular y el Habitat Urbano*', Programa Urbano, JUNDEP, 1989.

Tapia, Ricardo, '*Diseño participativo y vivienda progresiva en un campamento de radicación de Conchali*', Programa Urbano, JUNDEP, 1989.

INE, National Institute of Statistics, '*Compendio Estadistico*, Santiago, Chile, 1992.

Romeo B.

INIFOM. *Encuesta poblacional del municipio de La Paz Centro*. Nicaraguan Institute of Municipal Development, 1992.

Council of La Paz Centro *Caracterización del municipio de La Paz Centro*, 1990.

Maskrey, A. and Rochebrun, G. (eds) *Si Dios Hizo la Noche sin Luz: El marejo popular de tecnologiás*. IT Publications, 1990.

Sjomann, L., *Vasijas de Barro: La ceramica popular en el Ecuador*, 1992.

Paul Rivet Foundation, *Pompolio y su Pueblo*. An exhibition of pottery from Chordelo, Cuenca, 1988.

López Pinedo

Herrera Hidalgo, Fausto, *Cuaderno de capacitación*, Issues 1, 2 and 3, CEDISA, Tarapoto, Peru, 1987.

Dr Klement Mohles, *El Ahumado*. Editorial Acribia, Zaragoza, Spain, 1976.

Rengifo Ruiz, Max, *Projecto de Embutidos Aresanales en la Selva Alta del Peru*, Department of San Martin, CEDISA, Tarapoto, Peru, 1986.

Rengifo Ruiz, Max, *Estudio de la Elaboración de Janión y Chorizo*, CEDISA, Tarapoto, Peru, 1989.

Rojas Vargas, Yolanda, E., *Informe de Prácticas Pre-professional: Producción de Embutidos*, Tarapoto, Peru, 1988.

308

Canto Sanabria

Antunez de Mayolo, Santiago E., *La nutrición en el antiguo Peru*. Banco Central de Reserva del Peru, Fondo Editorial, Lima, Peru, 1983.

Baltazar, Pedro F., *Junin Documental del Peru*, Volume 11, Peru, 1985.

Cakebread, Sidney, *Dulces Elaborados con Azùcar y chocolate*, Editorial Acribia, Zaragoza, Spain, 1981

Charley, Helen, *Tecnologia de Alimentos*. Editorial Limusa, Mexico, 1989.

Herpen, Dorien Van, *Participación de las mujeres y los menores en la Agricultura de América Latina y el Caribe*, CIAT, Cali, Colombia, 1991.

La Crónica special supplement. *La Crónica*, Lima, Peru, 16 October 1989.

León, Jorge, *Plantas Alimenticias Andinas*. Technical Bulletin No 6. Inter-American Institute of Agricultural Science, Andean Area, Peru.

Muñoz, Leyton, *Alimentación y Nutrición*. National Agricultural University of La Molina, Lima, Peru, 1990.

Nutrition Association of Peru, Proceedings of the Fourth Peruvian Congress on Nutrition Carlos Collazos Chiriboga, Lima, Peru, 1986.

Perú Women's Association, *Manual de Capacitación para la Gestión Empressarial*, Lima, Peru, 1992.

Schmidt Hebbel, Hermann, *Ciencia y Tecnología de los Alimentos, Editorial Universitaria*, Santiago, Chile, 1973.

Tapia, Mario E.,*Cultivos Andinos Sub-Explotados y su aporte a la Alimentación, FAO*, Lima, Peru, 1990.

Palao Yturregui

Arriaga, Irma, *La participación desigual de la mujer en el mundo del trabajo*, CEPAL journal No. 40, Santiago, Chile, April, 1990.

Facio, Alda, *Cuando el género suena, cambios trae*, ILANUD, Costa Rica, 1992.

Grimberg, Mabel, *Cambio Tecnológico y Discriminación, la incorporación de la mujer en la fotocomposición*, Document included in the Third Argentine Congress on Social Anthropology, 23–7 July 1990.

Guzman, V., Portocarrero, P., Vargas, P., *Una neuva lectura: Género en el Desarrollo*. Entre mujeres Publications, 1991.

Molyneaux, Maxime, *Movilización y emacipación: Interesse de las mujeres, Estado y Revolución en Nicaragua*, Feminist Studies, Summer 1985.

Pimentel Sevilla, Carmen, *Familia y Violencia en la Barriada*. TIPACOM, 1988.

UNICEF, *Social adjusment: Towards essential development in Peru*, 1991.

Abad *et al.*

1. Abad, R. and Luis, M., *Tecnologia y Economia Popular*. Report presented at the International Seminar on Popular Economics, Caracas, November 1992.

2. Avalos, Ignacio, *Aproximación a la Gerencia Tecnológica*, Caracas, 1989.
3. Bethke, M., Klaus, *Desarrollo rural con y para mujeres El caso Tempoal, Veracruz*. Report presented at the 1st Latin American Programme for the Development of Social Managers, Caracas.
4. Fedecámaras, *El Estado Lara, la mejor selección para invertir en Venezuela*, Barquisimeto, June 1987.

Lahai

Massaquoi, J.G.M., 'Salt from silt in Sierra Leone' in Gamser, Matthew, S, Appleton, H. and Carter, N. (eds) *Tinker, Tiller, Technical Change: Technologies from the people*. IT Publications, London, 1990.